Sociologies of Disability and Illness

Also by Carol Thomas

FEMALE FORMS: Experiencing and Understanding Disability (1999)

Sociologies of Disability and Illness

Contested Ideas in Disability Studies and Medical Sociology

Carol Thomas

First published 2007 by
PALGRAVE MACMILLAN
Houndmills, Basingstoke, Hampshire RG21 6XS and
175 Fifth Avenue, New York, N.Y. 10010
Companies and representatives throughout the world

PALGRAVE MACMILLAN is the global academic imprint of the Palgrave
Macmillan division of St. Martin's Press, LLC and of Palgrave Macmillan Ltd.
Macmillan® is a registered trademark in the United States, United Kingdom
and other countries. Palgrave is a registered trademark in the European
Union and other countries.

ISBN-13: 978–1–4039–3636–3 hardback
ISBN-10: 1–4039–3636–6 hardback
ISBN-13: 978–1–4039–3637–0 paperback
ISBN-10: 1–4039–3637–4 paperback

This book is printed on paper suitable for recycling and made from fully
managed and sustained forest sources. Logging, pulping and manufacturing
processes are expected to conform to the environmental regulations of the
country of origin.

A catalogue record for this book is available from the British Library.

A catalog record for this book is available from the Library of Congress.

10 9 8 7 6 5 4 3 2 1
16 15 14 13 12 11 10 09 08 07

Transferred to Digital Printing 2010

For Jay

Contents

Acknowledgements

This book has not been easy to write. I am very indebted to friends, colleagues and research students, near and far, who have offered encouragement, practical assistance and a sense of certainty along the way. Special thanks go to Anne Grinyer, Jane Simpson, Eeva Sointu, Anthony Greenwood, Sheryl Coultas, Sue Yates, Rannveig Traustadóttir, Michele Moore, Karen Dunn, Penny Curtis, Bob Sapey, Donna Reeve, Hilary Graham, Christine Milligan, Tom Shakespeare and Len Barton. I am also grateful to other present and former members of staff in the Institute for Health Research at Lancaster University for their collegiality and forbearance, especially David Clark and Tony Gatrell. Palgrave Macmillan's referees and editors are thanked for their helpful comments on the first draft.

Deepest appreciation and thanks go, as ever, to Quentin Rudland and Jay Rudland-Thomas, as well as to Alun Thomas, Sally Thomas and Jim Davies, and Andrew and Sue Thomas.

Part One

Theoretical Perspectives

1

Introduction: Disciplinary Divides and Definitions

Sociologies of Disability, Impairment and Chronic Illness

The use of the term 'sociologies' in the title of this book may seem perverse to some. The formulation of 'sociology' in the plural is unfamiliar and has an ungainly feel about it. Sociologists have found it unnecessary to journey into the plural because their discipline has thrived on theoretical diversification and empirical variety. From another angle, the title may seem untimely in the wake of recent suggestions that 'sociology', whether in the singular or plural, should shed its disciplinary carapace altogether. Indeed, an important theme in sociologists' reflections on their discipline at the start of the twenty-first century was that the time had come to move into a 'post-disciplinary' space (Sayer, 2000a; Wallerstein, 2000; McClennan, 2003). Such an unfettered vantage point, it was argued, allows for the more imaginative tackling of questions of the day, especially those bound up with globalisation; post-disciplinarity facilitates the transcendence of the parochial foci of twentieth-century sociology (Urry, 2000).

Nevertheless, I refer to 'sociologies' in this discussion of ideas about disability and impairment, a discussion that treats chronic illness as a category of impairment (see definitions, below). My rationale is twofold. First, I wanted to focus on the ideas of writers who privilege sociological approaches, whether or not they self-identify as sociologists. My interest is in the work of scholars who have used sociological perspectives to explore disability, impairment and chronic illness. Second, the use of the term sociologies reflects the fact that in the United Kingdom (UK), these sociologically informed engagements fall into two main camps: disability studies and medical sociology. The perspectives employed amount to more than variations within a single sociology: two contrasting, indeed competing, sociologies of disability, impairment and chronic illness are involved, hence my title. For convenience, I shall refer throughout to these as 'disciplines', though medical sociology is, of course, a well-established sub-discipline within sociology, and *the sociology of chronic illness and disability* is a sub-field within UK medical sociology.

The boundary between disability studies and medical sociology is clearly drawn in the UK, particularly in the minds of academics working in the former. The development of ideas in disability studies in the 1980s and 1990s amounted to a head-on challenge to medical sociologists' claim to sole jurisdiction in any sociology of disability. The existence of a disciplinary 'divide' soon became apparent (Barnes and Mercer, 1996), one not characterised by a polite 'agree to disagree' arrangement. Exchanges have often been heated, with views expressed forcibly and curtly – especially those emanating from disability studies. The reasons for this relate to the political origins and orientation of UK disability studies, discussed at length in Chapter 3.

The disciplinary divide hinges on how 'disability' is understood as a social phenomenon. Despite sociologists' frequent dislike of the term 'paradigm', I have found it of use in the elaborate 'compare and contrast' exercise that follows: the organising principle of this book is that two overarching and contrasting sociological paradigms are in play. Sociologists in disability studies use a *social oppression* paradigm: to be disabled, or to be discursively constructed as 'disabled', is to be subject to social oppression. *Disablism* functions alongside sexism, racism, ageism and homophobia in society. Medical sociologists, I argue, theorise chronic illness and disability through the *social deviance* lens, and have done so in different theoretical guises for many years. Ideas about social deviance have infused medical sociologists' analyses of two main themes: societal responses to people designated chronically ill or disabled, and the social experience of living with stigmatised bodily states. Theoretical diversity is evident in both the oppression and social deviance paradigms.

This book explores this intellectual landscape as it manifests itself in the UK – though the ideas and perspectives discussed are of relevance to an international readership in disability studies and medical sociology. It offers a review of conceptual engagements with disability, impairment and chronic illness in the two disciplines, situating these within the theoretical perspectives employed, and examines three themes in detail: 'care and dependency', 'the impaired body' and 'lived experience'. Food for thought is provided for students at both undergraduate and postgraduate levels, as well as for researchers and writers specialising in disability studies or medical sociology. The book draws upon the work of many people, and is particularly indebted to writers in disability studies who have already explored aspects of the disciplinary divide in the UK, most notably Michael Oliver (1990, 1996a,b,c) and the publishing efforts of the Colin Barnes and Geoff Mercer partnership at the University of Leeds (Barnes and Mercer, 1996, 1997; Barnes *et al.*, 1999, 2002.

See also Abberley, 1987; Barton, 1996a,b; Swain *et al.*, 2003. For responses from medical sociologists, see especially: Bury, 1996a, 1997, 2000, 2005; G. Williams, 1996a,b, 2001; S. Williams, 1999).

Readers will soon find that the reviews and discussions in the pages that follow are not 'neutral' in character. I have approached this 'compare and contrast' exercise from the point of view of a disabled sociologist whose primary allegiance is to disability studies, and whose work within disability studies is known for its materialist feminist orientation (Thomas, 1997, 1999, 2001a,b, 2004a). This means, first, that some of the ideas expounded by medical sociologists on disability and chronic illness come in for heavy criticism, either explicitly or implicitly, and second, that most sympathy is expressed for ideas in disability studies that are 'gender sensitive' and realist in character. My approach is also informed by my long-standing respect for much of the scholarship that carries the 'medical sociology' imprint; indeed, this attitude is reflected in my own use of its interpretative tradition in research on living and dying with cancer (Thomas, 2005; Thomas and Morris, 2002; Thomas *et al.*, 2004).

My reasons and motivation for writing the book are as follows. First, I wanted to undertake a critical but open-minded review of medical sociologists' ideas on chronic illness and disability, past and present, from a disability studies perspective. As well as providing an informative account for readers on both sides of 'the divide', this would allow me to develop my own thinking on disability, disablism and what I call *impairments effects* (Thomas, 1999) – an unfolding process that has left its mark herein. Second, I wanted to produce an inclusive account of sociological perspectives and ideas currently to be found in UK disability studies – a discipline that has witnessed something of an explosion in thinking in recent years. My motivation was twofold in this regard: to convince students of medical sociology and other disciplines that there is more to disability studies than simplistic reiterations of 'the social model of disability', *and* to provide students of disability studies with an update on the rich and varied sets of ideas thrown up within the social oppression paradigm. Third, I hoped that a text such as this might encourage students and researchers in medical sociology to reconsider the ways in which their discipline has engaged with chronic illness and disability, and to look to disability studies for alternative views as well as new inspiration. This relates to a fourth reason: to encourage further dialogue across the disciplinary divide, building on work on this theme in the UK and North America (Barnes and Mercer, 1996, 1997; Barton, 1996b; Barnes *et al.*, 1999, 2002; Zola, 1991; Bury, 1997, 2000; Linton, 1998a; S. Williams, 1999; Albrecht *et al.*, 2001a; Hahn, 2001; Omanski and Rosenblum, 2001; G. Williams, 2001). Finally, I wished to form my own view on the potential for a singular but theoretically diverse 'sociology of disability'.

As the book took shape, the *living* nature of the relationship between disability studies and medical sociology became apparent: each discipline has played a role in moulding some of the features of the other in recent decades. This was brought to light through reading, in serial fashion, the books and papers that have documented examples of direct and purposive debate between disciplinary representatives in the last 40 years (e.g. Barnes and Mercer, 1996). Selected examples of such inter-disciplinary *episodes*, as I shall call them, play an important role in this book and are located in Chapters 4 and 6. Moreover, my reading of 'old' publications on disability in both UK and US medical sociology clarified my thinking on a seam of work that might be termed a nascent 'sociology of disability' – a collection of writings that place disability in macro-sociological context, coming close to 'social modellist' thinking at times. This sub-theme is introduced in Chapter 2.

Reflections on 'disciplinary change', on past and present, inevitably encouraged the posing of 'whither'questions. Today, both disciplines inhabit a 'new' political and policy landscape, reflecting the achievements of 'disability rights' activists and advocates in the last 30 years. A good example of this is presented by the recent publication of a report by The Prime Minister's Strategy Unit entitled *Improving the Life Chances of Disabled People* (Cabinet Office, 2004). The report proposes that disabled people in Britain should have full opportunities and choices to improve their quality of life and to be treated as respected and equal members of society (Cabinet Office, 2004: 7). How will medical sociology position itself in this altered socio-political landscape? Will sociologists 'of chronic illness and disability' plough the same old furrows, or move on to pastures new? The disability studies' focus is unlikely to change; fine words in official reports are held to be meaningless unless translated into *real* improvements.

Two Disciplines: An Introductory Sketch

Many of the writers who align themselves with disability studies in the UK have personal experience of living with disability and impairment (including chronic illnesses), though the discipline welcomes non-disabled individuals who support the interests of disabled people in all social arenas. As shall become clear in the chapters that follow, this disciplinary *embodiment* has certainly played an important role in the development of a radical sociology of disability. The *social model of disability*, a term coined by Michael Oliver (1983) in the early 1980s, is at the heart of UK disability studies, and the ongoing linkage with the British disabled people's movement remains a strong commitment (Barnes *et al.*, 2002). Although the social model is now hotly debated and contested – a consequence of theoretical diversification – it remains the central theme around which disciplinary adherents coalesce.

Disability studies is a relatively young discipline that now has an acknowledged presence in UK universities (from the 1980s); it feeds into courses and qualifications for students in the social sciences and the social care and health professions (Oliver, 1983, 1996a; Barton, 1996a; Swain *et al.*, 2003; Oliver and Sapey, 2005). Indicators of its advance in the academy include: the existence of a number of research centres and groupings specialising in disability research; the status and influence of the UK-based international journal *Disability & Society*; the popularity of international conferences hosted by the UK Disability Studies Association; the securing of Research Council funding for disability studies projects and the rapid growth of publications with the 'disability studies' nomenclature.

The majority of writers in disability studies consider sociology – understood broadly to include much that travels under the titles 'social policy', 'gender studies' and 'cultural studies' – to be the social science that offers theoretical and methodological resources of greatest relevance. However, a growing multi-disciplinarity is evident as other social sciences have made their presence felt, especially geography, history, psychology and political science. However, unlike disability studies in North America, the UK discipline does not have a sizeable humanities profile.

Medical sociology has a considerably longer history, and much has been written about its genesis and paths of development in the United States (US) and the UK (Stacey and Homans, 1978; Scambler, 1987; Bird *et al.*, 2000; Cockerham, 2004). Uta Gerhardt's authoritative *Ideas About Illness* (1989) traces the development of medical sociology back to the 1930s when interest was first expressed in the significance of the physical and mental health of individuals for the warp and weft of the social fabric (for an alternative account of medical sociology's origins, see Turner, 1987).

By the close of the 1950s, medical sociology was an established subspecialty in American sociology, a disciplinary practice that spread to Europe – with the first British medical sociology conference taking place in 1964. Subsequent decades saw the flourishing of medical sociology on both sides of the Atlantic, and the subspecialty established a strong presence in a range of university departments. The *Medical Sociology Study Group* makes up one of the largest and most active study groups in the *British Sociological Association*, and students and researchers in the field have access to a rich mix of relevant conferences, symposia, journals and newsletters. The title 'the sociology of health and illness' is preferred by many of those involved (for reasons noted in Chapter 2), but 'medical sociology' retains wide usage. Of course, medical sociologists do not inhabit an academic community in which personal lives are free from chronic illness or disability, certainly not, but these realities are rarely referred to in academic writing.

The UK disciplinary divide is less in evidence elsewhere, at least on the surface. 'Disability studies' is a more all-encompassing social scientific category in North America and the Nordic countries (Albrecht *et al.*, 2001a; Gustavsson, 2004; Meekosha, 2004; Kristiansen and Traustadóttir, 2004). Nevertheless, arguments between members of communities engaged in disability research and scholarship can be as sharp as those found in the UK, and radically minded writers have a great deal in common with British social modellists (see, for example, Hahn, 1994, 2001; Charlton, 1998; Fine and Asche, 1988; Linton, 1998a,b; Rioux and Bach, 1994).

Book Structure and Limitations

The book has two parts, and is best appreciated if the chapters are read sequentially. The two chapters in Part One deal with medical sociology and disability studies in turn; Part Two contains four chapters that compare the ideas at work in both disciplines. The complex reasons and motivation for writing the book, outlined above, mean that each chapter tries to serve more than one purpose. Sometimes the *emphasis* is on providing a critical review of long-standing ideas (Chapter 2), sometimes it is on generating a summative account of relatively new ideas (Chapter 3). Sometimes the focus is on documenting and exploring the contours of the disciplinary divide (Chapters 4, 5 and 6), sometimes this is twinned with reflections on what disability studies might usefully 'borrow' from medical sociology (Chapter 5), or vice versa (Chapter 6).

Chapter Outlines

Chapter 2, on medical sociology, reviews the interpretations of chronic illness and disability associated with structural functionalism, symbolic interactionism, phenomenology, conflict theories – including critical realism and Foucaldian poststructuralism. It also outlines the nascent 'soci-ology of disability' present in UK and US medical sociology from the 1960s, that is, a (fragmented) body of work distinguished by its concentration on disability *per se* and the use of macro-sociological perspectives, sometimes in combination with interpretative themes. Chapter 2 also serves as a 'theoretical traditions' backdrop for Chapter 3: although sociologists within disability studies set their ideas out in opposition to medical sociology, they inevitably make use of some of the same theoretical building blocks.

Chapter 3 examines the origins and development of sets of radical ideas about disability to be found in disability studies in the UK. It reviews theorisations of disability rooted in materialism, related conflict theories, poststructuralism and phenomenology. An important theme is the role played by feminist thinkers – of contrasting theoretical persuasions – in the shaping of the social oppression paradigm. The chapter also reflects on the meaning and application of the concept 'social oppression'.

Moving to Part Two, Chapter 4 contrasts approaches to 'care' and 'dependency' in medical sociology and disability studies, and suggests that the social deviance and oppression paradigms clash most forcibly in this area – despite the multiplicity of theoretical perspectives *within* each discipline. This chapter features four of the five inter-disciplinary *episodes* featured in the book.

The disciplinary divide is also manifest in theorisations of impairment and 'the body', the themes covered in Chapter 5. The chapter's first part demonstrates that debate on the impaired body in disability studies has travelled far beyond initial consideration of whether impairment should or should not be addressed *at all*: the body can no longer be declared 'missing'. The chapter moves on to review a selection of ideas used by medical sociologists whose work contributes to 'the sociology of the body', and closes with my reflections on how some of these ideas might be put to work in disability studies.

Chapter 6 explores the sociologies of lived experience found in disability studies and medical sociology – illustrated by inter-disciplinary *episode 5*. It also includes a section on research methods. The analysis shows that empirical research on the experiential has been pursued for contrasting purposes in these disciplines, but goes on to consider recent evidence of shifting intellectual boundaries and changing agendas. The implications of these developments are discussed, and I offer my reflections on where I would like to see them lead.

Chapter 7, the final chapter, tries to harness the whole, and considers the prospects for a singular *sociology of disability*.

Limitations

It is important to acknowledge some limitations and boundaries. First, reference has already been made to limitations imposed by the book's UK focus. Undertaking an international or cross-national comparison of sociologies of disability is a necessary but huge task, one beyond the scope of this volume. Second, space has not been available to link sets of ideas about disability, impairment and chronic illness to their wider historical, cultural and political contexts, at least not in any consistent fashion. That is, readers must take it as given that I consider *all* sociological knowledge to be 'situated' in time and place. Third, in its use of concrete examples to illustrate ideas, physical impairment gets more attention than sensory impairment, learning difficulty or mental health – and the illustrations used fail to take full account of age, 'race' and sexual diversity. Achieving an equal balance would have required much more time than I had at my disposal. Finally, although the sociological literature covered in this book is extensive, I have not been able to engage with all relevant publications. Readers attached to particular theoretical perspectives or authors may think that justice has not been done, but compromises had to be made and limits set, else the book would never have seen the light of day.

Key Concepts: Definitions

The remainder of this chapter discusses the meaning of key terms used in the chapters that follow. We start with social oppression and social deviance, concepts that are central to the distinctions drawn between disability studies and medical sociology, and move on to disability, disablism, impairment and chronic illness. Readers must keep in mind that the term 'disability' can and has been invested with different meanings, and that language is a key terrain of disciplinary divergence and contestation.

Social Oppression ... and Social Exclusion

Iris Marion Young, a US political theorist, offers helpful ways of thinking about 'oppression' in her book *Justice and the Politics of Difference* (1990). Her analysis explored the *social injustices* experienced by a number of social groups in contemporary societies, including disabled people, and captured the meaning of social oppression in the following summary statement:

> In [an] extended structural sense oppression refers to the vast and deep injustices some groups suffer as a consequence of often unconscious assumptions and reactions of well-meaning people in ordinary interactions, media and cultural stereotypes, and structural features of bureaucratic hierarchies and market mechanisms – in short, the normal processes of everyday life. We cannot eliminate this structural oppression by getting rid of the rulers or making some new laws, because oppressions are systematically reproduced in major economic, political, and cultural institutions. (Young, 1990: 41)

Young's inclusion of disabled people in her shortlist of groups subject to social oppression is testimony to the successful outcome of years of ideological struggle waged by disabled people's movements in the US and UK.

Today, social scientists often use the term *social exclusion* interchangeably with social oppression – a term that dates back to the mid-1980s (Alcock, 1997). The 'socially excluded' are people who, through no inherent failing, do not have access to rights or resources taken for granted by the majority.

To be excluded is to be treated unequally and thus disadvantaged. Excluded people usually belong to stigmatised minority groups, and their exclusion amounts to an unacceptable denial of full citizenship rights. Since the election of the UK Labour Party to Government in 1997, successive administrations have given the term official legitimacy – most obviously by setting up the *Social Exclusion Unit* – and routinely pronounce on maximising inclusion and minimising exclusion. Disabled people are officially recognised as belonging to a group unjustly 'shut out': bodies such as the UK *Disability Rights Commission* decree that disabled people must now be brought into the mainstream, and accepted on equal terms 'for what they are'.

Social Deviance

'Social deviance' is a key concept in the sociological lexicon. In *The Rules of Sociological Method* (1964, first published 1895), Emile Durkheim – a founding figure in the discipline – distinguished between 'pathological' and 'normal' forms of social organisation, and examined the functions fulfilled by 'deviant' cases in the maintenance of social order and coherence. From these roots, sociological interest in 'social deviance' grew and bifurcated, an intellectual odyssey that continues today – most notably in the fields of criminology and medical sociology.

A key staging post in the twentieth century was the 'functionalist' elaboration of Durkheim's social deviance perspective by the American sociologist, Talcott Parsons. In *The Social System* (1951), Parsons included the 'deviance' represented by illness, disease and disability in his analysis of the manifestation and management of social dysfunction (see Chapter 2, this volume). In so doing, he laid the foundations of medical sociology in the US, and secured his authority in the subspecialty. Parsons' ideas were, and remain, of great influence in North American and British medical sociology (S. Williams, 2005).

The longevity and transformation of the deviance perspective in medical sociology is captured by William C. Cockerham (2004: 142–3) in the *ninth* edition of his book *Medical Sociology*; he explains:

> The basis for describing illness as a form of deviant behaviour lies in the sociological definition of deviance as any act or behaviour that violates the social norms within a given social system. Thus, deviant behaviour is not simply a variation from a statistical average. Instead, a pronouncement of deviant behaviour involves making a *social judgement* about what is right or proper behaviour according to a social norm … . Conformity to prevailing norms is generally rewarded by group acceptance and approval of behaviour; deviation from a norm, however, can lead to disapproval of behaviour, punishment, or other forms of social sanctions being applied against the offender … . [S]ickness as

deviance is typically regarded as an undesirable circumstance for both the sick person and for society.

This statement also reflects the influence of symbolic interactionist thinking about illness as social deviance – developed in 1960s America and discussed in Chapter 2. Indeed, the 'illness as deviance' motif has survived the rise and fall in fashion and fortune of diverse theoretical perspectives in medical sociology. We shall see that communities of theorists and researchers have employed the deviance approach in contrasting ways, and learn that its use is far subtler in some traditions than others.

Disability: Usage in Medical Sociology

Medical sociologists generally work with the lay or commonsense meaning of 'disability', or with 'official' re-workings of the lay view. In Anglophone cultures, disability refers to 'limited activity' – not being able 'to do things', and a 'disabled person' is someone who has a medically certifiable 'condition' that prevents him or her carrying out the full range of age-related activities considered normal. This understanding of disability is deep-rooted and pervasive, and is reflected in the UK's Disability Discrimination Acts of 1995 and 2005 (DDA). To paraphrase the DDA: a person 'has a disability' if he or she has a physical or mental impairment that has a substantial and long-term adverse effect on his or her ability to carry out normal day-to-day activities.

The commonsense perspective assumes that an injury to the body – through illness, accident or 'developmental abnormalities' in gestation – is the cause of disability, of 'being disabled' and of 'disablement'. For any individual, the degree of her disablement, or the extent of his 'disabilities', depends on the severity and nature of the condition involved. Collectively, reference is made to 'people with disabilities'. Medical and rehabilitative services are believed to possess the scientific expertise required to identify with precision the failings of the body that 'cause disability', and to offer the best hope for corrective solutions.

In the main, medical sociologists' interests lie not in contesting or examining the meaning of the concept 'disability' *per se*, but in exploring the social dimensions and consequences of disability and its causes – at societal and individual levels. Some have made use of 'official' definitions such as the World Health Organisation's (WHO) International Classification of Impairments, Disabilities and Handicaps (ICIDH) (Wood, 1980). Indeed, a small number of medical sociologists played an important role in formulating the ICIDH in the late 1970s. The ICIDH, expressed the standard definition with greater precision: 'a disability is any restriction or lack (resulting from impairment) of ability to perform an activity in the manner or within the range considered normal for a human being' (cited in Bickenbach *et al.*, 1999: 1175). It follows that the prevalence of disability rises with age: because impairment increases with age so too does disability (or disablement). It also follows that disability is a universal phenomenon: 'The existence of impairment and disability are as old as the human body and early societies; they are a human constant' (Albrecht, 1992: 36). Medical sociologists have long recognised that disabled people are also subject to degrees of social discrimination and disadvantage, and some have made these *additional* limitations the subject for research (see Chapter 2).

The WHO's ICIDH schema now has a successor known as the ICF: the International Classification of Functioning, Disability and Health (WHO, 2001a). The ICF attempts to integrate social and lay/medical meanings of disability. It will be interesting to see if and how disability studies researchers and medical sociologists make use of this schema in years to come.

Disability and Disablism: Usage in Disability Studies

In the 1970s, disability activists in the UK challenged the common sense meaning of disability and its *individualising* essence and consequences – a story told in some detail in Chapter 3. The best-known outcome of this struggle to redefine what being disabled means is 'the social model of disability', formulated by Michael Oliver in 1983. In his words:

> In the broadest sense, the social model of disability is about nothing more complicated than a clear focus on the economic, environmental and cultural barriers encountered by people who are viewed by others as having some form of impairment – whether physical, mental or intellectual. The barriers disabled people encounter include inaccessible education systems, working environments, inadequate disability benefits, discriminatory health and social support services, inaccessible transport, houses and public buildings and amenities, and the devaluing of disabled people through negative images in the media – films, television, and newspapers. (Oliver, 2004: 21)

This shifts the focus to the imposition of limits on activity *from the outside*. As we shall see, writers and researchers in disability studies have worked to substantiate and elaborate *social* definitions and interpretations of disability ever since.

Disablism, a term introduced by Paul Abberley (1987), refers to the social beliefs and actions that oppress/exclude/disadvantage people with impairments. It is a term that is used widely in disability studies – one that belongs to the social oppression paradigm. Its meaning is easily grasped because its sister concepts – racism, sexism and ageism – are so familiar and well understood. The term is often used in this book, both when expressing my own views on the issues under discussion and when citing the arguments of others.

Impairment and Chronic Illness

As Chapters 3 and 5 reveal, there is much debate in disability studies on how to conceptualise and theorise 'impairment'. Nonetheless, many members of the disability studies community would concur with the definitional approach to impairment set out in the ICF (WHO, 2001a). On past form, is likely that most medical sociologists will agree with the ICF's treatment of the impairment category.

The ICF makes a distinction between two constituent elements of impairment – body functions and body structures:

> Body functions are the physiological functions of body systems (including psychological function) … . Body structures are anatomical parts of the body such as organs, limbs and their components. (WHO, 2001a: 10)

Impairments may be life-long or acquired, 'physical' or 'mental'. This approach to impairment is clearly *inclusive* of diseases that are commonly referred to as 'chronic illnesses' – an approach that I share. That is, I treat chronic illnesses/diseases as *categories of impairment* in this book.

It is widely accepted that the terms 'chronic illness' or 'chronic disease' refer to long-term and incurable medical conditions. Chronic illnesses may be relatively stable but are often degenerative, and are sometimes marked by acute episodes and exacerbation. Particularly prevalent in late capitalist societies are heart diseases, cancers and neurological conditions – associated mainly with later life. Medicine continues to offer little by way of curative or even ameliorative treatments for many chronic illnesses and their symptoms; indeed chronic illness 'frustrates the project upon which medicine's prestige rests' (G. Williams, 1991: 519). In the UK, chronic diseases became the major health scourge from the mid-twentieth century, largely replacing the infectious diseases so deadly to both young and old in earlier decades (Bury, 1997).

2

Theories and Traditions in Medical Sociology: Illness and Disability as Social Deviance

Introduction

Medical sociologists interested in 'chronic illness and disability' have a variety of theoretical perspectives at their disposal today. Each perspective has a history, a tradition, and has contributed to the shaping of the discipline's contemporary conceptual landscape in the UK. The purpose of this chapter is to review, in loose chronological order, the traditions that have informed ideas on chronic illness and disability in medical sociology since the mid-twentieth century.

My argument, at its simplest, is that *all* theorisations of illness and disability in medical sociology deploy the social deviance lens – whether sociological preoccupations lie with social order and structure *or* with social action and agency. Despite considerable theoretical diversity, it is reasonable to speak of an overarching *social deviance paradigm*. A flavour of this is found in Bryan S. Turner's introduction to his influential study of medical sociology: 'I shall be particularly concerned with the relationship between knowledge and power in the social distribution of health and illness, and as the basis for professional management of *socially deviant individuals*' (1987: 2, my emphasis). As we shall see, this paradigmatic approach accommodates disparate moral and political stances on disability and chronic illness. This contrasts with the *social oppression* paradigm in disability studies, which places sociologists unequivocally on the side of 'the oppressed'.

The chapter begins by outlining the roots of medical sociology in the US structural-functionalist sociology of Talcott Parsons, the pre-eminent perspective from the 1930s to the 1950s, then works through interpretative perspectives – symbolic interactionism, phenomenology and ethnomethodology, followed by theories that emphasise social conflict (including critical realism) and, finally, postmodernism and poststructuralism. It ends with a section entitled 'A Sociology of Disability … ?'. This considers a seam of work in medical sociology that engages with disability *per se* but is not organised into, or recognised as, a distinct sociology of disability. In the UK, this seam of work failed to develop in the shadow of the interpretive sub-field of research and scholarship known as *the sociology of chronic illness and disability*.

Although a very useful device for introducing and comparing theoretical perspectives, the categorisation and sectioning employed in this chapter may give the mistaken impression that medical sociologists can be neatly compartmentalised, and that one theoretical paradigm is cancelled out by the next on the scene. Compartmentalisation underplays the extent to which ideas are cumulative and cross-cutting, and can overstate the degree to which medical sociologists follow single theoretical tracks. While many writers do display a close and singular theoretical allegiance, others are more pluralist or eclectic in their approach – drawing on what are thought to be the best insights offered in two or more traditions. Readers must bear this in mind.

Structural-Functionalism

Interest in distinguishing the normal from the deviant or 'pathological' can be traced back to the work of Emile Durkheim in the late nineteenth century (1964 [1895]). As noted in Chapter 1, Durkheim recognised that definitions of the pathological play a crucial role in constituting 'the normal' in society, and vice versa. Sociological interest in the management of social deviance gathered momentum after the Second World War, in the wake of the Nazi holocaust, when sharp questions about sustaining 'normality' and 'sanity' were posed (Gerhardt, 1989: xvii). Talcott Parsons played a leading role in defining and attempting to explain these boundaries in the twentieth century, and his structural-functionalist theoretical approach laid the foundations of an emergent medical sociology. The writings of this US thinker have been hugely influential, and continue to be critically reviewed and re-evaluated (Turner, 1987; S. Williams, 2005).

Parsons' ideas about the social system were first formulated in 1939, but is most clearly spelt out in his book *The Social System* (1951). This drew sociological attention to medicine as a professional institution engaged in the social control and rectification of a form of deviance and disequilibrium in society: illness. Parsons sought a common explanatory perspective to engage with the various forms of social deviance that threatened the coherence of the social system, with society being conceived as analogous to a biological organism – a system of social structures interacting and co-existing in a *consensual* web of relationships. He saw a healthy populous as a necessary condition for an optimally functioning social system: healthy people could fulfil their roles as paid and unpaid workers. 'Normal' people functionally sustain the economy, family life and other core fibres of the social organism. Illness, especially mental illness, represents social deviance because ill people opt out of their productive and contributory social roles; their incapacity undermines the social structure.

From this perspective, the survival of the social system depends on the management and limitation of illness and the restoration of individuals' health. This is the social function of the institution of medicine. A key element of the doctor's *social* role is to sanction individuals' temporary adoption of a 'sick role' – a legitimate status allowing for the suspension of the ill person's normal social roles – but on condition that the doctor's orders are followed and a return to health sought and, where possible, achieved.

The Sick Role

When outlining Parsons' view, textbooks in medical sociology invariably forefront his formulation of the four characteristics of the 'sick role' – two rights and two obligations – the rights being conditional upon the fulfilment of the obligations. The rights are, first, to be exempt from punishment or approbation for failing to fulfil one's normal social roles and, second, to be exempt from carrying any blame for being ill and failing to fulfil one's duties. The two obligations are, first, to strive to get well as speedily as possible and, second, to seek the assistance of a medical professional and follow 'his' orders. If the ill person abides by the rules of the sick role then all will be well for the social system – the destabilising risk posed by illness is functionally managed and diffused.

What, the reader might ask at this point, has this got to do with *chronic* illness and disability? Surely Parsons' conceptualisation of illness as deviancy and of the rights and obligations of the sick role can only apply in situations where people experience *acute*, short-term, episodes of illness, since one cannot strive to restore full 'health' if one has a chronic illness or lives with the permanent loss of a limb or fully functioning organ? Indeed, one of the standard criticisms of Parsons' theory within medical sociology is that it is not applicable to chronic illness (Mechanic, 1959; Freidson, 1970).

However, Uta Gerhardt (1989), among others, argues convincingly that such a criticism is misplaced and represents a failure to understand Parsons' conceptualisation of the social significance of illness. In her view, the criticism fails to appreciate that Parsons' sociological preoccupations led him to abstract from empirical variations in disease and ill-health (acute, chronic, disabling and so forth), so that the sick role could be treated as a unitary social form. Such an abstraction, for the purposes of sociological theorising, did not mean that Parsons was unaware of variation in illness type and consequence. On the contrary, he made it clear in a later 'reply to the critics' paper that his ideas about illness and the sick role apply to acute *and* chronic illness:

> There are many conditions which are, in any given state of the art of medicine, incurable. For them the goal of complete recovery becomes impractical. However, recovery is the obverse of the process of deterioration of health, that is, a level of capacities, and in many of these chronic situations tendencies to such deterioration can be held in check by the proper medically prescribed measures based on sound diagnostic knowledge. (Parsons, 1975: 259)

Thus, Parsons adopts a relativistic stance: no matter how incapacitated one is by chronic illness or other impairment, one's social duties and obligations remain the same as those of the acutely ill. One must place oneself in the hands of medical professionals, follow their illness management regimens and seek to maximise health and capacity so that contributions to the functioning of the social system are made, in whatever way possible. Put another way, social recognition of 'legitimate sickness' is conditional upon ill people making a continuous effort to maximise their health and functioning, and upon their willingness to submit themselves unquestionably to the treatment regimens of medical professionals.

The Motivation to Become Ill

A related dimension of Parsons' thinking concerns individuals' *unconscious* motivations to become ill, that is, to slip into social deviancy unknowingly (Turner, 1987; Gerhardt, 1989; Lupton, 1997; S. Williams, 2005). In summary, Parsons was greatly influenced by Sigmund Freud's psychoanalytical perspective and applied it, in a sociologically amended fashion, to the process of becoming ill. It is proposed that in circumstances where the functioning of the superego is prone to breaking down, a person may engage in a deliberate though unconscious withdrawal from their 'normal' practice of obtaining social approval (and thus gratification) by carrying out their 'normal' role responsibilities (paid work, family functions, and so forth). That is, such a person may be motivated, albeit unknowingly, to become ill in order to escape role responsibilities, finding 'pleasure' and gratification in sinking back into a kind of early childhood dependency. In this way, becoming ill, and especially becoming mentally ill, is a form of 'strategic deviance', offering a way out from the social pressures brought to bear in industrial society. Parsons' suggests that some individuals, for psychological reasons rooted in their early familial life experiences, may even unnecessarily expose themselves to the risk of accident or infection. Thus, much illness in society is psychosomatic and this, in Parsons' view, must be managed therapeutically and controlled by medicine if society is to function effectively.

Gerhardt (1989: 47) draws out the implications of Parsons' perspective:

> The unpleasant or threatening aspects of suffering pain, being humiliated by not being able to walk, talk or use the toilet are not taken into account. The individual is visualised as one who, more through the force of social controls than through the free will of a rational being, wants to remain active and successful in an achieving society ...

> The second astonishing omission in Parsons' conceptualisation is the following: he fails to see the danger of impoverishment and deprivation in illness in modern (especially American) society. While realising how pleasant – albeit temporary – exemption from work (everyday roles) is for the well, he fails to notice the threat of hardships for those finding themselves unable to retain their income. It seems to have escaped his gaze that the individual wishes to remain respectable, and that patients may suffer loss of reputation associated with passivity and withdrawal from responsibility.

That medical sociology has at its foundation such a pathologising, victim blaming and problem-infused view of 'the chronically ill and disabled' is not generally highlighted in medical sociology textbooks. Gerhardt's assertion that contemporary medical sociology should take account of the real 'suffering' and social disadvantage experienced by chronically ill and disabled people takes us into the realms of symbolic interactionism.

Interpretative Sociology

In the late 1950s, sociology in the US was reinventing itself, marked by the declining fortunes of structural functionalism and a growing enthusiasm for *symbolic interactionism*, building on the 'Chicago School' ideas of George Herbert Mead (1934) and, later, Lemert (1951). In the 1960s, the research and writings of Howard Becker (1963) and Erving Goffman (1961, 1968), became well known – later joined in the 'health and illness' domain by the scholarship of Freidson (1970) and Strauss and Glaser (1970, 1975). 'Labelling theory' came to the fore, followed soon after by an interest in phenomenology and Garfinkel's (1967) ethnomethodology, discussed below. This fresh thinking widened the social deviance lens considerably by addressing questions of social *action* as well as those of social *order*. Particular attention was paid to the meanings at work in interactions between and among individual actors and groups, together with the symbols, signs, gestures and informal 'rules' in play (Blumer, 1969). Together, these ideas formed an *interpretative* sociology working at the 'micro' scale, a perspective that has had an important and lasting impact on British medical sociology.

Interpretative sociologists share with Parsons the view that illness represents a form of social deviance. Lemert's social pathology perspective was located in a long-standing American sociological pragmatism preoccupied with overcoming 'social problems' (Gerhardt, 1989; Albrecht, 2002). This line of thought grouped together the 'social problems' of physical sickness, 'mental disease', blindness and deafness with other problems such as divorce, illegitimacy, prostitution and drug addiction. However, what differentiated the interactionists from the structural-functionalists was their rejection of the idea that there is something inherent in a behaviour or personal attribute that made a person 'a deviant' (such as being ill, disabled, a prostitute, an alcoholic). Rather a social process of deviancy creation is involved, a process referred to as 'labelling'. That is, they advanced the view that any behaviour or personal trait has to be categorised as unacceptably different, as deviant, by figures with social authority for it to actually become a type of deviance. This occurs in and through *social interaction*. Individuals with certain characteristics (long-standing illness, blindness, and so forth) are subject to a *social reaction* when they present themselves before others in society, a reaction determined by criteria of cultural normativity. Put another way, there is diversity rather than innate pathology in human societies, and deviancy has to be conferred. This allows for the social meaning of particular illnesses and impairments to vary across cultures. In Lemert's (1951: 29) words:

> There is nothing intrinsic in a disfiguring scar or in extreme hairiness on the body of a woman which interferes in any way with physiological activity or with the potential fulfilment of social roles. Nevertheless a culture may *impute* a set of mythical physiological limits to such differentiae and thus cause them to become criteria for social exclusion and penalty.

> It is likewise true that those biological differentiae which have a demonstrable handicapping upon behaviour are overlaid with culturally conceived ideas as to how far the handicaps go. In fact, it is these cultural stereotypes which give the larger part of the social meaning to physical handicaps.

Alongside the view that chronic illness and disability ('physical' and 'mental') are socially constituted as forms of deviance, interactionists like Lemert, Becker, Goffman, Strauss and Glaser, departed further from the Parsonian perspective by beginning to sociologically examine the *experiences* of these 'deviants', and, indeed, to take the side of the 'underdog', the 'victim', the 'outsider' (Becker, 1963). The interest and sometimes the sympathy of these sociologists lay with the unfortunate and disadvantaged 'other', and they sought to understand the world from the victim's point of view. This focus on the subjective experience and life stories of individuals marked a significant break with the old sociology. Interactionists agreed with Parsons that medicine, and especially its psychiatric wing, represents a key institution of social control since it has the power to confer deviancy labels through its diagnostic practices, but unlike Parsons they saw the exercise of control as far from beneficent. Indeed, medicine and welfare agencies, despite their 'moral enterprise' facades, were viewed by many interactionist writers as oppressive institutions, relegating individuals to categories of persons who constituted lower orders of human existence. The anti-psychiatry movement of the 1960s had its roots in such critical perspectives (Pilgrim and Rogers, 1999).

Following Gerhardt (1989), it is helpful to distinguish between two illness models in the interactionist perspective: the 'crisis' and 'negotiation' models. It is the negotiation model that has been actively developed in the British *sociology of chronic illness and disability*, but it is helpful to consider the crisis model first.

Interactionism: The Crisis Model

The crisis model is associated with labelling theorists like Becker (1963), and includes the influential work of Goffman on mental illness, total institutions and stigma (1961, 1968). From a labelling perspective, chronically ill and disabled people, whether their conditions are designated physical or mental, are seen as the unfortunate and suffering victims of labels that carry stigmatising meanings – though some may escape labelling if contingent factors work in their favour. These negative meanings draw upon cultural stereotypes and images. Once successfully attached to an individual – almost invariably to permanent effect – she or he is thenceforth understood to be of inferior moral character. Freidson (1966), for example, envisaged the designation 'disabled' to constitute a life-long status of deviance; in his influential text, *Profession of Medicine* (1970), he argued that doctors had secured virtually exclusive jurisdiction over determining what can legitimately be called illness or disability. A person's 'normal' identity is stripped away and replaced with a devalued one such as 'the mental patient', the new identity becoming a 'master status'. In Robert Scott's *The Making of Blind Men* (1969) – an important study of disability in the US based on the interactionist model of social deviance and stigmatised labelling – people who develop visual impairments become 'blind' through a process of socialisation:

> The disability of blindness is a learned social role. The various attitudes and patterns of behaviour that characterize people who are blind are not inherent in their condition but, rather, are acquired through ordinary processes of social learning. Thus, there is nothing inherent in the condition of blindness that requires a person to be docile, dependent, melancholy, or helpless; nor is there anything about it that should lead him to become independent or assertive. Blind men are made, and by the same processes of socialization that have made us all. (Scott, 1969: 14)

Scott argued that organisations, agencies and programmes for the blind were at the very heart of this socialisation process: 'One of the most important, but least recognized functions performed by organizations of the blindness system is to teach people who have difficulty seeing how to behave like blind people' (ibid.: 71). For some people in the grip of this blindness system, the loss of a former 'normal' identity is brutal and complete (Scott's analysis is revisited in Chapter 4).

Scott's statements capture the idea, central to labelling theory, that the attachment of a deviancy label is followed by 'secondary deviance': the powerless labelled person internalises the meaning of their deviancy and begins to display symptoms and behaviours that reaffirm it in the minds of others and themselves (Goffman, 1961). That is, self-perception becomes fixed on being 'the mental patient', or 'the blind person', and deviancy is escalated. A 'career' characterised by amplified deviance is embarked upon. In this way, medicine and other welfare professionals have an iatrogenic effect.

Some feminist writings on women and mental illness in the 1970s echoed this emphasis on the social process of pathologising and labelling – but with a new focus on the gendered labelling of women's behaviour as 'mad' by a male-dominated psychiatric profession. This could account, it was argued, for the over-representation of women among 'the mentally ill' (see reviews by Busfield, 1988; Chesler, 1972; Ehrenreich and English, 1979; Ussher, 1991).

At the time when labelling theory was in the ascendancy, the treatments and therapies imposed by medicine and welfare agencies in industrial societies continued to involve the removal of large numbers of 'deviant individuals' from the community and their incarceration in hospitals, 'homes', 'special schools' or other institutions of segregation: Goffman's (1961) 'total institutions'. In such settings, the effects of 'treatment' upon deviancy escalation had free reign. Meanwhile, the 'normal' in society could rest assured that the 'unfortunate' were being 'cared for' – somewhere else.

Goffman's Stigma

Before moving to the negotiation model, more should be said about Goffman's influential book *Stigma. Notes on the Management of Spoiled Identity*, first published in 1963 (the 1968 version is quoted below). Indeed, Goffman's analysis of social stigma continues to carry considerable weight in medical sociology, and bridges Gerhardt's crisis and negotiation models.

Although *Stigma* considers people with a range of attributes, disabled people occupy pride of place. Goffman (1968: 23) was interested, primarily, in the way that interaction between stigmatised and 'normal' individuals was accomplished, that is, in the performance of social roles 'when stigmatized and normal are in the same "social situation," that is, in one another's immediate physical presence, whether in a conversation-like encounter or in the mere co-presence of an unfocused gathering' (Goffman, 1968: 23).

Using a collection of published experiential accounts, Goffman engages in a fine-grained analysis of the behavioural responses of 'normals' to the presence of individuals possessing 'discrediting' features – that is, individuals whose 'actual' social identities do not match the 'virtual' social identities expected of them. In turn, he explores the responses of discredited persons to the social awkwardness and discomfort they provoke in normals. In brief, Goffman viewed the stigmatised as having 'to manage' social interactions in the interests of those deemed normal; though by no means 'passive victims', the stigmatised are the ones who feel the weight of this social obligation.

Management strategies employed by stigmatised individuals may include absenting themselves from avoidable social encounters entirely, but, more commonly, involve managing 'the presentation of self' by means of information control: 'passing' (disguise and secrecy) and 'covering' (admitting to the stigmatised feature or attribute, but working hard to minimise its significance) (see also, F. Davis, 1961, 1963). Fulfilling their social obligation is, Goffman clearly believed, a burdensome and unfair reality of life for people who are *culturally* (not inherently) discredited, with profound significance for personal identity. Life is particularly constrained for people for whom 'passing' is not an option because their 'difference' is invariably visible to normals. This is not at all to say that 'passing' is a comfortable option, just that it is more appealing because the rewards of being considered normal are great: 'almost all persons who are in a position to pass will do so on some occasion by intent' (Goffman, 1968: 95). But the risk of exposure is an ever-present anxiety.

Goffman also explored the 'in' and 'out' 'group alignments' of stigmatised people, and considered the 'courtesy stigma' that attaches itself to those normals who, like parents of a disabled child, are closely associated with a stigmatised person.

Interactionism: The Negotiation Model

Scholarship in the 'negotiation' tradition retains the focus on the socially deviant status of 'the chronically ill and disabled', a status conferred in social interaction, but has a different appreciation of the impact that a medical diagnosis can have on a person. Research on chronic illness and dying by Strauss and Glaser (1970, 1975) in the US has played an influential role, as have their methodological ideas on 'grounded theory' (Glaser and Strauss, 1967). Their work stimulated an approach that suggested that a social process of *negotiation*, or bargaining, between patients and doctors is involved – though doctors exercise greater power in the exchange.

From this point of view, patients are not simply passive recipients of a doctor's diagnostic decree, as tends to be the case in the labelling perspective; rather, a succession of interactive phases is involved. Nor does the patient suddenly take up the disease label as a new master status; rather he or she enters a period of reflection upon, and re-negotiation of, his or her 'spoiled' identity. In this way, patients are endowed with greater degrees of agency than in the crisis model: the conference of a deviant status is not avoided, but can be actively managed. Researchers began to examine the features of this negotiation, as exercised by both doctors and patients. Various patient 'trajectories' were found to result. Rather than accepting and escalating their deviancy, patients actively pursue *normalisation* behaviours – a strategy designed to maximise their chances of acceptance as 'normal'.

Medical sociologists in the UK in the 1970s and 1980s undertook a range of empirical studies in this vein, examining doctor–patient interactions and the work of doctors and other professionals (Webb and Stimson, 1976; D. Hughes, 1977; Strong, 1979a; Atkinson, 1981; Silverman, 1981). As Gareth Williams (2001) has reported, some of this research was undertaken in collaboration with rehabilitation specialists and epidemiologists. Interest grew in 'living with illness', focusing not just on the patient experience but on the changed circumstances of 'significant others' – family members and close friends (Bury, 1982; Charmaz, 1983; G. Williams, 1984a; Anderson and Bury, 1988; Radley, 1989; Kelleher and Leavey, 2004). It is this body of work that gained recognition as *the sociology of chronic illness and disability*. A common feature is he study of groups of individuals who shared chronic disease diagnoses, or example, epilepsy, stroke, multiple sclerosis or rheumatoid arthritis Scambler and Hopkins, 1986; Kelleher, 1988; Robinson, 1988; Scambler, 989; S. Williams, 1993).

Michael Bury (1982, 1991) became a leading British figure in this esearch genre in the 1980s and 1990s. In a later review of the key themes, e reports that:

> … the intrusion of [..] symptoms on the fabric and quality of everyday life was emphasised, as were the attempts to manage it. The themes of maintaining a sense of order, self-identity and social interaction under conditions of considerable strain were evident. (Bury, 1997: 122)

hree aspects of the experience of living with and responding to chronic llness occupied centre-stage in Bury's own work: 'biographical disruption', he impact of treatment and the longer term adaptation to and nanagement of illness and disability (Bury, 1997: 123). Biographical isruption refers to the disturbing impact that the onset of chronic illness as on self-perception and *identity*, 'exposing the individual to threats to elf-identity and the potentially damaging loss of control' (Bury, 1997: 124). Bury (1991) wrote about the two dimensions of 'the meaning' of chronic llness: first, meaning as *consequence* – the impact of illness on practical spects of life and relationships, and second, meaning as *significance* – the ultural connotations and implications carried by particular illnesses, and he impact of these on self-assessment and identity (e.g. cancer as 'death entence').

The 'loss of self' became an important theme in writings on illness xperiences in Britain and North America. As Mildred Blaxter has ecently noted (2004: 195): 'Much of the sociological literature on chronic llness concerns the *effects* of health on the sufferer's identity: how people ecome struggling, or changed, or defeated, or surviving individuals'. Charmaz (1983: 168) talked of the 'diminished self', with 'former self-mages crumbling away without a simultaneous development of equally alued new ones'. Her research on 'debilitating illnesses' highlighted the suffering' associated with restricted lives and social isolation, and drew ttention to the ways in which different dimensions of living with chronic llness interact to diminish control over lives and futures (see Chapter 6, his volume). As Kelly and Field (2004) note, in contemporary society both elf-identity and ascribed identity are caught up in a complex mix of ontinuity and change instigated by chronic illness (see also Kelleher and Leavey, 2004).

The concepts 'coping', 'strategy' and 'style' have been widely used in racking the longer term 'adaptation' and 'normalisation' of the chronically ill person. People learn the careful *management* of symptoms to avoid stigma and maximise 'normalcy' (Goffman, 1968; Charmaz, 1983, 1991; Bury, 1997). 'Sufferers' become increasingly 'expert' in the self-management of their condition and its symptoms, and relatively less reliant on medical treatments and related professional interventions. Drawing upon material and emotional resources offered by family, friends and wider social networks, individuals make choices and are usually successful in forging re-stabilised and re-normalised lives. The reconstruction of an altered but acceptable 'self' is generally achieved. In this way, chronically ill and disabled people find ways of sustaining claims to 'cultural competence' and legitimate personhood.

As we shall find in Chapter 6, this perspective continues to retain its hold in the sociology of chronic illness and disability, especially in empirical research on 'living with illness'. Only a few of its key concepts and precepts have come in for critical review *within* medical sociology in recent years (see S. Williams, 2000; G. Scambler, 2004).

Illness Narratives

From the 1980s, interpretative research on chronic illness and disability gave increasing empirical, theoretical and methodological attention to *illness narratives* (see, for example, G. Williams, 1984a; Kleinman, 1988; Hyden, 1997; Bell, 2000; Blaxter, 2004). Building on extensive clinical work with chronically ill patients, Arthur Kleinman, an American psychiatrist and anthropologist, defined illness narratives as follows:

> The illness narrative is a story the patient tells, and significant others retell, to give coherence to the distinctive events and long-term course of suffering. The plot lines, core metaphors, and rhetorical devices that structure the illness narratives are drawn from cultural and personal models for arranging experience in meaningful ways and for effectively communicating those meanings ... The personal narrative does not merely reflect illness experience, but rather it contributes to the experience of symptoms and suffering. (Kleinman, 1988: 49)

Interest in illness narratives in medical sociology was part of a more general shift within sociology, as Plummer notes in *Documents of Life* 2:

> ... the past twenty years has seen considerable development in life story work, biography, narrative, lives, oral histories, subjectivity, telling tales – all of these have now developed into a wide network of research. (2001: ix)

One thread in illness narrative research recognised that it was by 'telling one's story' that patients integrated their symptoms into a new sense of self.

a new personhood. Gareth Williams (1984a) referred to this as 'narrative reconstruction'. A few sociologists who succumbed to serious illnesses themselves have written their own illness stories, combining personal experience with sociological interpretation (Murphy, 1990; Frank, 1991a; Couser, 1997).

The narrative theme was taken further by Arthur Frank in his influential book, *The Wounded Storyteller* (1995). Frank argued that people with serious medical conditions make sense of their lives by telling illness stories *through* their diseased bodies. In an embodied sense, they give voice to an experience that medicine cannot describe (ibid: 18). He identified three illness narrative types: the restitution narrative ('tomorrow I'll be healthy again'), the chaos narrative ('all is lost') and the quest narrative ('I'll use this illness to seek to improve myself, and others'). People may move between these narrative types during their illness journeys.

The 'narrative research' approach has been taken up enthusiastically in disability studies, though it has been used to uncover different dimensions of disabled people's lived experience, as discussed in Chapter 6.

Phenomenology and Ethnomethodology

In the 1960s and 1970s, the 'illness as social deviance' perspective was reinforced in a version of interpretative sociology known as phenomenology. Interest in phenomenology among medical sociologists echoed the parent discipline's interest in Alfred Schutz's (1953, 1954) 'life-world' phenomenology and Harold Garfinkel's (1967) ethnomethodological work on the structure of social actors' situated experiences and meaning constructions. Ideas from these sources retain their influence in British medical sociology, often in combination with ideas from other traditions.

For phenomenologists and ethnomethodologists, the task is to empirically study, document and interpret the subjective meanings that individuals employ and construct in the daily round of routine and taken-for-granted activities; society is the aggregation of these individually experienced social worlds or systems. Research in the anthropological tradition, it is claimed, can uncover the deeper moral imperatives that inform individuals' interactions with others. That is, normative patterns and rules of social behaviour that everyone is accustomed to, but largely unaware of, can be laid bare. Social meanings are sustained over time by being repeatedly enacted. If social interaction is to be possible and successful, then the actions of one person have to make sense to others, to be judged valid. This means that there is strong tendency towards *normalisation* in social behaviour.

Though illness and medicine were not at the forefront of their work, leading theorists like Garfinkel (1956, 1967) adopted the view that illness and disability constitute 'troubles' at the level of the underlying cultural 'pattern' or rule. Put simply, 'everyone knows' that being chronically ill or disabled constitutes 'a trouble'; these are deviant and devalued social states to be avoided at all costs and, if encountered, then remedied if at all possible. But this is to understate the case: being ill or disabled diminishes a person's *competence* – the essential presupposition of membership in society.

Chronically ill and disabled people are thus 'victims' of social meanings that render them incompetent disrupters of the social order; they are persons possessing diminished moral authority. As a consequence, 'the chronically ill or disabled', or parents of disabled children (Voysey, 1975), have to endure social suffering. They, like other categories of people who constitute 'trouble', are subject to 'degradation ceremonies' in social inter-actions (Garfinkel, 1956). Their only option is to engage in normalisation efforts. This means placing themselves, or being placed by others, in the hands of doctors and welfare professionals who work for socially sanc-tioned 'remedial and restorative' agencies.

Robert Dingwall's book, *Aspects of Illness* (2001), offers a contemporary British example of this approach. Dingwall presents a critique of both positivistic 'absolutist and scientific thinking' (ibid.: 123) and interactionist perspectives on illness (and disability), and sets out a 'social action' theo-retical framework for engaging with illness that places the notion of 'illness as deviance' at its very centre. Social action in illness contexts is viewed as a product of the meaning and knowledge that people (patients, doctors, others) attribute to it; systems of meaning and knowledge about illness are derived from individuals' social worlds – what is deemed normal, rational, reasonable, and so forth. Dingwall explains that his anthropologically oriented perspective is closely tied to the field of 'ethnoscience' – the study of classifications (ibid.: 123); this means that, from a sociological point of view, scientific medicine is just one of a range of socially constructed systems of 'folk' knowledge (ibid.: 51). On the question of responsibility and culpa-bility, Dingwall views this as variable: the degree to which a person is deemed responsible for their illness or disability is socially contingent.

What moral or political stance is taken by phenomenologists and ethnomethodologists on the disadvantaged and degraded social position of the chronically ill and disabled in society? In contrast to those interactionists who 'take the side' of the disenfranchised, Schutz and Garfinkel did not adopt a political or radical stance with regard to the social positioning of chronically ill and disabled people. The plight of these 'social inferiors' is simply reported to be a feature of the social meanings that feed and sustain social activity. This same posture is adopted by Dingwall (2001) in what amounts, in my view, to a sociologically 'clinical' account of chronic illness and disability: it is only in the book's closing lines that the reader is told that the 'cool and critical detachment' (ibid.: 150) of the sociologist should not mean that 'we' are 'blind' to 'the genuine distress of those whom we are seeking to study' (ibid.: 150). Dingwall's chapter entitled *Illness and Sufferers* is, indeed, cool and critically detached: the social scientist (the 'we') is the objective observer of the 'deviant other'.

Other studies that have utilised phenomenology and ethnomethodology in British contexts include Voysey's (1975) exploration of parents' accounts of family life with a disabled child and Bloor's (1995) analysis of life-worlds associated with HIV infection. Studies with other illness-related foci have looked at the nature and production of knowledge in medical science (Atkinson, 1981, 1995), and doctor–patient interactions (Bloor, 1976; Heath, 1981; Strong, 1979a) – some making use of 'conversation analysis'. Today, medical sociologists often refer to the 'phenomenological approach' in a rather looser way, to refer to a range of studies of the subjective experience of illness and its symptoms (Turner, 1987; Bendelow, 1993; Williams and Bendelow, 1998a).

The emergence of sociological analyses of 'the body' in the 1980s, discussed below and in Chapter 5, generated considerable interest in the theoretical writings of the French phenomenologist, Maurice Merleau-Ponty (1962). Merleau-Ponty is known for his ideas on the connection between meaning and the 'lived body' – on the 'sentient body-subject' and our 'being-in-the-world'. In contrast to Western philosophy's 'disembodied' approach to consciousness or mind, Merleau-Ponty (1962) understood human *perception* and 'being' to be an *embodied* phenomenon: our access to the world and to meaning is by way of our perceiving bodies. Meaning resides *in* the body, and the body is seen to reside *in* the world. His ideas have attracted medical sociologists, and a number of writers in disability studies, because they appear to overcome Cartesian mind/body dualism in a way that avoids poststructuralist 'discourse determinism', discussed below (see Williams and Bendelow, 1998a; Crossley, 2001a; Davidson, 2001).

Conflict Theories: Ideas that Challenge Medicine and Foreground Inequality and Social Conflict

In the 1970s, many sociologists gravitated towards perspectives that understood society to be characterised by social conflict and inequality. There was a shift in sociological focus: from interpretative interest in social action (back) to the imperatives of social order and control, from the micro to the macro social scale. Interest grew in theorising and researching the social control exercised by institutions that retained power by economic and ideological means, especially the capitalist state and its tentacles – including systems of health care. Medicine came in for sustained critique. Some theorists retained an interest in micro-social interactions such as doctor–patient relationships, but as a means to throw light upon the wider social structures and power relations in capitalist society (Waitzkin, 1979).

In the minds of 'conflict theorists', as they came to be known, it was society rather than individuals that could now be characterised as 'sick', as pathological. The 'deviant' status of the chronically ill and disabled, though not challenged *per se*, might now be viewed as an effect of capitalist social relations and the activities of powerful groups, including doctors. As we shall learn in Chapter 3, conflict theories of a materialist and Marxist character have played a crucial role in the development of disability studies.

Conflict theorists often adopted a radical political stance, siding with victims of inequality and the dispossessed. In the wake of the 1968 student revolts in France, the US, and Germany, Marxism became an influential force in sociology. Some conflict theorists developed a Marxian political economy of health care systems: in the US health care amounted to a powerful capitalist business enterprise, driven by the profit motive (Ehrenreich and Ehrenreich, 1970; Navarro, 1976; Waitzkin, 1983; for a UK perspective see Doyal, 1979, and G. Williams, 1991). Moreover, illness and disability could be understood to be a direct *product* of the capitalist economic system (through industrial accidents, poverty, and so forth).

Interest in the social mechanisms that sustained social power, group domination, social subjection, and inequality came to the fore. The concept *ideology* was widely deployed to explain the subtle but powerful means by which dominant groups or classes could retain their privileged position through their control of ideas and beliefs among the populace. That is, dominant groups made their own sectional interests appear to subordinates, and to themselves, to be universal interests – by determining the ideas presented in the media and to children in schools (Giddens, 1979; Althusser, 1984). Bourdieu (1977) expressed this theme by referring to 'symbolic violence'.

Conflict perspectives certainly secured their place in British medical sociology in the 1980s (see, for example, Morgan *et al.*, 1985), though attachment to interactionist and phenomenological perspectives remained strong (Bury, 1997). In this context, medical sociology ceased to see itself simply as a sociology *in* medicine (i.e. a discipline that assisted medicine by bringing sociological knowledge to the doctors' table) and began to position itself as a critical sociology *of* medicine.

Medicalisation

One dimension of the critique of medicine pursued by conflict theorists concerns its 'imperialist' tendencies. It was argued that the twentieth century has witnessed the systematic extension of medical power – a process of *medicalisation* whereby medical control and jurisdiction has crept, overtly and covertly, into areas of life previously untouched, for example, child-bearing and birthing, sexual activity, the management of emotions, 'lifestyle' behaviours such as smoking and exercise, and the 'management' of children and adults with 'disabilities' (Zola, 1972). The presence of medicalising forces in contemporary societies soon became axiomatic in medical sociology, though the medicalisation thesis has not been without its critics in recent decades (Strong, 1997b; S. Williams, 2001a).

In his analysis of iatrogenesis, a famous version of the medicalisation thesis, Illich (1975) proposed that medicine itself, as a *social* institution, created and thus *added to* the burden of illness in society. Others scrutinised medicine's claims to 'objectivity' and value-freedom; as a system of knowledge, medicine could be viewed as historically relative and systematically one-sided (Wright and Treacher, 1982). The influence Michel Foucault's ideas on bio/power, considered below, also began to be felt at this time.

As well as opposing the power of medicine at the general societal level, sociologists like Eliot Freidson (1970) critiqued the dominance of the doctor and the enforced passivity of the patient in the doctor–patient encounter; this subordination often contributed to patients' uncertainty, stress and anxiety, further undermining their health. Conflict between the parties could now be seen as inevitable, though usually effectively suppressed by the weight and sanctions of professional power (Morgan *et al.*, 1985; Gerhardt, 1989). This drew attention to the need for change in doctors' professional behaviours and styles of practice.

Given the themes reviewed above, it can be of no surprise that ideas about medicalisation have been taken up in disability studies, as we shall see in Chapter 3.

The Social Causation of Illness and Distress, and Health Inequality

Medicine's scientific credo that disease and disability are entirely biologically caused also attracted a sustained critique. The proposition that diseases had *social causes*, received support from the social epidemiologist, Thomas McKeown (1979). He established that it was societal change (especially improved diet and living conditions) rather than 'medical advances' that brought about the decline in the infectious diseases that had caused high infant, child and adult mortality rates in the nineteenth and early twentieth centuries. This encouraged the development of sociological research on the *social determinants* of twentieth-century chronic diseases and mental distress, including the influential work of Brown and Harris (1978) on the social factors precipitating depression.

In the UK, interest in the social causes and distribution of illness, 'disabilities' and death at the population level was further stimulated by the publication of a now famous report on health inequalities in 1980, known as the *Black Report* (Townsend and Davidson, 1982). The sociologist, Peter Townsend, played a key role in the team that produced this government commissioned *Report*, which showed that people of poorer socio-economic status had higher death rates and carried a greater burden of ill-health than people of higher socio-economic status. The *Report* concluded that the main explanation for this *health divide* lay not in the nature of medical treatment or the health care system, but in the material disadvantage experienced by people in lower social class communities – in short, in their relative poverty. A programme of research on health inequality funded by the Economic and Social Research Council (ESRC) in the 1990s came to the alarming conclusion that the health divide in the UK has widened rather than narrowed since 1980. Echoing the *Black Report*, this was explained by socio-economic polarisation within the UK population in the 1980s, fuelled by a significant growth in the rate of poverty (Marmot and Wilkinson, 1999; Graham, 2001, 2002). It follows that narrowing the health divide requires social and environmental change – especially the eradication of child poverty.

Peter Townsend's (1979, 1993) interest in poverty and its ill-effects was part of his personal policy-related agenda. This agenda included the social disadvantages experience by disabled people (Walker and Townsend, 1980), and Townsend became an important figure in UK disability politics in the 1970s and 1980s – a theme explored in *episode 1* in Chapter 4. His weighty book, *Poverty in the United Kingdom* (1979), contained lengthy sections on 'disabled people and the long-term sick' and 'handicapped children', covering a wide range of issues: disability definitions; the epidemiology of long-term illness and other impairments; the relationship between disability and age; the low social status, poverty and deprivation endured by disabled people in the community; their location vis-à-vis employment; and the problems of everyday living. He concluded that:

> In general, the greater poverty of disabled people is explained by their uneven or limited access to the principal resource systems of society – the labour market and wage system, national insurance and its associated schemes, and the wealth-accumulating systems, particularly home ownership, life insurance and occupational pension schemes; by the indirect limitation which disability imposes upon the capacities of relatives, pooling resources in full or part in the household or family, to earn incomes and accumulate wealth themselves; and by the failure of society to recognize, or recognize only unevenly or fitfully, the additional resources that are required in disablement to obtain standards of living equivalent to those of the non-disabled. (Townsend, 1979: 734–5)

Another related seam of research on the determinants of health in the social conflict tradition focused on the impact of social isolation on individuals' *well-being*, and on the beneficial effects of social support and participation in social networks. From this perspective, chronic illness and disability are viewed as 'stressors', and attention is focused on identifying social factors that can facilitate coping and adjustment (Gerhardt, 1989). Social support, including the provision of support by health care professionals (contra the medicalisation thesis), is thought to enable chronically ill and disabled people to improve their sense of control over their health, life circumstances and environment. Overall, the achievement of emotional equilibrium through social support and participation in networks of sustaining interpersonal relations is thought to provide a source of protection against stress and the development of disease. The mushrooming of interest in the concept *social capital* in the 1990s (building on Pierre Bourdieu's varieties of 'capital'), especially in scholarship on health inequality, is the most recent manifestation of this approach (Putnam *et al.*, 1993; Wilkinson, 1996; Cooper *et al.*, 1999). The social capital thesis suggests that individuals' health status is compromised if they possess low levels of social capital – that is, low levels of involvement in valued social relationships and networks. It is of note that the social capital thesis has not yet made its mark in disability studies, though it has obvious utility: low levels of social capital among disabled people may be one consequence of disablism.

A lasting effect of the exploration of social processes bound up with maintenance of *health and well-being* was the re-branding of medical sociology in the 1970s: this sociological sub-specialty became *the sociology of health and illness*, though the 'medical sociology' nomenclature has retained its currency.

Feminist Critique

During the heyday of the conflict theory paradigm in medical sociology, the voice of feminist writers and researchers, many of whom adopted a conflict theory stance, began to be heard. The 1970s saw the development of feminist thought in sociology more generally, a response in the academy to the impact of a rapidly growing and influential women's rights movement in North America and Europe: 1960s 'second-wave' feminism. This set the scene for themes in the conflict theory paradigm to be re-examined and re-formulated in the light of gender relations, patriarchal power and women's subordination. Through a feminist lens – whether 'radical feminist', 'materialist feminist' or 'liberal feminist' – medicine's social control functions appeared to play a critical role in sustaining women's oppression. That is, the control of women's emotional and physical health by a male-dominated medical profession – especially in psychiatry, obstetrics and gynaecology – bolstered patriarchal authority (Oakley, 1984; Showalter, 1987; Ussher, 1991; Doyal, 1995; Foster, 1995). A very large body of feminist work now exists on women's health, and on the relationship between gender and health, too sizeable to do justice to here (see Annandale, 1998, 2004; Lorber and Moore, 2002).

This important development in medical sociology, as in sociology more generally, played its part in shattering the belief that social class is the only social fault line that sociologists need engage with. Combined with the impact of social movements for black civil rights and 'gay liberation', feminists demanded that attention be paid to the social divisions associated with gender, 'race', sexuality, and more latterly, age. However, it is only in the last few years that 'disability' has been added to this list (see, for example, Lorber and Moore, 2002), a reflection of the impact of disability studies – especially 'feminist disability theory' (see Chapter 3, this volume). Feminist thinking, always marked by internal theoretical schisms, was fractured further by its encounters with poststructuralist social theory, discussed below.

Critical Realism

The most recent manifestation of conflict theory is found in a philosophical and social scientific perspective known as *critical realism*, though how many of its proponents would see themselves as inheritors of a sociological conflict theory mantle is uncertain (Bhaskar, 1989; Sayer, 1992, 2000a; Archer, 1995). Bhaskar's interest in realist ontology, and what he terms 'concrete utopian thinking' and 'overcoming injustice', is, however, without doubt.[1] In medical sociology, Simon Williams (1999, 2003) and Graham Scambler (2002) are among British theorists who have been drawn towards the critical realist paradigm because it offers, they claim, a coherent realist alternative to the growing influence of poststructuralism. Indeed, interest in critical realism has gathered pace in opposition to postructuralism's remarkable advance in the academy, though it remains only tentatively used within medical sociology to date.

Among other things, critical realism shares with Marxism and other materialist modes of thinking a philosophical understanding that phenomena exist whether or not we have conscious knowledge of them. Indeed, our conscious knowledge of things (matters of epistemology) cannot and must not be conflated with the actual existence of things (matters of ontology). Following Bhaskar, the collapse of the latter into the former is termed an 'epistemic fallacy'; poststructuralist social theorists, it is claimed, are routinely engaged in such fallacious thinking. Critical realists understand that there exist *mind-independent* generative structures and non-observable causal mechanisms (social, biological, and so forth); these exist and exert force whether or not they are detected by human minds (Bhaskar, 1989). This perspective has important implications for theorisations of 'bodies and their impairments', because it suggests that there is a 'reality' about human bodies and altered biological states, a reality that exists independently of society's categories of knowledge about these matters. I take up this theme in Chapter 5.

Poststructuralist Perspectives

Theoretical approaches variously referred to as postmodernist or postruc-turalist have been taken up with great enthusiasm in medical sociology – as in sociology and cultural studies as a whole. These are characterised by the use of *constructionist* epistemologies. The poststructuralist shift in medical sociology has brought questions of social order once more to the fore, and reasserted the relevance of the long-standing idea that illness constitutes social deviance. Ideas about the *social construction* of disease and illness through the exercise of *medical discursive practices* took hold in the sociological imagination, with Michel Foucault's publications proving to be particularly influential (1965, 1973, 1977). However, as discussed below, medical sociologists have not yet applied poststructuralist perspectives in any systematic way to the study of chronic illness or disability. In contrast, disability studies has witnessed the growth in poststructuralist disability theory in recent years, discussed in Chapter 3.

The Cultural Turn: An Overview

In the last quarter of the twentieth century, philosophical reflections on the nature of the times propelled 'critical social theory' in a new direction. Jean-Francois Lyotard's book, *The Postmodern Condition* (1984), first published in France in 1979, announced that social and cultural conditions were now postmodernist. This signalled a 'cultural turn' in social theory, involving the proclaimed abandonment of *modernist* 'grand narratives' – sets of ideas spawned in the eighteenth century's Enlightenment project.

Alongside Lyotard, other French philosophers sought to theorise the features of the late twentieth century social landscape, and the English-speaking world became familiar with 'poststructuralist' writers such as Gilles Deleuze, Jacques Derrida, Michael Foucault, and, later, Luce Irigaray (for her gender-infused poststructuralism). Common poststructuralist themes sprang from theorists' critical engagements with the writings of forerunning 'structuralist' thinkers like Saussure (1974) and Althusser (1971), and from their rejection of the earlier humanist tradition embedded in Sartre's existentialism.

Poststructuralists insist on the fragmentary, heterogeneous and plural character of social 'realities' and refuse to acknowledge the social actor as a 'rational knowing subject'; they inhabit anti-realist (or anti-foundationalist) philosophical territory. That is, poststructuralist thought includes a denial of our ability 'to know' a reality outside of ourselves – because we can only know what systems of cultural meaning and language permit us to know about our social being and physical surroundings. This relativistic and 'situated' character of 'knowing' applies, it is argued, to any system of knowledge: physics, medical science, Marxism, sociology – whatever. The idea that science has the capacity to establish objective truths or to act as a rational force for 'social progress' is thought to be an Enlightenment-inspired illusion. From poststructuralist epistemological foundations, these 'authoritative' systems of knowledge are no more than grand narratives:

> Scientific knowledge of the world is a form of narrative (a story) and like all narratives science depends on various conventions of language (a style of writing, for instance). Narrative is a set of events within a language and language is a self-referential system. Nothing occurs outside language. Therefore, what we know about 'the world' is simply the outcome of arbitrary conventions we adopt to describe the world. Different societies and different historical periods have different conventions and therefore different realities. (Turner, 1987: 10–11)

Academics are encouraged to dismantle the dominant narratives, or *discourses*, in play – through an intellectual process involving the *deconstruction of the text* (a mode of reading designed to expose a text's implicit, unacknowledged, premises) (Derrida, 1978).

Such ostensibly fresh and radical ways of thinking have had a major impact in the social sciences, as well as in the arts and humanities, and continue to command considerable influence in Europe, North America and elsewhere. Many feminist writers have readily embraced poststructuralism, despite Foucault's sidelining of power relations bound up with gender and patriarchy (see, for example, Shildrick, 1997). The 'cultural turn' encouraged the pluralisation of feminist theory, something widely celebrated in the 1980s and 1990s because it allowed 'differences' among women associated with 'race' and sexuality – to be fully acknowledged and explored; indeed, the universal category 'women' was deemed ripe for deconstruction.

Despite its far-reaching influence, poststructuralism has had many critics (e.g. H. Putnam, 1981; Nicholson, 1990; Best and Kellner, 1991; Gellner,

1992), and something of a backlash against poststructuralist thought has been gathering pace in the social sciences in recent years, most notably in the shape of critical realism (Sayer, 2000a).

Foucault and Bio-Power

The writings of Michel Foucault on the regulation of the body have been of particular significance in medical sociology. Indeed, Foucault's influence on the direction taken by medical sociology in the last two decades has been profound. Foucault's interests centred on the relationship between systems of knowledge – referred to as *discourses* – and power. In his view, the relationship between power and knowledge is so close that it is best captured in the expression *knowledge/power*.

In a number of historical studies, Foucault (1965, 1973, 1977) focused on the *changed* exercise of social power in late-eighteenth-century Europe, resulting in the enhanced control, regulation and disciplining of individuals and populations. In short, the capitalist/modernist era required the replacement of pre-capitalist mechanisms of 'rule' and control (direct forms of violence and physical containment, together with ecclesiastical threats of eternal damnation) with far more subtle but nonetheless effective disciplinary mechanisms. Central to the new form of power and control was what Foucault referred to as *bio-power* or bio-politics.

Bio-power governs the bodies and behaviours of individuals and populations through techniques of external surveillance and internal self-regulation. Individuals become subject to moral and practical regimes of observation and monitoring that shape their subjectivity and serve to produce social conformity and docility. These disciplinary regimes work, first, *upon* the individual's body, then, in time, from *within* the body. Medicine, deriving power from the status enjoyed by scientific knowledge, is among the authoritative social institutions that keep people under surveillance and promote self-regulation (Foucault, 1973; Armstrong, 1983, 1995; Turner, 1987, 1992). Indeed, medical discourses, and related welfare discourses, are central to what Foucault came to call *governmentality*: they constitute supremely effective coercive and normalising forces. Given the centrality of bio-power in the modern era, Bryan Turner (1984, 1987) championed the idea that sociology in general, and medical sociology in particular, required a 'sociology of the body'. The last 20 years have seen something of an explosion of interest in the construction of such a sociology, a theme discussed in Chapter 5 (this volume).

Foucault argued that medical discourses determine what is *abnormal* and *deviant* in body, mind and behaviour, and instruct on how abnormality must be prevented, treated and corrected. Taking this lead, medical

sociologists have engaged in detailed explorations of medical regimes and
practices (see Fox, 1993; Peterson and Bunton, 1997; Nettleton and Watson,
1998; Scambler and Higgs, 1998). Writers have argued that disease
categories are not fixed or certain. Rather, these are categories of knowledge
with boundaries that shift and form anew as medical science negotiates
new diseases and syndromes – examples in recent decades being HIV / AIDS,
Attention Deficit Disorder, Anorexia Nervosa and Post-traumatic Stress
Disorder. Echoing the conflict theorists' medicalisation thesis, poststructuralists suggest that medical discourses and their associated practices have
extended medicine's reach in a systematic fashion over time: medicine has
secured its influence in the education system, the media, in all Departments
of State – in short, in every social domain. So pervasive and saturating are
'public health' concerns in contemporary society that people are charged
with the self-regulation of their every movement – what to eat, how and
with whom to have sex, how to bring up children, and so on (Bunton *et al.*,
1995; Lupton, 1995). Rose (1990) refers to the associated development of
therapies of self-help as methods for 'governing the soul'.

What about 'the Disabled'?

Foucault's analysis of bio-power *suggests* that people marked out as abnormal stand to experience the full weight of close medical and welfare
surveillance and regulation, that is, to be especially subject to techniques of
bio-power. Among those deemed 'clinically deviant' are the 'congenitally
impaired', the 'mentally subnormal', the 'mentally ill' and the 'chronically
diseased' – categories of persons who have long endured the 'clinical gaze'
and therapeutic interventions designed to (re)establish as much 'normality'
as is possible. Indeed, the history of the institutionalisation of disabled
people would seem to cry out for Foucauldian-inspired analyses.

But medical sociologists working in the Foucauldian *oeuvre* have actually paid very little attention to the lives of chronically ill and disabled
people, or indeed to 'real bodies' in general; and for poststructuralists, the
default body has been the 'healthy' body. As Michael Bury (1997: 187–8)
has put it:

> As with gender, it should be noted that many mainstream sociologists have paid
> little or no attention to the implications of disability for their analyses of the
> body in late modern or postmodern cultures … 'the body' is all too often
> regarded as self-evident.

Bryan S. Turner (2001: 255) attributes the poststructuralist lack of interest in
the differential qualities of real bodies, and their lived experiences, to

Foucauld's anti-humanist 'block':

> Foucault rejected both phenomenology and existentialism to develop an under-
> standing of social and cultural relationships as products and discourses. The
> result was to expunge an interest in the actual phenomena of the experience of
> everyday life. Foucauldian poststructuralism has examined the enormous
> variety of discourses by which 'bodies' have been produced, categorized, and
> regulated … . At the same time, it denies the sensuous materiality of the body in
> favor of an 'antihumanist' analysis of the discursive ordering of bodily regimes.

Simon Williams and Gillian Bendelow (1998a) argue along similar lines in
their critique of poststructuralist 'body theory' in *The Lived Body*, but
despite their book's inclusion of a chapter on pain they also fail to engage
with chronic illness or disability *per se* (see Chapter 5, this volume).

Thus the social regulation of those living with chronic illness and
disability remains largely unexplored by poststructuralist medical sociologists;
it is merely hinted at in generalised and abstract theorising about medical
discursive practices. Only 'mental illness' has drawn the attention of some
(see Rose, 1990; Pilgrim and Rogers, 1999; Busfield, 2001). As we shall see
in Chapters 3 and 5, it has fallen to poststructuralist scholars in disability
studies to take up the challenge.

Finally, many medical sociologists have taken issue with the (complete)
lack of agency attributed to individuals in Foucault's early work on bio-
power. His anti-humanist ontology, it is argued, reduces the social actor to
a 'discourse dope', a docile body positioned by the play of powerful
discursive forces: that is, resistance to the exercise of bio-power is not an
option. The implication is that the relegation of people with chronic illness
and disability to categories of abnormality and deviance is unassailable. In
response, poststructuralism's supporters point to what they see as an
encouraging turn towards 'the self' in Foucault's later writings. That is, a
subjectivity capable of resistance through 'technologies' or 'practices' 'of
the self' is evident in Foucault's later thinking (see, for example, Foucault
1988; Turner, 1992; Peterson and Bunton, 1997; Shildrick, 1997). Once again,
however, medical sociologists have not unpacked the implications of this
for people living with chronic illness and disability.

A Sociology of Disability … ?

Before moving to this chapter's summary, I shall turn away from reviews of
theoretical traditions to consider a seam of work that could, perhaps, be
identified as *a sociology of disability*, as opposed to the interpretative *sociology
of chronic illness and disability* discussed earlier. I refer to sociological research,

published in the US and UK from the 1960s onwards, that is marked out by its concentration on disability *per se*, and by its engagement with macro-sociological themes centred on social order and control. Some of this work has also explored themes informed by social action approaches, making use of interactionist perspectives on labelling and stigma. Not to draw attention to this body of work holds the danger of undervaluing sociologically informed analyses of disability in medical sociology.

This nascent sociology of disability has remained fragmented in both medical and mainstream sociology, throwing light on Turner's (2001: 252) observation that 'Apart from the influential works by Erving Goffman [...] and Irving Zola [...], sociology has contributed surprisingly little in terms of systematic theory and research to the study of disability'. In my view, there are at least four reasons for the lack of development of a distinct sociology of disability in the discipline. First, the few sociologists who did turn their attention to disability were aligned to different theoretical camps and centres, circumstances that often militate against the formation of generic research groupings. Second, in the UK in the 1980s, the develop-ment of the interactionist *sociology of chronic illness and disability* dampened down medical sociologists' interest in macro-sociological approaches to the study of disability. Third, in the US in the 1990s, sociological research on disability was subsumed by the influential Gary Albrecht under the generic heading 'disability studies' – an all-inclusive and *multidisciplinary* field concerned with the social scientific study of disability (see Albrecht *et al.*'s *Handbook of Disability Studies*, 2001). Fourth, 'the sociology of disability' became the core business of a new discipline in the UK from the 1980s: disability studies. Disability studies has laid claim to *some* of the earlier sociological writings on disability (see Oliver, 1990; Barnes *et al.*, 1999).

The Corpus

The publications listed below are of particular note in my proposed group-ing, but by no means constitute a complete listing, not least because only books are included. It must also be noted that this literature cannot be neatly packaged as 'sociology' because some of the titles straddle social policy and political science.

The list of UK publications includes Mildred Blaxter's *The Meaning of Disability: A Sociological Study of Impairment* (1976), Alan Walker and Peter Townsend's edited collection *Disability in Britain: A Manifesto of Rights* (1980), Eda Topliss's *Social Responses to Handicap* (1982), David Locker's *Disability and Disadvantage. The Consequences of Chronic Illness* (1983) and Gillian Dalley's edited collection *Disability and Social Policy* (1991a). Peter

Townsend's section on disability in *Poverty in the United Kingdom* (1979), discussed earlier, should also be included (see also Townsend, 1993). Gareth Williams' (1991, 1996a,b) writings on disability (as opposed to his sociology of chronic illness) should also be added to the list, together with his review of the relationship between disability studies and medical sociology (G. Williams, 2001). In my view, Gareth Williams is alone among leading British medical sociologists for his serious and sympathetic engagement with ideas in disability studies.

The list of US publications starts earlier, in the 1960s. It includes Marvin Sussman's edited collection *Sociology of Disability and Rehabilitation* (1966), Robert Scott's *The Making of Blind Men* (1969), Constantina Safilios-Rothschild's *The Sociology and Social Psychology of Disability and Rehabilitation* (1970), Robert Murphy's *The Body Silent* (1990), and Gary Albrecht's edited collection *The Sociology of Physical Disability and Rehabilitation* (1982) and his later book *The Disability Business: Rehabilitation in America* (1992) (see also Albrecht and Verbrugge, 2000; Albrecht, 2002). The US list should also feature *The Disabled State* (1984) by the political scientist, Deborah Stone, given its focus on the social construction of disability. A Canadian social scientist who demands inclusion in any North American listing is Wolf Wolfensberger (1980, 1983, 1994; Wolfensberger and Thomas, 1983); his ideas on normalisation and social role valorisation have had a considerable impact on the official policies pursued in UK services for people with learning difficulty in the last two decades. Of course, Goffman's *Stigma. Notes on the Management of a Spoiled Identity* (1968), discussed earlier in the chapter, has influenced the thinking of all of the UK and US authors listed above.

Before discussing ideas to be found in some of these sources, particular note should be made of the sociology of disability advocated by the US writer, Irving Zola. How Zola's intellectual contribution should be categorised is a matter for debate since he was both a leading medical sociologist in the interactionist tradition (Zola, 1966, 1972, 1973, 1991) and a disabled activist in the disabled people's movement (see G. Williams, 1996b). In the 1980s and 1990s, he wrote analytically, politically and autobiographically about the social position of disabled people, using the language of social oppression rather than social deviance, and insisted on the need to connect policy and politics to the realm of personal experience and narrative (Zola, 1982a,b, 1989, 1991, 1993a,b, 1994). For example, his book, *Missing Pieces: A Chronicle of Living With a Disability* (1982a), is a sociological and personal account of life in *Het Dorp*, a 65-acre village in the Netherlands specifically designed to house 400 adults with severe impairments. Zola's insistence on the importance of articulating the personal experience of impairment and disability remains a matter for debate in UK disability studies, as we shall learn in Chapters 5 and 6.

Ideas in the Nascent Sociology of Disability

This section reviews a selection of ideas to be found in the some of the sources listed above; the work of authors not included here is noted in later chapters, or has already been mentioned in this chapter. As we shall see, the authors featured below come close to associating 'being disabled' with being socially oppressed.

In their different ways, Mildred Blaxter (1976), Deborah Stone (1984) and Gary Albrecht (1992) all focused on the social construction of 'disability' as a distinct category and status, offering accounts of the effects of medical and legislative definitional acts and procedures (without the assistance of poststructuralist constructionism). Each shall be considered in turn.

Mildred Blaxter (1976) undertook a year-long interview study of 194 people of working age who had been discharged from hospital with a permanent or long-term impairment. She documented the convoluted organisational character of the health and welfare services encountered by her respondents, and the (often negative) impact of administrative definitional practices upon their lives. Her study highlighted the complexities involved in being defined 'disabled', and the frequent mismatch between individuals' needs (related to money, employment, personal care, family and social life) and service responses. Blaxter combined an interactionist commitment to understanding the daily problems faced by disabled people, articulated from their own point of view, with an interest in the socio-structural forces that shaped their lives. The influence of labelling theory is certainly evident in her account, with disability viewed through the social deviance lens. However, Blaxter was at pains to avoid portraying individuals as 'passive victims'. The people surveyed:

> [H]ave been shown as creating their own social reality, but not – especially in their particularly vulnerable situations – as completely free agents. They have been fettered and constrained not only by their social environment but also by the two major systems of society within which their lives were structured: the system of medical care and the administrative system of welfare, employment and social security. (ibid.: 246–7)

Blaxter's study also serves to illustrate a distinct feature of an emerging British medical sociology in the 1970s: a strong commitment to making research relevant to health and welfare service providers so that efficacious public responses to need could be facilitated.[2]

The creation of disability as an administrative category by welfare states is central to Deborah Stone's (1984) analysis. In her view, official definitions of disability differentially manage tensions between 'need-based' and 'work-based' systems of distributive justice. Medicine's gate-keeping certification role was identified as crucial: medicine and the state jointly construct 'the disabled' as a distinct class of persons in modern society. The state maintains this through its distributive mechanisms, relegating to extreme disadvantage those with impairment-related needs who do not qualify. The 'disabled' category 'entitles its members to particular privileges in the form of social aid and exemptions from certain obligations of citizenship' (ibid.: 4). However, the state views 'disability' as prey to falsification – hence the responsibility of medicine to certificate and police it. The state seeks to make the authorised exemption from work on the grounds of disability both difficult to obtain and tightly controlled, because people would otherwise use it as a means to shirk their responsibility to earn a living (cf. Parsons, 1951). Stone was writing in the 1980s, a time of perceived crisis in welfare expenditure in industrial societies: admission to 'the disabled state' was coming under ever closer scrutiny.

The social construction of disability is also an important theme in Gary Albrecht's sociological scholarship. As suggested by the title of his book, *The Disability Business* (1992), his focus is on the power of profit-making businesses in the US to construct disability and shape the disability experience. Albrecht's detailed analysis of the American 'rehabilitation industry' amounts to a political economy of physical impairment:

> … the present analysis of the production of disability, the construction of a social problem, and the rehabilitation institutional response will be couched in terms of American democracy, capitalism, and the government bureaucracy. (ibid.: 13)

In this and later work, Albrecht demonstrates that 'disability' is hugely profitable for the rehabilitation and pharmaceutical industries (Albrecht and Bury, 2001). Through its commodification of the social problem of impairment, the rehabilitation industry participates in the social construction of disability by determining what does and does not count as legitimate disablement. As in Stone's (1984) analysis, medicine plays a key role: classifying individuals and determining their 'eligibility'. Moreover, 'Rehabilitation programs are social devices that allow physicians to maintain control over patients even after the patients leave the traditional hospital settings' (Albrecht, 1992: 128); that is, despite purporting to promote disabled people's functional independence, complex rehabilitation institutions and programmes 'generally perpetuate dependency' (ibid.: 267). In *The Disability Business*, Albrecht goes on to argue that disabled people and their advocates are, nevertheless, beginning to exert some countervailing pressure, not least through exercising their purchasing power. He describes the development of a 'consumer identity' among disabled Americans, bound up with their 'emergent consciousness as members of a minority group' (ibid.: 271).

This interest in the responses of disabled people to the rehabilitation industry conveys something of the broad sweep of Albrecht's influential sociology of disability. Indeed, he has produced a body of research and scholarship on disability that is unmatched for volume and scope in medical sociology on either side of the Atlantic. His political economy of disability, at home in the conflict theory tradition, is combined with a track-record in interactionist research at the micro scale (Albrecht, 1982). Albrecht celebrates the development of the US disability rights and independent living movements (DeJong, 1983; Scotch, 1984), but subjects them to a sociological critique. Writing in the early 1990s, he notes that the US disability rights movement took root in a favourable legislative environment, and warns against overstating the active involvement of ordinary disabled people in political campaigning.

Moving on, we find that some of the themes discussed by Albrecht are also to be found in Wolf Wolfensberger's interest in the 'organisational dynamics' of the human service industries (1980, 1983, 1994; Wolfensberger and Thomas, 1983). Wolfensberger proposed that these industries had a latent function: to generate employment opportunities for professionals and other workers by sustaining large numbers of dependent and devalued people. This led to his interest in ideas and policies developed in the Nordic countries on the *normalisation* of people with learning difficulty. Making use of the labelling theory approach, Wolfensberger (1983) became an advocate of the principle that professionals should encourage and assist such people to achieve as 'normal' a life as possible, though this did not necessarily mean their removal from socially segregated institutions. It was argued that normalisation – later referred to as *social role valorisation* – would facilitate the social acceptance of people with learning difficulty. That is, the occupation of valued social roles was thought to offer a strategy for overcoming discrimination.

Constantina Safilios-Rothschild's (1970) *The Sociology and Social Psychology of Disability and Rehabilitation* is an interesting analysis of social and cultural responses to disability, including collective societal responses in the form of rehabilitation services, welfare legislation, and employment policies and practices. It is clearly influenced by US labelling theory and writings on stigma and deviancy, but considers social reaction mainly at the macro-social scale. Her first chapter focuses on 'discriminatory practices' and 'prejudice' and explores how these vary historically and cross-culturally. This identification of disabled people as a group subject to systematic social discrimination sets the author's tone, though this is combined with a more traditional interest in 'the problems of adjustment':

> We have seen that there are deep-seated fears and aversions in the nondisabled about most types of disabilities – visible and non-visible, stigmatized and nonstigmatized. These fears and aversions are most probably at the heart of the prejudice against the disabled who share with other minority groups similar types of discrimination and isolation. Moreover, the disabled are labeled

'deviant' by society, and under their multiple social and physical handicaps, encounter serious difficulties in adjusting to their disability. (ibid.: 130)

Such themes are echoed in David Locker's (1983) *Disability and Disadvantage. The Consequences of Chronic Illness*. Locker's study in the UK was based on repeat interviews with 24 men and women with severe rheumatoid arthritis and explored two main themes:

> The first is that disabled people are disadvantaged because chronic illness and the limitations in activity it produces result in a loss of personal, material, and social resources, and the resources that remain are almost wholly consumed in the effort of coping with the illness and its effects. The second is that the resources disabled persons can muster and the problem-solving strategies they are able to construct are factors which intervene between impairment, disability and disadvantage. (ibid.: vii)

Locker combined analysis of the subjective experience of living with illness and impairment with what disability studies researchers would think of as experiences of disablism.

We turn, finally, to Robert Murphy's *The Body Silent* (1990) – a book quite different in character. This is an autobiographical account of Murphy's worsening impairment – increasing paralysis – associated with a spinal tumour. As an academic specialising in social anthropology, Murphy decides to engage in a sociological analysis of disability, weaving together personal experiences and intellectual enquiry, touching on issues of identity, embodiment, emotion, prejudice and discrimination, stigma, sexuality and gender. He borrows from anthropological perspectives to introduce the idea that disability could best be described as a state of social 'liminality' – a state of exclusion from ordinary life and a denial of full humanity: 'a kind of social limbo in which [the disabled person] is left standing outside the formal social system' (Murphy, 1990: 131). It is of particular note that Murphy considered but rejected the deviance perspective: 'Viewing disability as a subtype of deviancy confuses many issues, leading to a theoretical dead end for social scientists' (ibid.: 130–1).

Summary: Chronic Illness and Disability as Social Deviance

This chapter has shown that the 'illness and disability as social deviance' paradigm is remarkably persistent in medical sociology, surviving the changing fashions and fortunes of diverse theoretical perspectives. Medical sociology and medicine have shared an interest in categorising and studying the 'abnormal' represented by bodily impairment – the former engaging with it socially, the latter biologically.

The explanation for this, at its simplest, may lie in Bryan Turner's (1987: 5) observation that sociology itself, contrary to standard accounts, is closely bound up with medicine:

> ... my argument considers Foucault's comment that sociology had its origins in nineteenth-century medical practices (in particular medical surveys), that sociology and medicine are inextricably linked together, and finally that modern medicine is in fact applied sociology, and sociology is applied medicine.

Whatever the merits of this argument, and that is for others to debate, the longstanding social deviancy conceptualisation of chronic illness and disability can be seen as a mirror image of modern medicine's 'abnormality' and 'pathology' understanding of disease and impairment. From a post-structuralist vantage point, it would not be difficult to see medical sociology and medical science as intertwined grand narratives – each dissecting abnormality and deviancy, both bound up with the post-Enlightenment preoccupation with the normal and the abnormal.

This chapter has also shown, however, that care must be taken to distinguish between the ideas about illness as deviance associated with different theoretical traditions in medical sociology, and to recognise the contrasting moral and political stances taken by their advocates (whatever claims might be made to 'neutrality' or 'value-freedom'). Many medical sociologists have advanced ideas that are medico-centric and normative in character, but *some* writers have taken 'the side' of those constituted 'deviant' and come close to adopting a social oppression perspective. Moreover, careful attention to detail has uncovered an important seam of work by medical sociologists that suggests the existence of a nascent *sociology of disability*. That is, there is a body of work that has considered the social construction of disability in macro-social terms, but this did not coalesce or gather force in medical sociology. This has meant that writers in disability studies have been able to claim *some* of medical sociology's research, ideas and authors for their own discipline (see Oliver, 1990, and Barnes *et al.*, 1999, 2002).

From the point of view of disabled people and individuals living with chronic illness, very different replies would be forthcoming in answer to a question they are entitled to pose to medical sociologists: whose side are you on? Structural functionalism in the Parsonian mould offered a sociology that served the social system, in the face of all forms of deviance. Both acute and chronic illness were understood to pose a serious destabilising threat to society, a type of social pathology that should rightly be controlled and regulated by the medical profession. Indeed, in Parsonian thinking, the unconscious motivations of people to opt out of their social responsibilities by claiming to be seriously ill should be kept continually in check – if not by individuals' own superegos then by stronger external social forces.

Sociologists in the US who developed a symbolic interactionist interpretation of social deviance also included chronic illness and disability in their inventory of social problems. But in a radical move, the labelling theorists turned a critical sociological lens upon the *social reactions* that designated the 'deviant' status of particular behaviours and attributes. They recorded the degrading and dehumanising consequences for people labelled 'mentally ill' or 'physically abnormal', through detailed studies of the day-to-day lives of 'outsiders'. Interest was focused on how the world was experienced from the point of view of the 'underdogs'. In Britain, a less hard-edged version of interactionist theory laid the foundations for an influential interpretative *sociology of chronic illness and disability*, whose advocates display, in the main, a genuine interest in understanding and improving the lives of 'sufferers' and their families. Many also draw upon phenomenological and ethnomethodological perspectives to capture the *meaning* of living with chronic illness and disability. However, I have noted that Garfinkel and subsequent ethnomethodologists have not adopted a radical or supportive political stance towards 'the chronically ill and disabled' but have merely observed their 'social degradation'.

In contrast, the school of 'conflict theorists' in medical sociology – a loose mix of Marxists, political economists, critical social epidemiologists, feminists, critical realists and others – has unequivocally sided with the victims of inequality against the prevailing power of the capitalist state and its institutions. The damaging effects and injustices wrought by medicine have exercised the minds of some, while the social causes of disease and related disadvantage has occupied centre-stage for others. The plight of the chronically ill and disabled has been addressed in a variety of ways, but always through macro-sociological frames of reference. Interestingly, the illness as deviance theme is at its most muted in the conflict theory tradition. Rather, deviance (real or attributed) resides not in individuals but in the social structure. These observations are also true for many of the writers whose work I have grouped in 'the sociology of disability' category.

This brings us, finally, to the ideas of poststructuralists writers, and to Foucault's work and influence. Alongside criminality, illness has assumed pride of place in a philosophically driven sociology focused on the discursive construction and regulation of social deviance; deviance comes to the fore once again. Indeed, in the age of bio-power, medical discursive practices define normality and abnormality, and exert a supreme disciplinary and regulatory force upon 'the body'. But despite the *implication* that people with chronic illness and disability must bear a particularly heavy burden of regulatory social technologies and practices, medical sociologists in this tradition have almost entirely ignored the disability theme. Whatever the 'radical' moral pretensions of poststructuralist medical sociology and its championing of 'the sociology of the body', a theme discussed in detail in Chapter 5, it has been left to scholars in disability studies to take up the poststructuralist challenge.

3

Theories and Traditions in Disability Studies: Disability as Social Oppression

Introduction

Disability studies in the UK is built upon the idea that disability involves the social oppression of people whose impairments mark them out, or are discursively constructed as marking them out, as 'different'. Alongside sexism, racism, ageism and homophobia, disablism has been added to the catalogue of forms of social oppression. This contrasts with medical sociology, a discipline that has made social deviance the conceptual axis around which understandings of chronic illness and disability have been articulated.

If individual writers in disability studies do not make use of the term 'oppression', their starting point is nonetheless that disabled people are systematically disadvantaged, marginalised and excluded in society. Academics and activists in the UK who align themselves with disability studies, a discipline newly formed in the 1980s, have coalesced around *the social model of disability* (whether they argue in favour of it, or against), and share a strong personal and public commitment to advancing the civil rights and social interests of disabled people. Their moral and political stance is explicit: disablism, in all its forms, is condemned and opposed. Many writers and researchers in disability studies have first-hand experience of living with impairment and disablism.

The purpose of this chapter is to examine the theoretical traditions and key ideas that inform disability studies in the UK. Though multi-disciplinary in character, disability studies is heavily influenced by perspectives in sociology. Theoretically minded activists and academics have used sociological ideas to build a distinct and radical sociology of disability, sometimes through critical engagements with analyses of disability to be found in mainstream sociology, medical sociology or mainstream feminism (Finkelstein, 1980; Abberley, 1987; Barnes and Mercer, 1996; Barton, 1996a; Morris, 1996; Oliver, 1990, 1996c; Barnes *et al.*, 1999; 2002; Thomas, 1999). Indeed, the development of a new sociology of disability has been an explicit goal of some leaders in the field (Oliver, 1990, 1996a; Barton, 1996a; Barnes *et al.*, 1999, 2002). This chapter does not deal, however, with the detail of disagreement and argument between writers in disability studies and medical sociology. Disciplinary exchanges are covered in the five *episodes* of debate examined in Chapters 4 and 6, and in discussion about 'the body' in Chapter 5. The focus here is on the substance of ideas about disability and disablism that disability studies' writers have developed and make use of.

As might be expected of a younger and rapidly growing discipline, one motivated by a desire to advance the social interests of disabled people, the theoretical perspectives with greatest appeal are those considered most radical and socially progressive. Individual thinkers have turned, in particular, to Marxism and materialism, and to varieties of feminism and poststructuralism. The point of departure in this chapter is not, therefore, structural functionalism or interactionism, but Marxist and materialist variants of what mainstream and medical sociologists refer to as conflict theories, followed by reviews of post-structuralist disability theory. The discussion then turns to theoretical engagements with a number of important themes: the nature oppression, 'difference' and identity. Not surprisingly, writers in disability studies have engaged with some long-standing mainstream sociological and feminist debates in a condensed fashion, and this chapter inevitably has a much stronger flavour of ideas *in the making*.

Readers are reminded that the account of theoretical traditions and key ideas offered here is necessarily informed by my own materialist feminist orientation and involvement in the disability studies (Thomas, 1999). Moreover, those looking for a straightforward account of the social model of disability, or for a review of the history of the disabled people's movement, must refer to other sources (see, for example, Campbell and Oliver, 1996; Oliver, 1996a; Goodley, 2000; Fleischer and Zames, 2001; Swain *et al.*, 2003, 2004; Oliver and Sapey, 2005).

Where does chronic illness fit in? As outlined in Chapter 1, I treat chronic illness (or chronic disease) as a category of impairment in this book. As people with impairment, those living with declared or readily apparent characteristics of chronic illnesses share in forms of social exclusion and disadvantage experienced by those whose impairments have other qualities and features. That is, people with chronic illness are exposed to disablism – whether or not they self-identify as 'disabled'.

Materialist and Marxist Perspectives

A Social Interpretation of Disability

Conceptualising disability as a *social* phenomenon in UK disability studies does not have its origins in ideas thought up in university libraries or academic offices. On the contrary, the starting point is located in the daily life-struggles of disabled people in the 1960s, and in disabled individuals' oppositional encounters with a number of social scientists in the early days of political self-organisation (see *episode* 1 in Chapter 4). These distinctive origins of British disability studies, and the discipline's continued celebration of its links with campaigning organisations governed by disabled people, lie at the root of its current separation from medical sociology – the latter being a discipline born and nurtured in the academy.

These disciplinary origins involved the development of an innovative social interpretation of disability in the 1960s and 1970s by some highly motivated disabled people, many of whom lived extremely socially restricted and highly regulated lives in residential establishments (see Campbell and Oliver, 1996). They knew that fresh and radical ideas were called for, and were untrammelled by having been educated and trained in particular theoretical traditions in sociology or other academic disciplines. Indeed, the key thinkers of the day often had little formal education, and only one another upon whom to try out ideas. Given the times, the circumstances, and the personal biographies involved, it is perhaps not surprising that leading figures turned to Marxism for ideas and inspiration.

Paul Hunt was one of these innovators. In 1966, Hunt published *Stigma The Experience of Disability*, an edited collection of 12 essays written by disabled people. *Stigma* offers an insight into 'being disabled' in a decade that saw the stirrings of political consciousness and new forms of self-organisation among disabled people in the UK. It signalled the awakening desire to formulate a social understanding of disability in the face of the overpowering medical and professional control of disabled peoples' lives. Many in the British disabled people's movement today regard Paul Hunt, a wheelchair user with muscular dystrophy who lived out most of his life in residential care homes, as its founder (Campbell and Oliver, 1996). Hunt wrote the following in his own essay:

> Disabled people often meet prejudice, which expresses itself in discrimination and even *oppression*. ... Maybe it is invidious to compare our situation with that of racial minorities in any way. The injustice and brutality suffered by so many because of racial tension makes our troubles as disabled people look very small. But I think there is a connection somewhere, since all prejudice springs from the same roots. (1966: 152–3)

This statement tells us that looking for parallels between the social position of disabled people and other oppressed groups was at the core of attempts to develop a radical social interpretation of disability in the UK.

This search for a social understanding of disability matured in the years that followed, and 1976 saw the publication of a document entitled *The Fundamental Principles of Disability* by an organisation formed four years earlier by Paul Hunt, Vic Finkelstein and other like-minded disabled people: The Union of the Physically Impaired Against Segregation (UPIAS). In *Fundamental Principles*, disability was *redefined* by drawing a clear line between impairment and disability such that impairment was no longer *the cause* of disability. This held the potential for a *social relational* conception of disability to develop, that is, the idea that disability is a phenomenon brought into being in and through social relationships – at both structural and interpersonal levels:

> Thus we define impairment as lacking part or all of a limb, or having a defective limb, organ or mechanism of the body; and disability as the disadvantage or restriction of activity caused by a contemporary social organisation which takes no or little account of people who have physical impairments and thus excludes them from participation in the mainstream of social activities. Physical disability is therefore a particular form of social oppression. (UPIAS and TDA, 1976: 14)

With Hunt's early death, Vic Finkelstein, a wheelchair user who had moved to the UK in 1968 as a political exile from South Africa following his imprisonment and banishment for opposition to apartheid, continued to champion the oppression perspective, and viewed Marxism as offering the necessary political and theoretical tools. Looking back, Finkelstein (2001a: 5) recounts how disabled people were faced with a stark choice: 'you see disability fundamentally as a personal tragedy or you see it as a form of social oppression'. Finkelstein and his co-thinkers argued that non-impaired members of society and their social institutions oppress people with impairments in many ways: by excluding them from employment and the educational mainstream, by relegating them, as 'dependants', to residential care (and often to the openly repressive exercise of power and control by staff), by blocking their access to the built environment, and by ensuring their poverty through the inadequate provision of welfare benefits:

> Disability is something imposed on top of our impairments by the way we are unnecessarily isolated and excluded from full participation in society. (UPIAS, *Fundamental Principles of Disability*, cited in Finkelstein, 2001b: 1)

This meant that disabled people's political struggle should be directed towards changing society and winning control over their own lives (see also

Sutherland, 1981): it was a question of revolution rather than reform, or in Finkelstein's terms, a question of an emancipatory strategy rather than a compensatory' one. The ideas of Finkelstein and his fellow activists found their way into the academy when Finkelstein joined The Open University to work on the 'Handicapped Person in the Community' course, setting the seed that grew into disability studies (Campbell and Oliver, 1996: 6–7).

The Materialist Roots of Oppression

What are the social mechanisms involved in the social isolation and exclusion of disabled people? How does 'society' act as an oppressive disabling force? Finkelstein and Hunt did not produce a full theorisation of this, though that had been their intention.[1] In Finkelstein's *Attitudes and Disabled People* (1980), we can nonetheless discern the general direction of their theoretical path: towards a materialist analysis of the ways in which the social oppression of disabled people is fundamentally bound up with the social relations of production in capitalist society.

In *Attitudes*, Finkelstein (1980) introduced the idea that the social relationships embedded in 'disability', as opposed to impairment, arise as a product of the material conditions of life at a particular socio-historical juncture. This challenged prevailing ideas concerning the transhistorical or universal character of disability. A series of three historical phases in Britain (since the 1600s) was sketched out. Phase 1 preceded the establishment of large-scale industry and was marked by the inclusion of 'cripples' as one group among many in the lower orders of the social hierarchy, alongside 'beggars' and the poor. Phase 2 came about through the establishment of large-scale industrial production 'geared to able-bodied norms' (ibid.: 7; see also Ryan and Thomas, 1980). This nineteenth- and twentieth-century phase is characterised by the segregation of people with impairment from their communities with the growth of hospital-based medicine and the creation of large asylums, that is, their institutionalisation and construction as passive, needy, dependent dis-abled people. Contemporary social attitudes towards disabled people, and their grouping as an administrative category, stem from this era. Phase 3, a period only just beginning in the last quarter of the twentieth century, is one in which 'new electronic technology' (ibid.: 8) could enable the most severely physically impaired people to live independently in the community. This held out the hope that attitudes could be transformed, and the social oppression of disabled people overcome.

Michael Oliver (1990), perhaps the best-known figure in UK disability studies, advanced this materialist line of argument in his writings on the economic, political, cultural and spatial mechanisms that generated disability during the transition from feudalism to capitalism in the West. In

The Politics of Disability (1990), a founding disability studies text, Oliver elaborated Finkelstein's three phase sketch, suggesting that the development of disability should be rooted in an account of changes in the mode of production and in the associated 'mode of thought' – the latter involving the individualisation and pathologising of impairment by medicine and the encouragement of a 'personal tragedy' perspective. His argument made use of Marxist political economy in its analysis of the exclusion of people with impairment from capitalist production.

More recently, the Australian geographer, Brenan Gleeson, set out to provide a sophisticated and empirically grounded account of the origins of disability in Western societies, building on Oliver's insights. In *Geographies of Disability* (1999), Gleeson researched the realities of life for people with physical impairments in feudal England and in selected industrial cities in Australia and the UK, making use of what he termed an 'embodied historical-geographical materialism'. In brief outline, Gleeson proposed that 'disability' is produced through 'the socialisation of impairment' (ibid.: 31), something that varies in time and place. He interprets Marx's account of nature and the human body to mean that 'the individual body is socialised through a lifetime of encounter between the subject's organic physiology and his/her experiences of production and reproduction' (ibid.: 37). In feudal England:

> the structures of peasant existence did not expose any material reason why impaired family members could not have remained *in situ*, contributing to their household's sustenance ... . In feudalism, the impaired peasant body was, to a significant degree, an autonomous creator of social space. Disablement, as the antithesis of this power for self-creation, was not an attribute of the material structures surrounding, and underpinning, peasant life. (Gleeson, 1999: 97)

The spread of capitalist relations of commodity production and exchange, and especially the rise of factory production, involved the 'repression of certain forms of social embodiment' (ibid.: 39). The fate of many people with impairments (physical, sensory, cognitive or psychological) was sealed by a combination of developments: the wholesale uprooting of people from agricultural settings and their relocation in over-crowded and unsanitary urban centres, the enforced attendance of labourers for long hours at the workplace and the setting of minimum standards for levels of dexterity and speed of work. The outcome was that people with impairments were unable to sell their labour-power on equal terms. This created the conditions for their devaluation and removal from the community, in short, the emergence of a social differentiation that we now understand as 'being disabled'.

Displacement forces were sourced in three socio-spatial nodes: centrifugal pressures emerging from the home and workplace (especially the factory); and the centripetal pull of the institution. (ibid.: 125)

The institutionalisation of people whose social utility was discounted was the state-sponsored response, one that persisted long into the twentieth century. Medical science set about distinguishing categories among the 'abnormal' – to be collectivised in the course of the twentieth century into broad groupings such as 'the mentally ill' and 'the physically disabled'. Individuals who resisted nineteenth-century institutionalisation and took to the streets as traders or beggars felt the full force of social disapproval of their 'abject bodies' (Gleeson, 1999). Together, proletarianisation and urbanisation created oppressive socio-spatial conditions for physically impaired people. As a consequence, disablement is now 'deeply inscribed in the discursive, institutional and material dimensions of cities' (ibid.: 11).

In my view, the materialist theorisation of the transformations wrought by the transition from feudalism to capitalism by Finkelstein, Oliver and Gleeson has certainly offered a powerful means of understanding the historically and temporarily bounded nature of 'disability', and the social conditions that gave rise to, and continue to shape, disablism as a modern form of social oppression. However, this line of thinking and research remains underdeveloped. For example, very little attention has thus far been paid to themes such as gender and age; what were the consequences of these social transformations for women with impairments, and how do these social forces play out in contemporary society? Such questions remain largely unanswered.

Prospects for Liberation: Can Impairment Be Set Aside?

If being impaired constitutes the grounds for a specific form of social oppression in industrial capitalism, what do materialist and Marxist writers tell us about the prospects for the eradication of disablism? Looking to the future, the message *appears* to be that the full engagement of people with impairment in the economic sphere – in employment and labour – will bring an end to their social oppression. Surely this is the logical sequelae of the materialist analysis? This is a question considered in some detail by the late Paul Abberley (1996, 1997, 2002). While Abberley acknowledges that it is 'perfectly correct and necessary to explore and document the socio-economic determinants of the disablement of impaired persons' (1996: 68), he finds fault with what he calls its 'utopian' implications for the liberation of disabled people. In his view, the problem lies with the centrality placed upon participation in work as the criterion for social membership and citizenship:

> For Marxism, then, there is an identification of who you are with the work you do which transcend capitalism and socialism and enters the concrete Utopia of the future to constitute a key element of humanity, and a key need of human beings in all eras. (ibid.: 69)

Indeed, Abberley points out that this work-based model of social membership and identity is to be found in national and European social policies in the 2000s, policies designed to encourage the social inclusion of disabled people. More worryingly, it is a perspective on social membership '… integrally linked to the prevention/cure oriented perspective of allopathic medicine and to the specific instrumental logic of genetic engineering, abortion and euthanasia' (Abberley, 2002: 135).

In Abberley's view, the nature of impairment means that some people will never be able to participate in work, whatever socio-economic arrangements are in place. Even if the vast majority of people with impairment were absorbed into the workforce, there would always remain a residual non-employed group with severe impairment. Indeed the oppression of this remainder would probably intensify (Abberley, 1996: 71). The failure of materialists such as Finkelstein to recognise this is attributed, in part, to their lack of engagement with impairment *per se* (discussed in detail in Chapter 5). Although Abberley fully acknowledged the political significance of the severing of the causal link between impairment and disability in the UPIAS *Fundamental Principles* (1976), and the corresponding setting aside of impairment, he saw in this the danger of setting up false hopes for liberation. Rather than being ignored, or reduced to 'mere difference', impairment itself should be fully socially theorised:

> I wish to argue that we must talk more about impairment at the level of *theory* if we are to make sense of disability, since impairment is the material substratum upon which the oppressive social structures of disablement are erected (Abberley, 1996: 63, emphasis in the original)

Building on his earlier arguments, Abberley suggested that this would uncover the ways in which impairment makes the social oppression of disabled people distinct when compared with women, people from minority ethnic groups or other excluded groups (Abberley, 1987). Abberley looked to mainstream feminist thinkers such as Patricia Hill Collins (1990) for alternative theoretical perspectives on the nature of the social oppression of disabled people, since many feminists reject the male' work-based model of social membership and human identity. He also found favour with Honneth's (1995) ideas on the importance of securing access to the social conditions that make possible both identity formation and self-realisation as an autonomous individual (Abberley, 2002). Though not claiming to have found the answers, Abberley argued consistently for the development of theoretical perspectives on impairment and disability that have the potential, on the political plane, to unite *all* impaired people.

The Social Model of Disability

It is helpful to introduce the social model of disability at this point, the offspring of materialist ideas about disability advanced by Hunt and Finkelstein (Thomas, 2004a). In the 1980s, Michael Oliver (1983) talked about *social* as opposed to *individual* models of disability. He argued that the individual model is underpinned by a 'personal tragedy theory' of disability, and involves the medicalisation and concomitant individualising of the effects of living with impairment (Oliver, 1983). Medical sociologists are among those accused of working with versions of individual or medical models of disability (Oliver, 1996c).

In *Understanding Disability* (1996a), Oliver tells us that the social model formulation originated in his attempts, in the early 1980s, to explain to his students UPIAS's severing of the causal link between impairment and disability: it offered an easily accessible explanatory device. The social model asserts that disability is not caused by impairment but results from the social restrictions imposed upon people with impairment: '... ranging from individual prejudice to institutional discrimination, from inaccessible public buildings to unusable transport systems, from segregated education to excluding work arrangements, and so on' (Oliver, 1996a: 33). This has become known, in shorthand, as the 'social barriers' approach to the restricted activity experienced by people with impairment, the basis of their social oppression.

In the 1980s, the social model of disability quickly assumed a status of enormous significance in disability studies and the disabled people's movement in the UK (its 'big idea'), and disability activists and scholars overseas came to associate 'the British approach' with the social model. Disabled people and their organisations in the UK, most notably the British Council of Disabled People, recognised the social model's 'immediate connection to their own experiences' (Oliver, 1996a: 31) and utility in Disability Awareness Training, as did international groupings such as *Disabled People's International* (and *Disability Awareness in Action* today).

The importance of the social model of disability is that, as a model providing an alternative understanding of the experience and reality of disability, it has given disabled people a basis on which to organise themselves collectively. Using the social model as a basis for explanation, disabled people have been drawing attention to the real problems of disability: the barriers they face; the patronizing attitude they have to deal with; the low expectations that are invested in them; and the limits available to them. (Swain *et al.*, 2003: 24)

There is no doubt that the social model has also played an important role in shaping current policies pursued by major Charities, Government departments, and official agencies such as the *Disability Rights Commission*, in the UK. Indeed, Oliver (2004: 22) has recently commented – with mixed feelings – about the social model being 'colonised by a range of organisations, interests and individuals, some of whom had bitterly opposed its appearance less than ten years previously'.

But this is not to say that the model is uncontested. On the contrary, there has been a long and lively debate about the model's conceptual and practical utility, both within disability studies and disability politics. As will become clear later in this chapter, there have been calls, in several quarters, for its rejection or revision. Critics frequently conflate the model's purported failings with the perceived limitations of materialist or Marxist thinking (for both attacks and replies see Morris, 1991; French, 1993; Crow, 1996; Oliver, 1996a, 2004; Oliver and Barnes, 1998; Thomas, 1999, 2004a,b; Shakespeare and Watson, 2001; Corker and Shakespeare, 2002a; Swain *et al.*, 2003).

It is tempting, at this point, to get further drawn into the minutiae of debate about the social model, but to do so would run counter to the principle purpose of this chapter: to outline the theoretical traditions that inform UK thinkers in disability studies. It is important to remember Oliver's caution: 'the social model of disability is [...] not a substitute for social theory, a materialist history of disability nor an explanation of the welfare state' (Oliver, 1996a: 41). However, in Finkelstein's (2001a: 6) words 'Sadly a lot of people have come to think of the social model of disability as if it were an explanation, definition or theory, and many people use the model in a rather sterile formalistic way'.

Disablism Today: The Materialist Legacy

Materialist and Marxist perspectives have provided a theoretical framework and impetus for studies of disablism in contemporary societies; indeed, these would be of very limited value were it otherwise. Of course enormous social changes have taken place over the course of the last two centuries in late capitalist societies, transforming life in important ways, for everyone. Yet, from a materialist point of view, the drive to accumulate capital continues to direct the economy, and to shape cultural and political institutions, ideologies and practices. Change and continuity are companion themes. For example, although disabled people have witnessed the dismantling of systems of 'care' based on the large-scale residential institutional model, a huge army of 'health and welfare' professionals continue to exercise significant power and control in disabled individuals' lives (discussed below and in Chapter 4).

What, then, has changed and what remains the same in the fortunes of disabled people? The discipline's materialist founders have encouraged today's researchers to break with 'official' disability classifications and research schemas like the WHO's ICIDH, and to turn their attention to the social mechanisms involved in the exclusion and marginalisation of people with impairment in a wide range of social arenas in contemporary society. These include, for example: employment (Barnes, 1991; Roulstone, 1998, 2000; French, 2001); education (Riddell, 1996; Corbett, 1998; Barton and Slee, 1999; Swain *et al.*, 2003; Armstrong and Moore, 2004); housing (Stewart *et al.*, 1997); health care, 'community care' and independent living (Morris, 1993a, 2004; Zarb and Nadash, 1994; Priestley, 1999; Swain *et al.*, 2003; Finkelstein, 2004; Sapey *et al.*, 2005) travel, transport and the urban environment (Imrie, 1996; Gleeson, 1999); family, household, childhood and childbirth (Thomas, 1997; Robinson and Stalker, 1998; Davis and Watson, 2001; Priestley, 2003); and the media and other arenas of cultural representation (Hevey, 1992; Darke, 2004; Wilde, 2004).

Of course, only a small minority of the authors just cited would characterise themselves as materialists. Nevertheless, given the lineage of the social model, it is the case that this engagement with a wide range of disabling social barriers is heavily informed by the materialist tradition in British disability studies. The composite picture painted by this and related research draws attention to the changing social position of groups among people living with impairment, whether these are distinguished by gender, 'race', sexuality, age, impairment type or social class. Some groups have fared better than others in recent decades, but, overall, people with impairments continue to experience inequality, disadvantage and exclusion when compared with their non-disabled counterparts.

Disability studies scholars in other countries have undertaken similar studies, uncovering the multiplicity of social restrictions imposed upon people with impairment (see, especially, Charlton, 1998). Just a glance at recent volumes of the international journal *Disability & Society* gives a clear indication that the British materialist tradition resonates with many scholars in North America (see *Disability Studies Quarterly*), the Nordic countries (see the *Scandinavian Journal of Disability Research*), Australia, New Zealand, Japan, and elsewhere. And in a development much to be welcomed, British disability studies scholars have extended their attention beyond their shores (E. Stone, 1999; Priestley, 2001; Holden and Beresford, 2002; Thomas, 2004a).

Critics of Marxism, and of its historical materialist philosophical under-pinnings, often charge it with crude economic determinism. It is no surprise, therefore, that writers who favour a materialist approach are keen to complement *the economic* with *the cultural* in their analyses of disability (see, for example, Oliver, 1990; Barnes, 1996; Gleeson, 1999; Barnes and Mercer, 2001). Consciousness, ideology and other forms of cultural expres-sion are viewed as social 'products' that come to exert an independent social force. And in response to feminist criticism (Morris, 1991, 1993b), topics such as reproduction and domestic life, together with 'the experiential' in general, are now acknowledged to be important themes with which to engage (Gleeson, 1999; Thomas, 1999; Priestley, 2003). My own materialist feminist analyses (Thomas, 1997, 1999, 2004b) fit into the debates on these and related questions.

The materialist argument that disability and disablism are historically and spatially determined rather than transhistorical and universal in character has found support in anthropological and cross-cultural studies. Such studies have highlighted the very different cultural attitudes and social positioning (both positive and negative) associated with bodily and behavioural 'difference' in traditional non-Western and pre-capitalist societies (Haffter, 1968; Sheer and Groce, 1988; Connors and Donnellan, 1993; Ingstad and Reynolds-White, 1995; Braddock and Parish, 2001; Hubert, 2001; Ingstad, 2001). Studies examining the history of 'alternative' communities set up by disabled people and those identifying as 'Deaf' also lend support to the materialist argument. One well-known example is Nora Groce's *Everyone Here Spoke Sign Language* (1985) – a study of a community of deaf and hearing people in Martha's Vineyard in Massachusetts. The community contained a high proportion of people with congenital deafness, one in which deaf and hearing people used both sign and spoken languages as a norm. Such studies show that disablism does not thrive in social contexts where people with impairments are attributed value and purpose (see also Padden and Humphries, 1988, and L. Davis, 1995).

The Critique of Professional Dominance and State Welfarism

One of the most important themes in the study of disablism from a materialist perspective – or at least in the name of the social model of disability – is the control that health and social care professionals exercise in the daily lives and destinies of adults and children with impairments and 'mental illness', a theme discussed at length in Chapter 4.

It is argued that principal among professionals who exercise control are octors – located at the apex of a professional hierarchy that includes ccupational therapists, physiotherapists, social workers, and teachers and sychologists in the 'special needs' sector of education. Many other rofessions and 'specialisms' are involved (Finkelstein, 1980, 1981; Barnes, 990; Oliver, 1990, 1996a; French, 1994; Abberley, 1995; Beresford, 2000, 002; Swain *et al.*, 2003; Oliver and Sapey, 2005). If 'cure' fails or is not an ption then medicine turns its attention to directing rehabilitation services a an attempt to maximise physical and psychological functioning, and/or facilitate the prosthetic disguise of impairments. In addition, medicine llocates a proportion of its expertise to legitimising the assessment of the ong-term 'care needs' of disabled people by a range of PAMs (Professionals .llied to Medicine) and social workers (French and Swain, 2001). However, inkelstein (1991) views the medicalisation of disability as only one aspect f the overarching state 'administrative' control of disabled people's lives. le summarised the tremendous growth in the number and social power of rofessionals and care workers in the twentieth century as follows:

> Since [1900] the number of workers, professional and lay, in industrial societies who work in the field of disability has increased enormously. Almost every aspect of the life of a person who is disabled has its counterpart in a profession or voluntary organisation. Potential and real control over the life of a disabled individual is a modern fact. This has resulted in the attitude that the disabled individual is obviously particularly dependent upon others for help. The growth of professional expertise in the field has also meant that these helpers have had an almost absolute monopoly in defining and articulating the problems of disability to the public at large. (Finkelstein, 1980: 1)

From a materialist perspective, this professional dominance is a conse- uence of the exclusion of the majority of people with impairments from ne labour-force with the rise of industrial capitalism. In nineteenth- and ventieth-century Britain, this economically surplus and problematic pop- lation was segregated from the social mainstream through their removal charitable and state-sponsored institutions ('homes', hospitals, 'special hools'), run by a burgeoning class of 'carers' and professionals. This had least two important effects on a societal scale. First, for two centuries cial structures and behaviours in towns and rural communities eveloped with only the 'normal', 'able-bodied', person in view. This shaped nd consolidated a material environment and set of mainstream social insti- itional arrangements fit only for the non-disabled (Gleeson, 1999). Second, ealth and welfare professionals became key social forces in promulgating nd sustaining the ideological mantra that people with impairments are *pendent* individuals, that is, people 'in need' who can only 'take from'

rather than 'give to' society, and whose individual disadvantage is directl
attributable to impairment. Such ideas quickly became culturall
normative. Indeed, 'these ideologies are so deeply embedded in socia
consciousness generally that they have become naturalised 'facts' (Olive
1990: 80). Charities *for* disabled people have fed off this construction o
disabled people, using 'pity' as their fund-raising motif. Dependency o
professionals and state welfare has been the structured result (Drake, 2001
However, K. Davis (1994) and Oliver (1990), among others, have pointe
out that professionals and care workers are really the true dependants: thei
jobs, incomes and careers depend on disabled people.

From this materialist perspective on the social construction of dependenc
it is not at all surprising that many disabled children and adults continue t
view themselves as a burden upon others; their self-identity is frequentl
infused with a sense of purposelessness, worthlessness and self-blam
(Oliver, 1990). Nevertheless, Chapter 4 will show that the struggle wage
by disabled people's movements for *independent living* has met with
remarkable degree of success in the last two decades; and it is now a polic
requirement that UK state authorities and professional groups take accoun
of the views of disabled people.

Combining Theoretical Perspectives

Some materialist thinkers in UK disability studies now find it useful t
advance a more theoretically eclectic approach. A useful example is Mar
Priestley's (2003) adoption of the sociological 'life course' perspective, on
that uses a range of theoretical perspectives to bring together both struc
tural and cultural themes. In *Disability: A Life Course Approach* (2003), h
considers disabled lives through a generational lens, moving from 'wom
to tomb'. This framework offers a fresh way of bringing contemporar
debates and controversies into focus – from the genetic screening o
embryos to prevent 'abnormal births' to the ethical dilemmas bound up i
physician-assisted suicide. Priestley's approach uncovers the ways i
which disabled people share a marginal and dependent social status wit
other social groups designated a 'non-adult' (infants, children, teenager
'the frail elderly'), and directs attention to groups relatively neglected i
disability studies – disabled children, young adults and older adults.

Priestley suggests that both society's generational system *and* disability
disablism can be thought of as products of modernity – that is, of a socia
epoch that has given centrality to adult work and employment (ibid.: 196
However, 'modernist life course trajectories' – structured around class, ge
der and age – are now being undermined by the *individuation* characteristi
of post-modern societies, and the foregrounding of matters of *consumptio*

ather than production (ibid.: 197). This may enable some disabled people to challenge disablism, and to move closer to full social participation and equality. However, he warns that these same developments may simultaneously serve to deepen the exclusion of disabled children and older people.

Poststructuralist Perspectives in Disability Studies

The Cultural Construction of Disability

The influence of poststructuralist perspectives in the social sciences and humanities has been echoed in debates in UK disability studies in recent years. This influence is much deeper and of longer standing in North American disability studies, most notably among writers in the humanities – a wing of disability studies that has, as yet, no counterpart in British universities (see Wendell, 1989, 1996; L. Davis, 1995, 2002a; Garland-Thomson, 1996, 1997a, 2005; Linton, 1998a,b; Rioux and Bach, 1994; Mitchell and Snyder, 2000; Breckenridge and Volger, 2001; Snyder *et al.*, 2002; Meekosha, 2004). The previous chapter outlined some of the defining features of poststructuralist thinking, and reviewed the considerable impact that its Foucauldian variant has had on medical sociology in the UK; readers are referred to that discussion for background information. What have these constructionist perspectives added in understanding disability and impairment in disability studies? The consideration of this question in this section draws upon ideas in both British and North American scholarship.

A shift from a focus on materialist to poststructuralist thinking in disability studies involves a move away from an approach which accords central theoretical significance to the economic (albeit with full acknowledgement of the importance of the cultural domain). Attention now concentrates almost entirely on culture, language and discourse, albeit with acknowledgement of the significance of economic factors. The ideas of Michel Foucault (1965, 1973, 1977) have been extremely influential (Tremain, 2005). Many of the poststructuralist writers in disability studies who feature below would also characterise themselves as feminist, and frequent use is made of themes in postmodernist feminism(s) introduced by Judith Butler (1993) and Donna Haraway (1991). 'Queer theory' (Seidman, 1996) is a related source of inspiration.

From a poststructuralist perspective, the Marxist attempt to uncover 'the roots' of disablism in the political-economy of the capitalist mode of production is rejected as an example of modernist meta-narrative. In contrast, the social exclusion or oppression of people designated 'disabled' and 'impaired' is understood to be an effect of new forms of power – bio-power (or bio-politics), to use Foucault's terminology. Disability is a *constructed* category in the sense that it comprises a set of social meanings woven together within and across powerful scientific discourses and the popular 'imaginary' (Lacan, 1977). The task of disability studies theorists, it is argued is to deconstruct these dominant social discourses and cultural representations, whether medical, academic, literary or popular.

Mairian Corker[2] and Tom Shakespeare's *Disability/Postmodernity Embodying Disability Theory*, published in 2002, brought together an international collection of essays. This was followed, in North America, by Shelley Tremain's *Foucault and the Government of Disability* (2005). The appearance of these texts underlines the arrival of 'strong' constructionis perspectives in disability studies, and offers a contrasting set of ideas about disability to those found in the well-established materialist tradition, with its 'social model' flagship. Derrida, Foucault, Baudrillard and other poststructuralist theorists are turned to for new ways of understanding disability and the social oppression of 'disabled people'. However, as is characteristic of approaches that foreground 'difference' and refuse essentialism we are not dealing here with a single approach – a 'postmodernist disability studies' – because authors in this genre generally resist labels that shoehorn them into singular theoretical categories. Nevertheless, opposition to the dominance of materialist ideas in UK disability studies, with its purported rejection of the value of poststructuralist insights, does constitute common ground, as does the assertion that poststructuralism can bring much needed theoretical ballast to the developing discipline:

> In British disability studies, 'postmodernism' has become a dumping ground for anything and everything that appears to challenge the orthodoxy of neo Marxism, historical materialism and the social model. The assumption of this volume is that this failure to engage with post-structuralist and postmod ernist thought is to the detriment of disability studies. (Corker and Shakespeare 2002b: 13)

Corker and Shakespeare acknowledge, however, that the movement into the terrain of poststructuralist theorising does bring with it complex ideas which are difficult to express in a straightforward and accessible fashion and recognise that this may create tensions between disability academics and grass-roots activists. They see this as an unavoidable necessity, and a considerable challenge.

What's in a Name?

Writers influenced by poststructuralist ideas in disability studies have written a great deal about the everyday and scientific terminology used to define and categorise 'disabled people', and the role that language plays in sustaining disablism (or *ableism* as it is termed in North American disability studies) (Linton, 1998b). Indeed, the political power bound up with naming' and the control of terminology and language has been of fundamental importance to disability rights activists and their movements everywhere (Zola, 1993a; Swain *et al.*, 2003; Haller *et al.*, 2006). Words now widely understood to be offensive in English-speaking countries, such as 'handicapped', 'cripple', 'dumb', 'deformed', 'retard' and 'spastic', are examined for their stigmatising qualities and genealogies, though the transgressive reclamation of 'cripple' and 'freak' by some disabled people and their movements is celebrated.

However, points such as these about terminology are not what distinguish the poststructuralist contribution. Poststructuralists draw attention to the underpinning binary thinking that informs and constructs such terminology. It is argued that critiques of Enlightenment-inspired 'grand narratives' exposes the either/or formulations that are replete in scientific and other culturally dominant discourses: individual/society, society/nature, mind/body, normal/abnormal, diseased/healthy. Such Cartesian dualisms, now deeply embedded in both academic disciplines and everyday thinking, are thought to play a critical role in sustaining the oppression of disabled people (Corker and Shakespeare, 2002a; Snyder *et al.*, 2002; Tremain, 2005).

The method of epistemological deconstruction is used to subvert these 'fortresses of unexamined assumptions and received opinions' (Jeffreys, 2002: 31). This reveals that one half of the binary divide only holds meaning because an 'Other' side is assumed; every articulation of the one inscribes the existence of the other: 'Disability' is meaningless without 'normality', and vice versa. Moreover:

> A Derridean perspective on disability would argue that though they are antagonistic, 'normativism' needs 'disability' for its own definition; a person without an impairment can define him/herself as 'normal' only in opposition to that which s/he is not – a person with an impairment. Disability is not excluded from 'normativism': it is integral to its very assertion. (Corker and Shakespeare, 2002b: 7)

Some Effects of the Disabled/Normal Binary Divide

A great deal is made of this insight in poststructuralist analyses of disability. It demands an examination of the social experiences of people who occupy *both* sides of the divide rather than pursuing an exclusive focus on disabled people. For example, in the humanities it can be used to unpack the purpose fulfilled by the extremely common, in fact pervasive, portrayal in novels and films of 'evil', undesirable or tragic characters as disabled (Garland-Thomson, 1996, 1997a; Mitchell and Snyder, 2000; Snyder and Mitchell, 2001):

> ... visible degeneracy, impotency, congenital deformity, festering ulcerations, and bleeding wounds all provide the contrastive bodily coordinates to the muscular, aesthetic, and symmetrical bodies of the healthy citizenry ... . The materiality of metaphor via disabled bodies gives all bodies a tangible essence, in that the healthy corporeal surface fails to achieve its symbolic effect without its disabled counterpart. (Mitchell, 2002: 28)

The presence of the disabled figure symbolically affirms the hero's status through a subtle celebration of the latter's normality. In this way, disablism is bolstered: readers and viewers who unthinkingly identify as 'normal' are deeply reassured in their recognition of themselves as fully human (for UK variants of this argument see Shakespeare, 1997a, 1999a; Darke, 2004; Wilde, 2004).

As this implies, the disabled 'other' play a part in sustaining the psychic well-being of those deemed normal in society through shoring up their ontological security. Indeed, people with evident impairments serve as dumping grounds for the projection of 'normal' people's deep-rooted fear of illness, frailty, incapacity and mortality (Shakespeare, 1997a; Marks, 1999). In this way, psychoanalytic considerations take diseased/healthy and disabled/normal dualisms in new directions within deconstructionist thought (Corker and Shakespeare, 2002a).

Deborah Marks (1999) uses psychoanalytic theory to explore aspects of the oppression of disabled people by professionals, 'carers' and non-disabled people in general. She suggests that such groups erect personal 'defences' that may result in expressions of hostility and anger towards disabled people; in some people such negative emotions run alongside an altruistic desire to care and 'to help'. Indeed, there is often a complex attraction to and repulsion from disabled people bound up with fear, guilt and many other emotions.[3] This perspective allows the discriminatory treatment of disabled people to be understood not simply as the result of ignorance, self-interest or indifference but 'also as a reflection of unconscious fears and fantasies' (Marks, 1999: 24; see also Price and Shildrick, 2002). The psychic response of disabled people to such hostility and rejection often results in what the disabled activist, Micheline Mason, terms 'internalised oppression':

> Internalised oppression is not the cause of our mistreatment, it is the result of our mistreatment. It would not exist without the real external oppression that forms the social climate in which we exist. Once oppression has been internalised, little

force is needed to keep us submissive. We harbour inside ourselves the pain and the memories, the fears and the confusions, the negative self images and the low expectations, turning them into weapons with which to re-injure ourselves, every day of our lives. (Mason, cited in Marks, 1999: 25)

The Normal/Abnormal Dualism

From a humanities perspective, Lennard Davis, American English and disability studies scholar, has analysed the historical construction of the concept 'normality', and the consequence that this powerful discursive category has had for people we now identify as disabled (L. Davis, 1995, 2002a,b). His cultural analysis constitutes an interesting parallel with materialist theorisations of the historical development of 'disability' and disablism, discussed above.

Davis argues that the concept 'normal' only made its appearance in Western society in the early- to mid-nineteenth century (the word only appeared in the English language around 150 years ago):

Before the rise of the concept of normalcy ... there appears not to have been a concept of the normal, but instead the regnant paradigm was one revolving around the word ideal. If people have a concept of the ideal, then all human beings fall below that standard and so exist in varying degrees of imperfection. The key point is that in a culture of the ideal, physical imperfections are seen not as absolute but part of a descending continuum from top to bottom. No one, for example, can have an ideal body, and therefore no one has to have an ideal body. (L. Davis, 2002a: 105)

The culture of the ideal was linked ideologically to structures of kingship and feudal society, to a period in history when people with physical impairments were not distinguished as a group but lived out their lives in communities of individuals bearing degrees and variations of human imperfection (L. Davis, 2002a). The displacement of the 'ideal' by a normal/abnormal dichotomy, and the concomitant creation of 'the disabled' individual and group, was bound up with developments in numerical science in the early nineteenth century: statistics and the concept of the bell curve – the 'normal curve'. These developments introduced the idea of the embodied norm, and bodies and body practices became standardised and homogenised. Those at the curve's extremes constitute the 'abnormal'.

Thus, there is an imperative on people to conform, to fit in, under the rubric of normality. Rather than being resigned to a less-than-ideal body in the earlier paradigm, people in the past 150 years have been encouraged to strive to be normal, to huddle under the main part of the curve (ibid.: 105).

Disablism (termed 'ableism' by Davis) thus acquires ideological support with profound consequences for people categorised 'disabled' Nevertheless, Davis (2002a) sees hope for change because political, socia and linguistic practices are amenable to alteration.

The creation of centralised nation-states, the standardisation anc homogenisation of language practices and behaviours, the establishment o white and male bodies as reference points for humanity, and medicine': drive to 'fix' the abnormal, are all features of the Enlightenment inspirec move to normalise (ibid.). Moreover, Jackie Leach Scully (2002) describe: the normal/abnormal dualism as fundamental to today's medical *meta-nar rative*: the 'molecular model', a model that encompasses genetic science.

Foucault's Bio-Power and 'Disabled' Subjectivity

These observations on the construction of social distinctions and categorie: in the wake of modernist epistemological dualisms clearly owe as much tc Foucault as to Derrida. Shelley Tremain (2005), a writer in Americar disability studies, is convinced that Foucauldian scholarship represents ar approach of tremendous significance and potential, especially the applicatior of Foucault's ideas on bio-power and governmentality. She summarises he: claim as follows:

> The importance of critical work on bio-power (bio-politics) to analyses o disability cannot be overstated. For during the past two centuries, in particulai a vast apparatus, erected to secure the well-being of the general population, ha: caused the contemporary disabled subject to emerge into discourse and socia existence. Among the items that have comprised this expansive apparatus ar asylums, income support programs, quality of life assessments, workers compensation benefits, special education programs, regimes of rehabilitation parallel transit systems, prostheses, home care services, telethons, shelterec workshops, poster child campaigns, and prenatal diagnosis. These (and a host o other) practices, procedures, and policies have created, classified, codified managed, and controlled social anomalies through which some people hav been divided from others and objectivized as (for instance) physically impaired insane, handicapped, mentally ill, retarded, and deaf. Foucault argued that in recent times, practices of division, classification, and ordering around a norn have become the primary means by which to individualize people, who come t be understood scientifically, and who even come to understand themselves ii this mode. (ibid.: 5–6)

This passage tells of the enormous potential for studies on the historical anc contemporary technologies involved in the construction, regulation anc subjectification of differentiated groupings among 'the disabled'. As yei such studies are few in number but are, in my view, much to be encouraged (see, for example, McFarlane, 2005).

Critiques of the Social Model of Disability, and the Question of Impairment

The social model of disability, so central to disability studies in the UK for the reasons outlined earlier in this chapter, has been pilloried by poststructuralist writers for being a new form of privileged knowledge – though its role in politically mobilising disabled people has not been denied (Corker, 1998; Corker and Shakespeare, 2002a; Tremain, 2005). Their critique has focused on the UPIAS assertion that *impairment* (characteristics of the body) could/should be separated from *disability* (social restrictions imposed upon people with impairments), a distinction that Oliver (1983) went on to place at the heart of the social model. From a poststructuralist perspective, such a separation is not tenable. It establishes a new impairment/disability dualism belonging to a modernist world-view – in this case, a Marxist totalising meta-narrative. This version of binary and reductionist thinking is held to mirror the Cartesian biology/society and mind/body dualisms that run through medical and other scientific discourses (Corker and Shakespeare, 2002b: 15).

Bill Hughes and Kevin Paterson (Hughes and Paterson, 1997; Hughes, 1999, 2005) have played an influential role in the debates that have ensued in the UK, but their solution to the social model's biology/society dichotomy takes a different turn. Poststructuralist 'solutions' are rejected in favour of the development of a *phenomenology* of impairment and 'the body', based on Merleau-Ponty's (1962) philosophical ideas (see Chapter 2, this volume):

> The impaired body is a 'lived body'. Disabled people experience impairment, as well as disability, not in separate Cartesian compartments, but as part of a complex interpenetration of oppression and affliction. The body is the stuff of human affliction and affectivity as well as the subject/object of oppression. The value of a phenomenological sociology of the body to the development of a sociology of impairment is that it embodies the addition of sentience and sensibility to notions of oppression and exclusion. Disability is experienced in, on and through the body, just as impairment is experienced in terms of the personal and cultural narratives that help to constitute its meaning. (Hughes and Paterson, 1997: 334–5)

These poststructuralist and phenomenological observations on 'body matters' are returned to in Chapter 5.

Theoretical Engagements with Gender, Difference and Oppression

We now move into territory that has been influenced by poststructuralist thought in recent years, but was dominated by feminists with materialist, socialist feminist or other realist theoretical perspectives in the 1980s and 1990s – many influenced by autobiographically based accounts, stories and poems published by disabled women and their allies. This section begins with feminist writings on the relationship between disability and gender, then considers ideas on how to theorise social oppression *per se* and the interface between forms of oppression.

The Gendered Character of Disability

Feminist thinkers of all theoretical persuasions continue to play a role of great significance in shaping disability studies in the UK, as they do in North America, the Nordic countries and Australasia (e.g. in the UK: Morris, 1991, 1996; Riddell, 1996; Corker, 1998; Moore *et al.*, 1998; Marks, 1999; Thomas, 1999; French, 2001; Corker and Shakespeare, 2002a; In other counties: Fine and Asche, 1988; Wendell, 1996; Garland-Thomson, 1996, 1997a, 2005; Abu-Habib, 1997; Meekosha, 1998; Linton, 1998b; Traustadóttir, R. and Johnson, 2000; Kristiansen and Traustadóttir, 2004; Smith and Hutchinson, 2004; Tremain, 2005). Many *feminisms* are now in play, echoing the theoretical diversification and fragmentation that has unfolded in mainstream feminism since the 1980s (Adkins and Skeggs, 2004; Gilles *et al.*, 2004).

Feminists in disability studies work on two interrelated fronts: first, bringing theory and research practices from mainstream feminism into disability studies, and using these to build new perspectives and knowledge; second, critiquing mainstream feminism for its failure to take disability and disablism seriously, and intervening in debates in an attempt to influence the development of feminist theory and research. One important result is that disability studies now takes it as given that 'disabled people' do not constitute a homogeneous social group. Rather, experiences of disablism and living with impairment are understood to be bound up with other cultural markers of social 'difference': gender, 'race', sexuality, age and class.

In the UK, Jenny Morris – one of the most influential writers – built on the work of activists and authors such as Jo Campling (1981) and Micheline Mason (see above) to show that the forms and impacts of disablism are invariably refracted in some way through the prism of gender locations and gender relations: being disabled is a *gendered* experience (Morris 1991, 1993c, 1996). In my own research, disabled women's written and spoken narratives confirmed the gendered character of disablism and its effects: women's narratives only acquired meaning when reference was made to the gender norms that make up their social worlds (Thomas 1999, 2001b). That is, whether or not lives follow conventional gender pathways (and most do), disabled women tell their stories with explicit or implicit reference to the public narratives that define 'what it means to be a woman'. A smaller but growing body of research literature on the lives of disabled men also confirms the gendered character of disability and disablism (Gerschick and Miller, 1995; Robertson, 2004; Smith and Sparks, 2004), as does research on disabled women's experiences in resource poor countries (Abu-Habib, 1997, see also Charlton, 1998; Priestley, 2001).

However, taking heed of the fragmentation in mainstream feminism when it began to engage with 'race' and sexual difference, feminists in disability studies have avoided bracketing disabled women into one undifferentiated social grouping: care is taken to acknowledge important differences *among* disabled women (and men) associated with age, impairment type, sexuality, 'race' and class (Stuart, 1993; Begum *et al.*, 1994; Corbett, 1994; Wendell, 1996; Brownworth and Raffo, 1999; Traustadóttir and Johnson, 2000; Kristiansen and Traustadóttir, 2004). Moreover, some poststructuralist feminist writers refuse to accept *any* attempt to categorise and group people because reference is inevitably made to the purported qualificatory and foundational properties of 'subjects' (Corker, 1998; Fawcett, 2000; Corker and Shakespeare, 2002a; Price and Shildrick, 2002; Tremain, 2005).

The Personal and the Political

An important feature of Jenny Morris's writings in the 1990s was her refusal to leave unchallenged the normative social distinction made between 'the personal and the political', a distinction that she saw replicated in the work of leading male social modellists (Morris, 1992b). Morris applied the feminist slogan: 'the personal *is* political', referring to the (realist) mainstream feminist argument that the personal/political or private/public dualism is a product of the relationship between gender and economic orders in the capitalist era (e.g. Walby, 1990, 1997).

Thereafter, debate about the significance of 'the personal' and 'the experiential' has been at the heart of disagreements between feminists and some leading male writers within UK disability studies, a debate to which I have contributed (Thomas, 1999, 2001a). Feminists reject the accusations made, for example, by Finkelstein (1996) and Oliver (1996a), that a focus on 'personal experiences' can by politically diversionary or provide sustenance for the reviled 'personal tragedy' approach to disability.

One consequence of feminists' success in opening up the 'black box' on 'private life' is that family dynamics, parenting, childcare, childhood, sexuality, sexual relationships and domestic violence now constitute well-established domains for research and theorising in UK disability studies – domains of research in which feminist ideas inform a variety of approaches (see, for example, Morris, 1996, 1997a, 2001; Shakespeare *et al.*, 1996; Robinson and Stalker, 1998; Thomas, 1999; Davis and Watson, 2001; Goodley and Lawthom, 2006). Another important consequence is that 'being impaired' is no longer something that is completely set aside. Feminist writers like Jenny Morris (1996), Liz Crow (1996) and Sally French (1993) have won a place for scholarship on the *lived experience* of impairment and the emotional impact of disablism, a development that is discussed at length in Chapter 5.

Psycho-Emotional Disablism

Turning to my own ideas, my materialist feminist interest in 'the personal' and the experiential led to the naming of 'psycho-emotional dimensions of disability' in *Female Forms: Experiencing and Understanding Disability* (Thomas, 1999). This concept is now in common usage in disability studies.

To restate my case: *psycho-emotional disablism* involves the intended or unintended 'hurtful' words and social actions of non-disabled people (parents, professionals, complete strangers, others) in inter-personal engagements with people with impairments. It also involves the creation, placement and use of denigrating images of 'people with impairments' in public spaces by the non-disabled (Hevey, 1992; Garland-Thomson, 1996, 1997a). The effects of psycho-emotional disablism are often profound: the damage inflicted works along psychological and emotional pathways, impacting negatively on self-esteem, personal confidence and ontological security. Disabled people can be made to feel worthless, useless, of lesser value, ugly, burdensome (Reeve, 2002, 2006). Moreover, impairments may themselves be affected in problematic ways by the impact of psycho-emotional disablism.

Put another way: social barriers 'out there' certainly place limits on what disabled people *can do*, but psycho-emotional disablism places limits on who they *can be* by shaping individuals' 'inner worlds', sense of 'self' and social behaviours. Moreover, there is an interacting and compounding relationship between psycho-emotional disablism and the imposition of restrictions on activity in employment, education and other social arenas (Thomas, 1999). This dimension of disablism should not be mistaken for either the 'inevitable consequences' of being impaired (a medical model view) *or* what Oliver (1996a: 48) has called 'the personal restrictions of impairment' or 'private troubles'.

The theoretical and empirical exploration of this form of disablism obviously requires an engagement with individual subjectivity and personal experience, something that feminists' insistence on paying attention to 'the personal and private' made possible in disability studies. Its recognition allows for the reformulation of the pioneering UPIAS definition of disability:

> Disablism is a form of social oppression involving the social imposition of restrictions of activity on people with impairments and the socially engendered undermining of their psycho-emotional well-being.

Another concept that I introduced in *Female Forms* has also been taken up by others in UK disability studies: *impairment effects* – a concept that I discuss in Chapter 5.

Theorising Oppression, and the Intersection of Forms of Oppression

Returning to the theme of disability and gender, how have writers attempted to theorise the intersection of disablism and sexism? Some have taken the most obvious 'double oppression' or 'multiple oppressions' approach: that is, disabled women are viewed as doubly disadvantaged, in an additive or layered sense, by the impact of both sexism and disablism (examples are found in Lonsdale, 1990; Begum, 1992; Lloyd, 1992, 2001). In this view, deeply embedded cultural ideas about femininity and disability act in tandem to cement the marginalised and purportedly 'pitiable' position of disabled women – because both promote notions of passivity, dependency and frailty. However, Morris, among others, rejects such an over-simplified 'double whammy' approach because it often serves to individualise disability: 'the attention shifts away from non-disabled people and social institutions as being the problem and onto disabled women as passive victims of oppression' (Morris, 1996: 89). Ossie Stuart (1993) and Ayesha Vernon (1997) have argued along similar lines in relation to 'race' and disability, with Stuart opting for the 'simultaneous oppression' approach. Overall, such attempts to theorise the interrelationship between dimensions of social oppression have proved to be of limited value.

Some writers came to understand that the problem lay with the inadequacy of the underlying theory (or theories) of social oppression in disability studies (Abberley, 1987). Early activists and thinkers had simply borrowed the concept of social oppression from other social movements: the term appeared to offer an entirely appropriate means of characterising the social mechanisms involved in the appalling treatment of disabled people in society (Hunt, 1966). The 1990s witnessed an increase in the number of writers who turned to scholars outside the discipline for ideas that might assist in understanding both oppression *per se* and the intersection of different forms of oppression.

The writings of the US political theorists Iris Marion Young (1990) and Nancy Fraser (1989, 1995, 2000) on social justice and the nature of oppression in liberal societies have found particular favour, though their ideas have not been adopted uncritically (Gleeson, 1999; Danemark and Gellerstedt, 2004). Young and Fraser both seek to transcend the Welfare State 'distributive paradigm of justice' – a liberal individualist approach that has its focus on patterns of possession of material goods and social positions. And both offer general theories of oppression in democratic states, together with the analytical means to compare the oppression of disabled people with other disadvantaged and marginalised sections of the community, thereby uncovering similarities and differences. Fraser does not address disability *per se*, whereas Young includes movements for disability rights in her analysis of social groups that advance emancipatory claims for justice and an end to their oppression (others being feminists, Black activists, American Indians, gay men and lesbians, and older people). Young observes that 'there exists no sustained theoretical analysis of the concept of oppression as understood by these movements' (1990: 9).

I shall focus here on Young's analysis of social oppression. She rejects the idea that a singular *essential* definition of oppression can be given, either in general or in the form of distinct systems of oppression for specific groups; nor does she claim to provide a *comprehensive* theory of oppression – see the citation of her statement on the meaning of oppression in Chapter 1 (this volume). Rather, she offers an analysis of five 'faces' of oppression that can function as criteria to determine whether, and in what ways, individuals and groups are oppressed. These are: *exploitation, marginalisation, powerlessness, cultural imperialism* and *violence*. Individuals and groups experience these to varying degrees of intensity and in different combinations. This approach enables the position of disabled women, or of black disabled gay men – or people with any combination of group affinities – to be considered in a fluid and nuanced fashion, and allows for similarities and overlaps within and between social groups. Young makes use of both materialist and postmodernist theoretical perspectives to elaborate these dimensions of oppression: the first three all occur by virtue of the division of labour in capitalist societies, the fourth and fifth draw on poststructuralist and psychoanalytic approaches. This approach leads her to conclude that achieving justice demands both the satisfaction of material needs *and* the cultural empowerment and inclusion of excluded groups.

It is helpful to summarise these five faces of oppression because this schema will be referred to in other chapters:

Exploitation: This form of oppression 'occurs through a steady transfer of the results of the labor of one social group to benefit another' (Young, 1990: 49). Young applies Marxist political economy to look at examples – such as the capitalist super-exploitation of 'Blacks and Latinos' in the US.

Marginalisation: This form of oppression involves the placement of people on society's margins: 'Marginals are people the system of labour cannot or will not use' (ibid.: 53). Young views this as working along social lines of distinction drawn up for 'race', disability and age, in particular. 'Marginalization is perhaps the most dangerous form of oppression. A whole category of people is expelled from useful participation in social life and thus potentially subjected to severe material deprivation and even extermination' (ibid.: 53). Individuals become 'dependent' in ways that undermine their perceived moral agency and citizenship: these latter qualities require autonomous and independent subjects. The result is not just serious issues of distributive injustice, but also 'the deprivation of cultural, practical, and institutionalized conditions for exercising capacities in a context of recognition and interaction' (ibid.: 55).

Powerlessness: This type of oppression occurs in employment and other social settings where power and authority are exercised by some upon others. Those who lack power and authority are inhibited from developing their own capacities, lack decision-making latitude and autonomy, and are exposed to disrespectful treatment because of their lowly status.

Cultural imperialism: This involves the universalisation of a dominant group's experience and culture, and its establishment as the norm. Those not in the dominant group are marked as deviant and inferior 'Others'. 'Cultural imperialism involves the paradox of experiencing oneself as invisible at the same time that one is marked out as different ... the oppressed group's own experience and interpretation of social life finds little expression that touches the dominant culture, while that same culture imposes on the oppressed group its experience and interpretation of social life' (ibid.:60).

Violence: This form of oppression combines systematic physical violence and its lesser though profoundly damaging expressions – harassment, intimidation or ridicule. It is fuelled by hatred and fear. In Young's view, groups most obviously exposed to unprovoked physical violence are minority ethnic groups, women, and gays and lesbians. The perpetrator of violence seeks to damage, humiliate or destroy the victim.

Readers only have to reflect for a moment to realise that every facet of disablism discussed in this chapter can be located within this schema – irrespective of the theoretical perspective brought to bear. Young's opinion is that marginalisation and cultural imperialism are the forms of oppression that operate most forcibly in the lives of disabled people, and many in disability studies would agree. However, research and argument also points to the presence of exploitation, powerlessness and violence – with violence involving verbal humiliation and ridicule as well as sexual abuse and physical violence (see Sobsey, 1994; Kennedy, 1996). In Gleeson's materialistically informed application of Young's criteria to disability, both exploitation and marginalisation are key, with both being 'partly achieved and reproduced through discriminatory mainstream cultures and political structures' (Gleeson, 1999: 131). Using Young's five faces of oppression, we can see that disabled people whose ascribed identities mark them out as also belonging to *other* disadvantaged social groups will experience different degrees and combinations of these faces of oppression.

Difference, Identity and Identity Politics

One of the points frequently made by disability studies writers is that the boundary separating disabled and non-disabled people is not sealed or fixed, because accident, injury and the onset of chronic illness can propel the non-disabled person into the world of 'the disabled' at any time: being 'able-bodied' is, for most, only a temporary state. Chapter 2 examined the ways in which medical sociologists in the interpretative tradition have researched this boundary crossing. Their focus has been trained on how individuals who become chronically ill 'cope with' and 'manage' their new socially 'deviant' status, and how they endeavour to reconstruct their shattered identities. The discussion in this section outlines different approaches to identity matters.

Writers and activists in disability studies have paid a great deal of attention to individuals' identities (both 'self-identity' and 'ascribed identity'), to identity politics and to the nature of social movements – not least because the potential for marshalling forces to press for social and political change is at stake. As many have documented, the 'social model' interpretation of disability, discussed above, offered the means of forging a self-determined group identity among a significant proportion of disabled people, irrespective of their impairments (Campbell and Oliver, 1996; Swain *et al.*, 2003). Individuals could join together on the basis of their shared experiences of *disablism*, making common cause for social change and the removal of disabling barriers.

The history of the disabled people's movement in the UK is testimony to the potential for individual radicalisation and collective mobilisation that was unleashed by the social oppression paradigm. However, it was not long before disabled writers and activists began to draw attention to 'difference' and exclusions. In the same way that the universalising potential of the category 'women' was interrogated by black and lesbian feminists, resulting in feminist and 'women's movement' fragmentation, the category 'disabled people' and the potential for an all-encompassing 'disabled people's movement' came into question. As discussed above, disabled feminists exposed the gendered nature of disablism. Others have drawn attention to differences among disabled people associated with sexuality, 'race', age and type of impairment, and questioned whether the interests of these groups are served by the movement and the social model (Walmsley, 1991; French, 1993; Stuart, 1993; Appleby, 1994; Corbett, 1994; Harris, 1995; Morris, 1996; Abberley, 1997; Vernon, 1997; Corker, 1998; Robinson and Stalker, 1998; Priestley, 2003; Sherry, 2004). Shakespeare (1996) and Watson (2002) have both reflected on the fact that the majority of people with impairments do not self-identify as disabled, and some dissociate from the label. In their claim to linguistic minority status, Deaf people involved in Deaf culture often reject the 'disabled' label (Corker, 1998). Perhaps the disabled people's movement cannot represent most or all disabled people? Perhaps a disability identity politics is a chimera?

Debates on these questions have been wide-ranging – in the UK and elsewhere – though two contrasting lines of argument can be discerned. The first is that a resolution is possible through the accommodation of 'difference'. That is, the disabled people's movement and disability studies should fully recognise and accommodate all groups of people designated 'impaired', including people with learning difficulties who currently sit on the margins (Apsis, 2001; Dowse, 2001). Whatever social characteristics disabled people possess, the possibility remains for them to use the social model of disability to unite against disablism. This approach tends to rest on a 'trait' or 'categorical' approach to identity, wherein personal identity can be read off from individuals' social characteristics; it gives rise to the possibility of an identity or 'standpoint' politics. Taking this further, there is appeal in the North American references to 'feminist disability studies' (Smith and Hutchinson, 2004; Garland-Thomson, 2005) and 'queer disability studies' (McRuer and Wilkerson, 2003).

The second line of argument, pursued by some poststructuralist thinkers, contrasts starkly. From this perspective the pursuit of disability identity politics, like all forms of identity politics, is a dangerous strategy because it rests on, and *reinforces*, the abnormal/normal binary divide that has been discursively constructed by regimes of bio-power. This suggests that rather than liberating disabled people, identity politics ties them to the 'Other' category ever more firmly. Instead of 'celebrating our differences', disabled people should deconstruct and transgress all of the unifying categories that position them – 'disabled', 'women', 'gay', 'black' or whatever – because such categories *always already* ascribe a superior status to their normative opposites – 'normal', 'men', heterosexual', 'white'. *Essentialist* epistemologies should be exposed and overcome.

One example of the first line of argument involves an ongoing debate about whether or not people with mental health problems can and should call themselves 'disabled'. From his perspective as a 'psychiatric system survivor', Peter Beresford (2000, 2002; Beresford *et al.*, 2002) has written with passion on this theme. He sets the scene by describing how the mental health users/survivors movement is attempting to develop ideas on mental distress that challenge the powerful psychiatric view of 'mental illness' (mental illness as individual pathological deficit that leads to defective thoughts, behaviours and emotions). The question posed is: should they adopt, in an amended form, the social interpretation disability developed by the disabled people's movement and disability studies, or take another road? Beresford's view is that ongoing dialogue between survivor activists and representatives of the disabled people's movement is much to be welcomed, and that the social model of disability could be adapted so that a 'social model of madness and distress' is articulated: 'The social model of disability suggests a different lexicon to mental health service users, based on ideas of support, personal assistance and non-medicalised provision' (Beresford, 2002: 583).

Beresford (2000) outlines three areas of common ground between survivors and disabled people. First, psychiatric system survivors – however they self-identify – are grouped together with physically impaired people, and thus constructed as 'disabled', by state legislation and policy makers in health and social care services. Second, it is not uncommon for survivors to have physical impairments, sometimes related to the damaging effects of the drug and other 'treatments' meted out by professionals. Third, both disabled people and psychiatric system survivors are subject to discrimination and oppression. However, the forging of a common identity is undermined by unwillingness among some psychiatric system survivors to personally identify as 'disabled' or 'impaired', and by an unwillingness among some disabled people to include people with mental health problems in their ranks (Beresford *et al.*, 1996; see also McNamara, 1996; Gabel, 1999; Mulvany, 2000). Overall:

> There are many unresolved issues for us to explore with each other as survivors and disabled people. We need to be sensitive to both our differences and similarities and our developing understanding of what these actually are. We have to respect our distinct identities and movements, each with its own history, culture, ideas, agenda and ways of doing things. At the same time, we clearly have in common our enforced inclusion in a pathologising administrative category and our common oppression – in social model terms – our shared disability. (Beresford, 2000: 171)

Other examples of the first line of argument are found in the work of some feminist writers. Jenny Morris (1991, 1996) asserts that disabled women, whatever their impairments, do constitute a group with distinct interests and demands who should occupy a more central position *within* a gender-sensitive disability movement. Though more wary of an essentialist charge, the Canadian, Susan Wendell (1996), also concludes that despite the great diversity among disabled people there remain grounds for a shared 'disabled' identity and politics associated with overlapping experiences of social oppression (see the discussion in Thomas, 1999).

However, many feminist and other writers follow the second, constructionist, line of argument: that identity and minority group politics is highly problematic (Fawcett, 2000; Goodley, 2000; Corker and Shakespeare, 2002; Price and Shildrick, 2002; Tremain, 2005). They assert that there is no core 'self' that gives rise to a singular 'disabled' identity, nor to a pluralised identity that takes account of one's gender, 'race', sexuality, and so forth. Rather, personal identities are ascribed through discursive practices, and are always multi-faceted. Any group category is inevitably normative and exclusionary. As Tremain (2002: 44) explains:

> Many feminists have long since realized that a political movement whose organizing tools are identity-based shall inevitably be contested as exclusionary and internally hierarchical. A disability movement that grounds its claims to entitlement in the identity of its subject can expect to face similar criticisms from an ever-increasing number of constituencies that feel excluded from, and refuse to identify with, those demands for rights and recognition. In addition, minorities internal to the movement will predictably pose challenges to it, the upshot of which is that those hegemonic descriptions eclipse their respective particularities ... My argument, therefore, is that disability activists and writers must develop strategies for advancing claims that make no appeal to the very identity upon which that subjection rests.

In my view, the alternative 'strategies' for social and cultural change suggested by poststructuralists tend to be vaguely formulated. Price and Shildrick (2002: 73), for example, say, rather enticingly, that 'the move to postmodernism is one that opens up the positivity of transformatory possibilities', but this is not concretised in a way that I find convincing. Similarly, Tremain (2002) is merely suggestive of the potential for resistance to regimes of bio-politics, referring us to Foucault's later writings on technologies of the self. Strategies also vary in the strength of their opposition to forms of identity politics; sometimes a compromise position is sought (see, for example, Fawcett, 2000). In their introduction to *Disability/Postmodernity*, Corker and Shakespeare (2002b: 15) hold on to the possibility of a liberatory struggle by 'disabled people': '... the goal remains the same: to contribute to the emancipation of disabled people, whoever they are, and whatever they decide that emancipation means, and to the development of inclusive societies'. In this way, they advocate a *strategic postmodernism* rather than a *radical postmodernism*, so avoiding a nihilistic stance towards identity-based social movements and struggles.

In searching for a middle ground that relies neither on a 'trait' or 'categorical' approach to identity nor on the poststructuralist deconstruction of all identity categories and the denial of a self and a subject, some writers have turned to ideas concerning self-identity as reflexively and *narratively* constructed (Watson, 2002). This approach credits individuals with the possession of agency, conceives of identity as fluid, and locates identity in biographical context. The work of Anthony Giddens (1991: 53) is often cited: 'Self-identity is not a distinct trait, or even collection of traits, possessed by the individual. It is the self as reflexively understood by the person in terms of her or his biography'.

But it is Margaret Somers' (1994) ideas on the narratively constructed self that finds favour with some in disability studies, including myself (Thomas, 1999). This suggests that people with life-long or acquired impairments make sense of their experiences and who they are by continually weaving stories about themselves that draw upon the public and cultural narratives they are exposed to about 'people like them/us' (negative and positive). Individuals' social circumstances (familial, educational, socio-economic, and so forth) differentially expose them to these public and cultural narratives, with only a minority currently having the benefit of being in touch personally and collectively with positively transformative narratives associated with the disabled people's movement. This perspective can explain why many disabled people do not or will not identify as 'disabled'; they often articulate negative self-identities: in their 'disabled' states of being (as children and/or adults) they tend to be isolated, alone, marginalised and exposed solely to medicalised and culturally denigrating narratives about what 'being disabled' means.

However, as John Swain and Sally French have warned, care must be taken not to overstate such negative outcomes (Swain and French, 2000; Swain *et al.*, 2003). Swain and French – a mainstay partnership in UK disability studies – build upon the social model perspective to argue for an 'affirmative model of disability'. This reflects the fact that many disabled people can and do reject a 'tragedy' view of their lives; ways are found to 'celebrate' their impairments and disabled status. They suggest that disabled individuals often find that there are advantages and benefits associated with living with impairment, such as an improved quality of life on giving up the occupational 'rat race'. Their research has found that involvement in Disability Arts is one important route to a positive self-identity.

Summary: Disability as Social Oppression

The volume and range of ideas about disability and disablism reviewed in this chapter demonstrates that disability studies in the UK has achieved a great deal in a short space of time. The social oppression paradigm, first advanced in the 1970s, has been taken in contrasting and imaginative directions by materialist, poststructuralist and phenomenological writers – with feminist scholarship playing a key role. All writers and activists in the discipline share a stated commitment to advancing disabled people's social inclusion and full citizenship; this has given disability studies in the UK its distinctive and distinguishing character.

Building on the ideas of disability activists, materialist scholars have theorised disability and disablism as outcomes of the way fundamental activities are organised in society – especially, but not exclusively, activities in the economic domain in the industrial era. In their view, the roots of the social marginalisation and spatial segregation of people with impairments are located in the historical development of capitalist commodity production and exchange. These socio-economic developments gave rise to social relationships between 'the normal' and 'the impaired' that systematically disadvantaged and disempowered the latter. The foundations were laid for medicalised systems of 'treatment and care' that subjected disabled people to professional control and enforced dependency, first in institutional regimes and later in systems of 'community care'. These perspectives have also unleashed a great deal of research detailing the social exclusion of disabled people in all social arenas in the contemporary era. Materialists have been sensitive, however, to the charge that their approach ignores or attaches insufficient significance to the role that cultural practices and processes play in shaping disablism. Their response has been to insist that attitudes, discourses and ideological representations are critical to disablism, though there is an insistence that these are materialised through the social practices required to meet basic needs.

This acknowledgement of the significance of the cultural has not satisfied those disability studies scholars who have supported the 'cultural turn' in the social sciences in recent decades. They have found poststructuralist theoretical perspectives, particularly Foucauldian and feminist variants, to be of much greater interest and utility. The cultural, the discursive and the linguistic have assumed pre-eminence in poststructuralist theorisations of disability *and* impairment. Materialist perspectives are dismissed as modernist grand narratives – systems of thought imbued with conceptual dualisms: abnormal/normal, disabled/non-disabled. The deconstruction of such binary thinking comes to the forefront. Many faults are found with the social model of disability – the offspring of the UPIAS materialist interpretation of disability, with a key failing purported to reside in the model's impairment/disability distinction. This, it is argued, merely replicates the problematic modernist biology/society dualism. Poststructuralists have interrogated the category 'impairment', and set about exposing what they see as its entirely socially constructed character, a theme taken up in Chapter 5.

This chapter has also discussed theoretical engagements with a number of other key themes: the gendered character of disability and disablism, the nature of the social oppression, and the question of identity. Feminist writers of all theoretical persuasions have led in this work, and in so doing have brought to light new dimensions of disablism. Their insistence on the importance of personal experience, and on the need to transcend the personal/private divide, set the stage for research on so-called private matters, on psycho-emotional disablism, and on living with impairment.

The gendering of disability soon led to the consideration of differences and similarities among and between disabled and non-disabled people associated with 'race', sexuality, type of impairment and age. It followed that the intersection of forms of oppression required theorisation, and this, in turn, highlighted the need for a more sophisticated understanding of oppression *per se*. The ideas of the North American political theorist, Iris Marion Young, have been particularly favoured in this regard. All writers and activists agree that identity and identity politics are themes of crucial significance to disabled people, at both individual and collective levels. Overall, there is no doubt that disability studies has established its presence and disciplinary credentials in the academy in the UK.

Part Two

Contested Terrain

4

Care and Dependency:
A Disciplinary Clash

Introduction

This chapter compares the ways in which writers in disability studies and those in medical sociology have approached the themes of care and dependency. This encompasses disciplinary perspectives on the social actors and social institutions that have assumed positions of authority and power in the lives of disabled people in the name of treatment, care and welfare – whether individuals' ascribed impairments are associated with chronic illnesses or other impairment states and conditions. To reflect the fact that it is sociological thinking in the discipline of social policy as well as medical sociology that is of relevance in this chapter, the term medical sociology will be temporarily replaced with the formulation *the sociology of health and social care*. The discussion builds on the introduction of such themes in Chapters 2 and 3. Although approaches in the UK are the focus, many of the observations and arguments have more general relevance.

Readers should be aware from the start that this chapter provides neither a comprehensive account of health and social care policy, legislation or professional practice in the UK, nor a detailed review of any particular policy or practice.[1] Rather, my purpose is to explore significant perspectives and their socio-political outcomes in relation to the concepts care and dependency. Questions of interest are: is there any common ground among sociologists in the disciplines under review, or do we encounter very distinct conceptual pathways? What do different theoretical perspectives within these disciplines bring to our understanding of care and dependency? Do feminist analyses based on differential disciplinary alignments lead to different conclusions?

Use is made of a standard distinction between 'formal' and 'informal' care. Formal care involves health and social care services (statutory, commercial, charitable or voluntary) using salaried professionals, waged employees and/or volunteer workers. Informal care refers to unpaid care

provided in familial, wider kinship, neighbourhood and friendship
networks. However, as will become evident later in the chapter, recent
policy changes in the UK associated with 'direct payments' are undermin
ing the long-standing dichotomy between formal and informal care, espe
cially in the provision of home-based support in community settings
(see Ungerson, 1997a, 2004; Twigg, 2000). Other relevant concepts and
themes include 'need', health care, social care, community care, welfare
personal care, support, personal assistance and independent living. I
should be borne in mind throughout that the concept 'disability' is defined
and applied in different ways in disability studies and the sociology o
health and social care (see preceding chapters).

We start with a discussion of the meaning of dependency and care at a
relatively abstract level. This provides an overarching conceptual
framework for thinking about the 'needs' of disabled people, and offers the
means by which contemporary disciplinary approaches can be compared
The observations made are derived from a rich mix of ideas to be found in
disability studies, feminism, sociology and social policy. Few, I venture
would disagree with the line of argument in this first section.

The second section reviews approaches to be found, respectively, in the
sociology of health and social care and in disability studies.

The chapter's third section considers a number of documented clashes of
perspective between representatives of these disciplines on issues of care and
dependency. These four *episodes* of debate serve to crystallise disagreements
and agreements, if any can be found – by structuring the discussion around
notable foci of contestation. They bring this chapter's themes 'to life', and in
so doing convey some of the passion and conviction that has accompanied
dialogue about dependency and care – particularly on the part of disability
studies' writers and activists. That passion is ignited is, of course, no surprise
because care and dependency themes get to the heart of disabled people'
struggle for social inclusion; indeed, they bear on the struggle for life itself
Structuring the third section in this way, with lengthy quotations and chapte
notes, also allows something of 'the story' to be told about the relationship
between the disciplines of interest in the UK, though constraints of space
mean that what is actually a complex story can only be sketched out. Light i
certainly thrown on the dynamics involved in the development of disability
studies as an independent discipline in British universities.

'Need', 'Care' and 'Dependency': Rising Above Everyday Ideas

However 'the body' is conceived by sociologists, few would disagree that
bodies have 'needs' if they are to survive from one day to the next. It cannot

be disputed that the following are essential to the sustenance of life: water and food, shelter from hazards and the protection of clothing. One could go on to list other basic needs for survival in contemporary society, and many more come into view if we think about bringing new bodies into the world, or about how young bodies are to grow and flourish. Our embodied selves also require ongoing emotional sustenance – to receive and give personal appreciation, affection and love – if we are to be 'fully human'. When the body falls ill, few would contest that it needs 'treatment' and 'care', and when it is dying it is thought to require 'palliative care'.

Documenting and philosophising the 'needs' of the embodied human is an ongoing endeavour, as is identifying variations in the ways these needs express themselves in different times and places at societal and individual levels (Doyal and Gough, 1991). Turning the coin around, much has and remains to be said on the simple and complex systems and arrangements that are in place in any society to *meet* the embodied needs of individuals and populations. Only one thing is constant: social relationships and interdependency are always involved. No one is an island, to use that well-rehearsed phrase. Bodies are 'lived' in social interconnection and interdependency: we are *all* dependent upon others (D. Stone, 1984; Young, 2002). Patterns of inequity, another constant, come to be structured into these relationships; in our own society these are recognised most readily using the language of class, gender, 'race' and age.

In contemporary Britain our embodied needs are many and varied, far exceeding those required for basic survival, conditioned as they are by economic and cultural standards and expectations that have become normative in advanced industrial and service societies in the twenty-first century. Complex social structures and systems are in place to meet these needs in the late capitalist era. Most are driven and governed by private market mechanisms, some take the form of tax-funded state services and payments – the legacy of ever changing 'state welfare' provision in the twentieth century, some are found in the 'not for profit' voluntary and charitable sectors, others rely on so-called private institutions – family and wider kinship networks, together with arrangements based on friendship and neighbourliness. Familiar terms distinguish landmarks and features on this social and spatial terrain: manufacturing and service industries, the shopping mall, the retail sector, transport systems, the media, the education sector, health services, social care services, the residential care sector, welfare benefits, voluntary organisations, charities, 'the home', 'the family' and 'the community' – by no means an exhaustive list, nor one in any order of significance. If one were to attempt to map the social relationships involved in meeting the full range of needs through these structures and systems it would become immediately obvious that all members of society are embedded in a labyrinthine network of relationships, now global in scale (Young, 2002). We think only of a limited number of these as providers of 'care', principally health and social care services, residential care, the voluntary sector and the family; the settings of greatest familiarity include: hospitals, general practices, 'care homes' and 'the home'.

From such a perspective it is possible to appreciate that, at any stage in the life course, disability and impairment (including chronic illness) simply bring into being particular and varying configurations of needs, as does being non-disabled and 'of normal health'. If one thinks in terms of scales of need – leaving aside for the moment the social exclusions and socially constructed 'needs' exacted by disablism – being an adult with an impairment(s) may mean that one has a greater than average need for assistance with daily tasks such as dressing, washing, cooking and travelling to the shops. But a non-disabled businessman may need the assistance of others to a far greater degree in the course of regularly criss-crossing the globe in aeroplanes, 'living' in hotels and restaurants for much of the year, and returning home from time-to-time to see his wife who runs the house and brings up the children. Despite this, our culture attributes 'neediness' and 'dependency'[2] – devalued, sometimes stigmatised, states of being – to the person with impairment, and celebrates the businessman's 'self-sufficiency' and 'independence'. 'Needs' in the abstract are rendered meaningless, and 'having needs' becomes a negatively valued quality attributed only to particular social groups.

Central to the impaired person's devalued status is the perception that impairment causes 'childlike' needs to be present, together with a presumption that disabled people do not work, either for a wage or on an unpaid basis in the home, and are financially dependent upon state welfare. Central to the businessman's celebrated status are the markers of adulthood: having an apparently 'normal' adult body that facilitates 'independence': forms of childhood dependency are left behind, 'good money' is earned and the services of others are purchased. Underlying both evaluations, of course, is the question of pecuniary give and take – credit and debit. In an economic and social system governed by commodity exchange values, judgements of individuals' social worth rest fundamentally on their waged or non-waged status, and whether they, on balance contribute to the social purse rather than draw from it; 'welfare dependency' is highly stigmatised (Fraser and Gordon, 2002). These criteria of social value are intensified in periods when Governments are steered by conservative ideologies and discourses ('Thatcher's Britain' in the 1980s being a case in point). Those who 'give' more than they take (as individuals, or in family units), or at least break-even, win social approval; those who 'give' nothing, or 'take' more than they 'give', enter the realms of 'dependency', become 'social problems' – undermining their claims to full citizenship.

Among 'the dependent', distinctions have long been made between 'the deserving' and the 'undeserving' (indeed, since the Poor Law of 1601), that is, between those who make 'legitimate' or 'illegitimate' claims for material assistance and other services. In the social imagination, disabled people are grouped and placed among the dependent and 'incapacitated' in society; they can qualify as 'deserving' of care services and welfare benefits only insofar as their impairments and chronic illnesses are acquired through no fault of their own, and so long as their 'needs-based' claims for assistance are 'genuine' and 'reasonable'. These are the principles that underpin the mixed economy of 'welfare provision' for disabled people in the state, family, charitable and commercial domains. The fact that disabled individuals who do not earn a wage or 'work' may contribute to society in other ways – for example, through art, writing, participating in community life or by giving affection and joy to others – counts for little or nothing (Young, 2002; Swain *et al.*, 2003).

The result is that we are accustomed to living in a society in which the universality of need and individuals' mutual interdependency is eclipsed, and 'independence' and 'self-sufficiency' have grown in value over the decades (Giddens, 1991). State ideology, professional discourses and public narratives all sustain cultural norms professing that it is only 'the disabled', 'the sick', 'the old' and 'the very young' who are dependent and have need of care and support. Disabled people have been constructed as a particularly 'needy', dependent and pitiable group throughout the capitalist era in British society; indeed, physical, sensory and intellectual impairment, and 'mental illness', are considered to be *direct causes* of dependency. This has underpinned and given legitimacy to the exercise of forms of authority and control in disabled people's lives. Interestingly, 'the disabled' and 'the old' tend to be treated as mutually exclusive categories although impairment rises with age and is concentrated in the 60 years and older age groups (Priestley, 2003).

The corollary of the above is that the meaning of 'care' has come to encompass a relatively narrow range of social practices involved in 'looking after' those deemed dependant. Public narratives on caring recognise that this involves varying degrees of duty, obligation, vocation, professionalism, affection, love, expertise, common sense and 'plain hard work' – depending on who is giving the care, whether they are paid or not, whether the carer is 'family', and where the caring takes place. Informal caring in 'home-space settings' (Milligan, 2003) is thought to combine the work activities of caring ('caring for' someone) and the affective aspects of caring ('caring about' someone – giving love and affection). Paid or professional caring – nursing and nursing assistance being archetypal – is expected to have a much heavier emphasis on caring work and tasks, though it is thought proper and desirable for such carers to feel and express concern for the well-being of their charges, that is, to engage in what sociologists have come to call emotional labour or emotion work (Hochschild, 1983; James, 1992; Bendelow and Williams, 1998; S. Williams, 2001b). People who 'care' are at once revered for being virtuous and displaying altruistic qualities, and at the same time are frequently taken-for-granted, especially if unpaid. Women rather than men are believed to be in possession of 'caring' qualities, and to be the 'best carers' – stemming from their roles as wives and mothers. Indeed, care work in society *is* profoundly gendered, a feature connected in feminists' minds to its taken-for-granted and unpaid or low paid character (Finch and Groves, 1983; Graham, 1991; Thomas, 1993; Ungerson, 1997a). Health care professionals at the top of the status hierarchy, especially doctors, are considered to be skilled in the curing and treating rather than 'just caring', and are remunerated accordingly (these include clinical psychologists, physiotherapists, occupational therapists and nurse specialists) (M. Stacey, 1988; French and Swain, 2001).

The foregoing observations on the nature of need, dependency and care provide a backdrop for a review of perspectives on care and dependency to be found, first, in the sociology of heath and social care, and second, in disability studies.

Disciplinary Engagements with Care and Dependency: The Sociology of Health and Social Care

Dependency and the Need for Care as Self-Evident

Sociology and social policy are disciplines that thrive on critique of the culturally normative. Few features on the social landscape escape critical scrutiny. It is rather curious, therefore, that the dependency of 'chronically ill and disabled people' has been treated as self-evident, as has 'the suffering that illness brings: 'Certainly physical dependency, if not also social and economic dependency, can result from illness' (Charmaz, 1991: 80). That is the sociology of health and social care, taken as a whole, has accepted and shared in the deeply rooted cultural assumption that chronic illness and disability give rise to social dependency – with the degree of dependency depending on the nature and severity of medically defined conditions and their symptomatic effects. This is true even of hardened poststructuralists who usually waste no time in their search for grand narratives to deconstruct in medicine and regimes of health and social care.[3]

This contrasts with the sociological treatment of another purportedly 'dependent' social group: 'old people'. In recent decades, sociologists and

)cial policy analysts have produced sophisticated analyses of the social
)nstruction of dependency in old age from a variety of theoretical
:rspectives (Walker, 1980; Townsend, 1981; Phillipson, 1982; Arber and
vandrou, 1993; Featherstone and Hepworth, 1998; Vincent, 1999).
)owever, such analyses rarely extend to questioning the 'inevitability' of
:pendency resulting from chronic illness and disability in old age.

The considerable power of sociological critique has been directed
sewhere: towards the nature of the *social responses* (structural and
dividual) to the dependency that chronic illness and disability are
:sumed to engender. Of course, the experience of 'living with' chronic
.ness has also been the subject of research, a theme discussed in Chapter 6.
rimary among *response* themes are systems and practices of 'treatment'
id 'care'. This social response focus does not mean, however, that the
;ency of ill and disabled people is denied, negated or ignored. We know
om Chapter 2 that interactionist sociology, especially in its 'negotiation'
)rm, has made a special study of how patients (clients, service users)
:ercise their agency in medical and care service contexts.

That chronic illness and disability are seen to generate the need for
)rmal and informal care – varying in degree by individual circumstance,
id resulting in differential levels of social dependency – means that most
)ciologists of health and social care would insist, in common with other
embers of the liberal intelligentsia, that the receipt of high quality treat-
ient and care by those in need is a basic human right, one that should be
:fended against political, financial, organisational, professional, or any
:her form of threat. Today's academics in the Richard Titmuss and Brian
bel-Smith tradition take things further by offering up their intellectual
id research skills to state-funded Research Councils and other agencies in
1 endeavour to assist society in discharging its responsibility to support and
ire for chronically ill and disabled people. This usually takes the form of
·search designed to bring about incremental change in existing services
ther than to institute radical change in provision; 'evaluation research' is
·pical – assessing the efficacy and effectiveness of new or existing services.
:w sociologists have placed themselves at the forefront of political
impaigns for *alternative* forms of care provision.

'ealth and Social Care Responses: Theoretical erspectives and Recurrent Themes

)r some 50 years, the critical perspectives that medical sociologists have
)plied to social responses to need and dependency in the medical and
)cial care arena have been moulded by observing illness and disability
.rough the *social deviance* lens – the Parsonian legacy (see Chapter 2).

However, different theoretical perspectives have generated markedl
different versions of the deviance theme, and are associated with contras
ing moral and political standpoints on medicine and the trials c
patienthood. Critiques of medicine can be sharp and damning – mos
notably in traditions associated with labelling interactionism, conflict the
ory and poststructuralism; or the positions adopted can be medico-centric

To recap briefly on the theoretical terrain covered in Chapter 2: Parson:
(1951) structural functionalist school of thought had no difficulty in accep
ing medical jurisdiction in matters of illness and disability; the solutio
offered by the 'sick role' to the management of the threat posed to the soci:
fabric by dependency in illness was deemed entirely appropriate – bot
'functional' and humane. It followed that the exercise of authority an
control by doctors and other health and social care professionals in the live
of chronically ill and disabled people was a socially expedient means c
dealing with the 'social problem' they represented. In marked contras
interactionist labelling theorists refused to see the exercise of medical powe
as benign. Their focus on the secondary deviance trajectory set in motion b
doctors' 'mental illness' (and other) diagnoses highlighted the plight of inst
tutionalised patients and fuelled the anti-psychiatry movement in the 1960
The rise to prominence of poststructuralist thought in later years took th
critique of medical power in new directions. Foucault's bio-politics investe
medical knowledge and its representatives with the capacity to disciplin
and regulate both sick and healthy bodies. The Foucauldian patient an
social care client appears unable to resist medicine's discursive authorit
though Foucault's positioning of patients as 'discourse dopes' is disputed b
some of his followers. In short, interpretations of the power and control exe:
cised by doctors and related figures of authority in the social worlds of th
chronically ill and disabled are multiple, and range from the functionall
beneficial to the problematically subjugating.

An impressive body of literature has accumulated on health and social ca:
responses to illness and disability – a literature too vast to review her
A perusal of medical sociology textbooks[4] reveals that particular attention h:
been paid to the following social response themes, at both macro an
micro-social scales: the doctor–patient (or professional–lay) relationship, an
the subordinate position of patients in this dyad; the power of medicine and i
impulse to medicalise (in both its conflict theory and Foucauldian variants); th
organisation of health and social care, including rehabilitative services, an
the systems of governance that pertain; the development of complementar
and alternative therapies; the changing authority, roles and divisions c
labour among professions in health and social care; the gendered nature c
formal and informal care; the challenge posed to medicine by lay healt
knowledge, and the growth in 'expertise' among patients living wit
chronic illness and disability. A glance at social policy textbooks reveals

reoccupation with analyses of state policies, legislation and service provision, including the success or failure of particular services, the character and
effects of professional practices and the nature of services in the non-statutory
sectors. These themes in medical sociology and social policy are often
examined theoretically and empirically in the spirit of reforming services in
the interests of 'users' – to redressing the power imbalance between doctors/
service providers/service industries and patients/clients/'users'.

The Doctor–Patient Relationship

Constraints of space permit only a brief review of one of these social
response themes: the doctor–patient, or 'lay-professional', relationship. The
clinical encounter between doctor and patient has long been a core interest
in medical sociology:

> The position of doctors and patients exemplifies, in particular, the central place of
> professional authority and its acceptance or resistance by people who encounter
> it. The doctor–patient relationship is not only a major aspect of modern health
> care experience but also a critical lens through which the impact of scientific,
> technical and rational authority on everyday life is observed. (Bury, 1997: 79)

Sociological studies in this field have tended either to observe doctors
interacting with patients or to examine medical training and socialisation,
especially with regard to 'communication with the patient' (see discussion
in May *et al.*, 2005). In the 1960s and 1970s, British researchers were
absorbed with patient 'compliance', with the assessment of whether services were used appropriately by patients, and with understanding miscom-
munication in doctor–patient exchanges (Gerhardt, 1989; Bury, 1997). That
is, sociologists' research efforts were designed to help doctors and the
health care system deal with matters of actual or potential patient deviance
('for the good of all'); the influence of Parson's functionalism with its 'sick
role' duties and responsibilities was clearly in evidence. As this consensual
sociology gave way to variants of interactionism, phenomenology, conflict
theory, feminism, and poststructuralism, the doctor–patient relationship
became a focus for re-thinking and critique. Scholars using conflict theory
or poststructuralism interpreted the actions of medical professionals as a
means through which the social power of medicine is imposed (Freidson,
1970; Turner, 1987). In contrast, empirical work in the negotiation wing of
the interactionist tradition stressed the active and influential role that
patients could play in this medical encounter (Bury, 1997).

As time moved on, sociological analyses took note of the altered context
in which interactions between doctors and patients occur. According to
Bury (1997: 81), the most notable of these contextual shifts are: the rise of

chronic illness as the leading cause of morbidity, associated with popula
tion ageing; the tendency for patients to be more knowledgeable about anc
'expert' in managing their conditions than in the past; the relative declin
in patient deference towards doctors associated with a weakening of trus
in medicine and medical authority; and the impact of legal and ethica
challenges to the autonomy and authority of doctors. These changes hav
meant that, over time, some power is perceived to have shifted fron
doctors to patients, though the overall balance continues to favour medica
professionals (see Annandale *et al.*, 2004).

The 'Sociology of Disability'

Perhaps sociologists who have engaged with disability *per se* have been mor
likely to question cultural assumptions about the dependency and 'car
needs' of disabled people? The review of a seam of work that I characterisec
as a nascent 'sociology of disability' in Chapter 2 suggests that, overall, th
answer to this question has to be 'no'. However, a critical stance towards th
nature of social responses to dependency needs is certainly evident.

We learned, for example, that a focus on service responses to chroni
illness and disability occupies centre-stage in Gary Albrecht's sociology c
disability. His work is best known for its political economy of the profil
driven rehabilitation industry in the US, captured in the title of his book
The Disability Business (1992) (see Chapter 2, this volume). This led Albrech
to recognise that medically dominated rehabilitation services play a centra
role in producing and constructing disability by drawing the boundaries c
eligible disablement. Moreover, his analysis revealed that rehabilitatior
programmes allow doctors to maintain control in disabled people's live
beyond rehabilitation interventions; despite purporting to promote func
tional independence, professionals actually perpetuate dependency
However, Albrecht does not question the assumption that chronic illnes
and disability (defined in the ICIDH sense, as limited activity resultin
from impairment) cause individuals to have unavoidable degrees c
dependency and need of care. Rather, *medically constructed* disability i
understood to impose a layer of meaning upon this bedrock of need suc
that only some people 'count' as disabled and qualify for services.

One study that does question the dependency status of disabled peopl
is Robert Scott's *The Making of Blind Men* (1969), another North America
sociological analysis of disability, based on extensive empirical researc
with both blind people and professionals/workers in 'organisations for th
blind' (see Chapter 2, this volume). Scott offers a damning sociologica
critique of the social creation of dependency in the name of 'care' an
'rehabilitation', all the more remarkable for the fact that his research wa

ointly sponsored by the *New York Association for the Blind* and the *Russell Sage Foundation*. Scott's labelling theory perspective (Scott and Douglas, 972), led him to conclude that individuals who developed visual impairment are socialised into archetypal 'blind' behaviours by organisations set up assist them. It is worth quoting his observations at length:

> The personal conceptions that blinded persons have about the nature of their problems are in sharp contrast with beliefs that workers for the blind share about the problems of blindness. The latter regard blindness as one of the most severe of all handicaps, the effects of which are long-lasting, pervasive, and extremely difficult to ameliorate. They believe that if these problems are to be solved, blind persons must understand them and all their manifestations and willingly submit themselves to a prolonged, intensive, and comprehensive program of psychological and restorative services. Effective socialization of the client largely depends upon changing his views about his problem. In order to do this, the client's views about the problems of blindness must be discredited ... . In short, blind persons who are acceptable to the agency for the blind will often find that intake workers listen attentively to their views but then dismiss them as superficial or inaccurate. (Scott, 1969: 77–8)

Scott goes on to outline the assumptions and theories about blindness and its amelioration shared by people who work for the 'blind agencies', including the sheltered workshops, and reports that while some people with visual impairment escape the grip of these organisations and live independently (difficult without resources) others become 'professionally' blind or 'true believers': 'True believers are blind people for whom workers' beliefs and assumptions about blindness are unquestioned ideals toward which they feel impelled earnestly to strive' (ibid.: 87).
However:

> The sequestering of blind people from the community by blindness agencies is not accomplished without certain psychological costs both to the community and to workers in the agencies. A deep-seated, abiding sense of guilt often develops in both groups, stemming from the recurring suspicion that blind people (or any other unwanted groups, for that matter) may not always find the arrangements provided for them compatible with their needs and aspirations. There is a gnawing doubt in the minds of many that the blind may not desire only the company of others who are blind; that they may not have entirely lost a desire or ability to be independent; or that they may continue to desire the freedom to make vital decisions affecting their own lives.

This is a rare example of a critical analysis of the social construction of dependency in disability contexts in the sociology of health and social care. Attention is directed towards the workings of social institutions, albeit with a particular focus on the attitudes of individuals that work within those institutions rather than wider structural and political context in which the institutions operate:

> Blind men are not born, they are made; the challenge to an organized intervention system such as work for the blind is to render the process by which this occurs both rational and deliberate. (ibid.: 121)

One wonders what shape the academic landscape might have assumed if more sociologists had taken Scott's path. His approach shares common ground with those found in disability studies.

Disciplinary Engagements with Care and Dependency: Disability Studies

Antipathy to 'Care' and 'Dependency'

Working within the social oppression paradigm, writers in disability studies have adopted radically different perspectives on matters of care and dependency to those found in medical sociology and social policy. The cultural assumption that being impaired (including being chronically ill) inevitably leads to dependency, and that people with impairments are, by definition, 'in need of care', is challenged in the strongest terms. All taken-for-granted categories are contested, and the terms 'care' and 'dependency' are refused, as is the term 'sufferer'. This does not mean that disabled people's requirements for resources, support systems, 'services' (in the generic meaning of the term) and medical treatment are denied (Oliver, 1996a). On the contrary, such 'support needs' – to use Jenny Morris's (2001) phrase – are deemed essential, though hugely variable according to individual circumstance, and can be matters of life or death. It does mean that forms of 'treatment' and 'care' that have been financed, organised and provided by charities, the state and other agencies *for* disabled people over the past 200 years are rejected and condemned: that is, the care system is viewed as central to disablist structures and practices in society.

This is for two principal and connected reasons. First, it is argued that traditional forms of social response have allowed doctors and other health and social care professionals to assume paternalistic positions of power and control in the lives of disabled people, so undermining or negating disabled people's capacity for autonomy and self-determination. However strong and widespread the 'to help and do good' motivations of professionals, the effects are perceived to be the same: the subordination of disabled people to professional rule. This is equally true of professionals striving to 'normalise' the lives of people with learning difficulty in line with Wolfensberger's

983) 'social role valorisation' strategy (see Chapter 2, this volume; happell, 1992; Swain and French, 1999; Goodley, 2000). Second, profesonals and their institutions are held responsible for creating and exacerating dependency among disabled people by denying them the means by hich to govern their own lives. Professionals have achieved this both rectly through their work practices with individual disabled people, and directly by generating, sustaining and spreading a social ideology, now eeply rooted, that portrays disabled adults and children as 'ill', in need of re, incapable of living independent lives: in short, a social problem inkelstein, 1980, 1991; Sutherland, 1981; Morris, 1993a, 1995; Oliver, 996a; Oliver and Barnes, 1998; Shakespeare, 2000; Drake, 2001; Corker and nakespeare, 2002; Swain and French, 2003). From this perspective, profesonals and the social institutions they serve can be seen to contribute to ree of the five faces of oppression outlined by Iris Marion Young (1990), iscussed in Chapter 3: first, the social *marginalisation* of disabled people is olstered, second, the *powerlessness* of disabled people is exacerbated, and, ird, the discourse of disabled people's dependency is sustained through rofessionals' *cultural imperialism*. A fourth dimension of oppression in oung's schema is also reported to have come into play in the history of are services' for disabled people: coercion through actual or threatened *olence* and abuse – in the forms of neglect, psychological cruelty, or hysical or sexual assault (see also, Sobsey, 1994).

An important theme in disability studies is that the residential instituons that operated from the late eighteenth century until well into the ventieth century to house categories of people in socially segregated ettings – 'the blind', 'the deaf', 'the insane', 'the lame', and so forth – have layed a critical role in the historical creation of disabled people's dependency eal and ideological) (Borsay, 2005). This 'warehousing' version of the eation of dependency is thought to be alive in today's residential 'care' istitutions, and to have been merely reinvented and repackaged under the uspices of 'community care' (Oliver, 1996a; Oliver and Barnes, 1998; riestley, 1999; Swain *et al.*, 2003; Oliver and Sapey, 2005). Moreover, inforal 'family care' is thought *not* to be exempt from dependency creation: is variant of 'community care' by no means guarantees greater dependence and autonomy for disabled people (Morris, 1993a). Indeed, it ever has: 'family care' has been the main form of care provision roughout the industrial era, albeit in the shadow of institutional 'care' ntil recent decades, and is often performed under the direction of rofessionals (Borsay, 2005). John Swain *et al.* (2003: 80) draw attention to roups that are particularly vulnerable to 'dependency creation' today:

Disabled young people, particularly those with learning difficulties, may be over controlled by their parents and carers and denied opportunities for experimentation

and choice. People with learning difficulties may find it difficult to initiat
change and parents and carers may be reluctant to do so because of upheava
risk and threat to existing sources of support.

Theorising Dependency

While disability studies writers agree that disabled people's dependenc
upon doctors, professionals, care workers and informal carers is sociall
constructed, they disagree on how this has come into being and on th
forms of power involved. In essence, Marxists and materialists viev
dependency as economically founded, that is, a consequence of the exclu
sion of people with perceived impairments from the labour force in th
period of capitalist industrialisation, and the continued denial of the
access to paid labour in subsequent years. This resulted in the enforce
reliance of people with impairments upon others for material subsistenc
and personal support (family, charities, state services), and the
consequent subjection to coercive regimes of professional control an
dependency creating practices (see Chapter 3, and: Finkelstein, 198(
Barnes, 1991; Beresford *et al.*, 1996, 2002; Oliver, 1996a; Oliver and Barne:
1998; Swain *et al.*, 2003).

Poststructuralists, especially those influenced by Foucault's thinkin
consider the surveillance, regulation and disciplining of the 'disable
body' by professionals and others in authority – the nub of dependency
to be an achievement of bio-power (or bio-politics), from the late eigh
teenth century. Bio-power is viewed as a devastatingly effective an
ubiquitous form of power exercised by medicine in modern and pos
modern societies, capable of instituting the *self-regulation* of dependenc
among disabled people (Shakespeare, 2000; Corker and Shakespear
2002; Tremain, 2005) (see Chapters 2, 3 and 5). Once allocated t
an 'abnormal' category by medical professionals, individuals become sut
ject to medical and state control in the name of 'treatment', 'care' an
'welfare'. Their 'dependency' is continuously performed and re-inscribed
in the bio-medical and related institutional arenas, and in wider cultura
discourses.

Feminist writers, using a variety of theoretical perspectives, have draw
attention to the ways in which the gender order impacts on the structures an
experiences of service provision and professional practice – whether in inst
tutional or community settings (Morris, 1995, 1996; French, 2001; Thoma
2001; McFarlane, 2005). This has alerted disability studies to the need to cor
sider how dimensions of social 'difference' play out in the social constructio

f dependency (see, for example, Begum *et al.*, 1994). Deborah Marks (1999, ee Chapter 3) is among the few to have offered psychoanalytic interpreta-ions of the motivations and practices of the 'caring professionals'.

ndependent Living

'urning to solutions, disability studies writers in the academy have sought •oth to press for radical change in existing professional practices and velfare state policies, and to support new forms of living and support .rrangements initiated by disabled people. Finkelstein (1991), for example, •utlined the need for a new class of professionals, immersed in disability ulture – 'PACs' (Professionals Allied to the Community) – in place of the 'rofessionals Allied to Medicine that we have today. However, the difficulty n bringing about change in the professions has not been underestimated. 'rofessional power and dominance is understood to be ingrained in and •olstered by historically deep-rooted structures, and to be officially sanctioned .nd jealously guarded (French and Swain, 2001). Sally French (1994, 2001) 1as argued that the greater involvement of disabled people in the profes-ions as trained practitioners might improve professionals' responsiveness .nd utility from the point of view of service users, though this would equire the dismantling of the many barriers that currently discourage or >revent disabled people from becoming professionally qualified, or that >revent individuals sustaining their professional roles if they become mpaired during their working lives.

The struggles for *independent living* (or integrated living, as it is some-imes called) waged by disabled people's movements in the US and the UK 1ave proved to be much more successful routes to change than attempts to eform professional practice.[5] Fundamental to the independent living idea .re the principles of *control*, *choice* and *self-governance*: that is, disabled peo-•le must have control of their own lives, and must have choices available hat make control and self-governance meaningful (Morris, 1993a).

This notion of independent living challenges the culturally normative neaning of 'independence' – echoing themes discussed early in this chapter. n the words of the disabled activist, Simon Brisenden:

> [Disabled people are victims of an] ideology of independence. It teaches us that unless we can do everything for ourselves we cannot take our place in society. We must be able to cook, wash, dress ourselves, make a bed, write, speak and so forth, before we can become proper people, before we are 'independent' … . [The independent living movement uses the word 'independent'] in a practical and commonsense way to mean simply being able to achieve our goals. The point is that independent people have control over their lives, not that they perform every

task themselves. Independence is not linked to the physical or intellectual capacity to care for oneself without assistance; independence is created by having assistance when and how one requires it. (Brisenden, 1989, cited in Morris, 1993a: 23)

Jenny Morris believes independent living is possible for people with all types of impairment:

The [independent living] movement is clear that its aims and aspirations are as relevant to those with intellectual impairments, to older people (including those with conditions such as Alzheimer's Disease), and those who are survivors of the mental health system, as they are to the stereotype of the fit, young male paraplegic. (Morris, 1995: 74)

From this perspective, freedom from professional control and authority is considered central and essential, as is freedom from reliance on charity. Making choices means having access to financial and other resources to secure the assistance necessary to live in a self-determined way – at a decent standard of living. 'Assistance' may take the form of *personal assistance* (obtaining the help of another person for the completion of tasks like personal bathing and washing, dressing, cooking, household laundry, and transportation), or the use of assistive technologies, or the securing of adaptations to buildings and vehicles. Independent living is associated with a 'civil *rights* not welfare *needs*' philosophy, extending beyond matters of 'living conditions' to encompass the exercise of choice and control in all social arenas, in the spirit of obtaining full citizenship (Morris, 1993a; Oliver 1996a; Priestley, 1999). As Jenny Morris (2004: 428) puts it: 'Independent living itself is a means to an end: it is a way of people accessing [...] human and civil rights'.

Celebrated examples of disabled people's success in creating an infrastructure for independent living are Centres for Independent Living (CILs) (alternatively entitled 'Centres for Integrated Living'). The first recognised CIL was established in Berkeley, California, in 1973, involving a personal assistance scheme under the control of its disabled users. Ten years later there were more than 200 CILs in the US, offering advice and new styles of user-controlled services to local disabled people (Crewe and Zola, 1987). Parallel developments occurred in Sweden, Denmark and the Netherlands in the 1970s and 1980s (Priestley, 1999). In Britain, attempts to move towards independent living developed in tandem with the implementation of the state's deinstitutionalisation policies in the 1980s: the closure of residential institutions (long-stay hospitals and units for 'younger' disabled people) and the relocation of former 'patients' and residents to 'community care' settings. In this context, some disabled people's organisations inspired by the emerging social model of disability at home and independent living movements abroad, sought to establish schemes and projects for independent living, rather than succumb to community care arrangements designed by statutory services or the voluntary sector (in the charity tradition). The landmark *Derbyshire Centre for Integrated Living* (DCIL) was the first of its kind in Britain, campaigned for and established by the Derbyshire Coalition of Disabled People (DCDP). The DCDP developed its plans around seven core areas – the need for: information, counselling, housing, technical aids, personal assistance, transport and access. It achieved a landmark negotiated partnership with local statutory services.

> The Coalition's vision for DCIL was twofold. On the one hand, it would begin to redefine the form and content of welfare delivery, going beyond the provision of 'care' and concerning itself instead with the removal of barriers to integrated living. On the other hand, it would begin to alter the social relations of welfare production by establishing mechanisms of joint control between the local state and disabled people themselves. (Priestley, 1999: 76)

Other CILs have followed, varying in their mode of organisation and provision. Personal assistants (PA) as opposed to 'carers' have become key to independent living arrangements, with PAs working under the direction of disabled persons. There are now a wide variety of independent living and personal assistance schemes, usually associated with the provision of *direct payments*. At present, there is a statutory duty (Direct Payments Act, 1996 and subsequent legislation) placed upon local authorities to offer cash payments to disabled individuals to enable them to purchase the PA services they are assessed as requiring. Payment arrangements are backed up by advisory and supplementary support initiatives for the new breed of disabled 'employers' (Barnes *et al.*, 2000).

Notwithstanding these gains and developments, and the potential offered for meaningful autonomy, the move towards independent living in the UK has not been easy or straightforward, and the picture continues to change daily:

> … user-controlled services were relatively slow to develop in the UK. This is mainly because, unlike America and many other countries across the world, Britain has a veritable farrago of state-run services and a large and well-established voluntary sector. Most of this provision is controlled and run by non-disabled professionals of one sort or another. In several respects, therefore, the problem for the British disabled people's movement was less to do with creating services and more to do with controlling them. (Barnes, 2002: 315)

Researchers have established that disabled people who aspire to attain full or enhanced degrees of independent living have encountered barriers in their path, not least those set up by Local Authorities who issue direct payments; many – including older people and members of minority ethnic communities – are unaware that such alternatives to traditional care services are either available or represent realistic options (Morris, 1993a, 2004; Bignell and Butt, 2000; Rummery, 2002; Vernon, 2002; Pearson, 2004; Riddell *et al.*, 2005). Thus, as in other domains of social life, independent living is not an area free from inequities associated with gender, 'race', age, sexuality, class – and impairment type (Morris, 1995; Riddell *et al.*, 2005).

Finally, on a qualifying note, Tom Shakespeare (2000) has pointed out that CIL-type independent living arrangements may not appeal to all disabled people. Some may prefer what he terms 'low-intensity support' (see Shakespeare, 2000 for examples), and others may prefer traditional family care arrangements. Nor is independent living free from dangers – the potential exploitation of the labour-power of PAs as a new class of 'domestic servants' being the most obvious: 'It would be deeply unfortunate if the liberation of disabled people from dependency contributed to the exploitation of another disempowered section of the population'(Shakespeare, 2000: 68). This concern is taken up in *Episode* 3, below.

Episodes of Debate and Disagreement

We now move from an overview of disciplinary engagements with care and dependency to consider a number of documented clashes of perspective. The discussion is structured around notable *episodes*, as I shall call them, of direct debate between representatives of the social oppression and social deviance paradigms. The four episodes selected for inclusion in this chapter have occurred during the last 40 years and have involved a number of leading figures – protagonists let's say – in their respective fields, and are marked by particularly sharp and concise expressions of view and political stance – thus getting to the nub of the matter. Episodes include: recorded face-to-face discussions and arguments in meetings, seminars and conferences; published critiques and counter-critiques in journals and books; and edited collections designed to showcase debate 'across the divide'. Despite the 'past' status of these episodes, the fundamental attitudes to dependency and care expressed have strong echoes in today's debates and disagreements. *Episode* 5 – focusing on the lived experience of disability and impairment – is located in Chapter 6.

Episode 1 – The Fundamentals: Debate Between UPIAS and The Disability Alliance

The first episode concerns a debate that took place at a meeting in November 1975 between representatives of two campaigning organisations: UPIAS and

The Disability Alliance (TDA). As discussed in Chapter 3, UPIAS and its leading members, Paul Hunt and Vic Finkelstein (disability activists of a materialist persuasion), played a critical role in laying the political foundations for the emergence of disability studies as a distinct academic discipline in the UK. *The Disability Alliance* was a broadly based coalition of organisations – both 'for' and 'of' disabled people – that came together in 1974 in pursuit of a comprehensive income for disabled people (see Campbell and Oliver, 1996, for further information). It was formed because an earlier organisation – the *Disablement Income Group* (DIG) – had failed to make progress towards securing such an income. Peter Townsend, a sociologist in the critical theory tradition (see Chapter 2) with social democratic politics and a strong campaigning instinct, was one of the founders of TDA. Townsend is perhaps best known for his research on poverty and old age, and as a member of the group that produced the *Black Report* on health inequality (Townsend and Davidson, 1982), but has maintained a long-standing and related interest in disability. He belongs to a generation of sociologists that produced a cadre of policy advisors to the post-Second World War Labour Party, and to some Labour Ministers in the 1960s and 1970s (SPA News, 2002).

The meeting of UPIAS and TDA in 1975 took place a few years after the *Chronically Sick and Disabled Persons Act* (1970) had given disabled people rights to certain community support services,[6] and at a time when the UK programme of de-institutionalisation was underway. It thus occurred at a critical juncture: the attitudes adopted on questions of need, dependency and care could propel disabled people in contrasting directions.

Hunt, Finkelstein and Townsend were all named 'speakers' (with five others) at the meeting, an event involving 20 people in all. Such details are known because the discussion was meticulously recorded by UPIAS. A summary of the dialogue in 'stage script' form, together with pre-circulated and follow-up 'Commentary' papers produced by both organisations, was published in the now landmark document *Fundamental Principles of Disability* (UPIAS and TDA, 1976).[7] The agreed purpose of the meeting was: to consider ways 'in which disabled people can become more active and involved in their own affairs' (ibid.: 1976: 3). Debate revolved around the nature of the *Alliance* and the conditions under which UPIAS (an organisation founded and led by disabled people) could be persuaded to join it. UPIAS members insisted that their organisation would only join if agreement could be reached on some fundamental principles about the nature of disability and the way forward for disabled people; these had been set out in the UPIAS *Policy Statement* paper, circulated prior to the meeting. *Fundamental Principles* records that UPIAS speakers returned repeatedly to these principles in the course of the discussion:

Disability is a situation, caused by social conditions, which requires for its elimination, (a) that no one aspect such as incomes, mobility or institutions is treated in isolation, (b) that disabled people should, with the advice and help of others, assume control over their own lives, and (c) that professionals, experts and others who seek to help must be committed to promoting such control by disabled people. (UPIAS, in UPIAS and TDA, 1976)

We see captured in these lines the newly formulated social interpretation of disability, and UPIAS members' key concerns of the day: disability is caused by the way that society treats people with impairments (*not* by impairment *per se*); social change on *all* fronts is required, not just on the income question;[8] disabled people must win control over their own lives; and the control that health and social care professionals have over disabled people's lives must be come to an end. In the spirit of these principles, the occupation of leading positions in the *Alliance* by non-disabled 'experts' (as they were termed) was seen as very problematic by UPIAS members – representing 'more of the same'.

Fundamental Principles records that Townsend had announced his full support for the UPIAS principles in advance of the 1975 meeting, and had even asked to become an Associate Member of UPIAS. At the meeting itself, however, Townsend would not be pinned down on these principles, and repeatedly asserted that the best way to advance the social position of disabled people was via the 'incomes' route, under the auspices of the *Alliance*. The following extracts from *Fundamental Principles* – combining reported speech and direct quotations – give a flavour of the exchanges that took place:

> FINKELSTEIN: Forming an umbrella organisation has not touched the fundamental issues, and unless you raise and investigate these questions – 'what is disability, and how come we are impoverished in the first place' – you are not going to deal with the causes of disability, and it may well be that your approach will help to perpetuate them. (ibid.: 7)

> PETER TOWNSEND said that statements of policy, etc, were 'open to different and acceptable meanings'. But PAUL HUNT reminded him that they were talking about absolutely fundamental principles, and PETER TOWNSEND then replied, 'You must understand, a social scientist who is asked to make a declaration about cause and effect takes up a very complicated position about factors which are associated as to make it difficult, in lay terms, to distinguish cause from effect – I have to make that point'.

> VIC FINKELSTEIN interrupted to say, 'That's just not acceptable, because it's implying that disabled people can put their necks out by making a declaration of what we feel is cause and effect, but you as a social scientist can't'. (ibid.: 8)

The outcome of the meeting was that no agreement was achieved on the UPIAS principles, and UPIAS declined to join the Alliance. Peter

Townsend, the representative of mainstream sociology and a social policy advisor, and Paul Hunt and Vic Finkelstein, disability activists, went
their separate ways thereafter. The rest, to coin a phrase, is history.
Indeed, this book might not have been necessary if things had turned out
differently.

Reflecting on the event years later, Vic Finkelstein said in an interview:

> ... when someone like Peter Townsend didn't come out in full support of the
> Union. If he'd been more foresightful he should have supported us. They
> [Alliance] really should have supported us. We had a lot to bring – if they'd
> thrown in their lot with us it would have been a different situation altogether.
> (Finkelstein, in Campbell and Oliver, 1996: 83)

From a 2006 vantage point, I think it true to say of Townsend's 1970s stance
that a leading British sociologist of health and social care has never again
come so close to forging links with radical disabled thinkers on a *social* interpretation of disability, nor to being so prepared to debate political strategy
in such a direct way. Townsend was certainly genuine in his view that disability should be understood as a social question. This is evident in another,
related, example of his connection with Paul Hunt: Townsend wrote the
Foreword to Hunt's (1966) collection of disabled people's essays, published as
Stigma. The Experience of Disability (see Chapter 3, this volume). And he also
appreciated that disabled people laboured under the weight of professional
and 'care' service dominance. In his *Foreword*, Townsend wrote:

> [The *Stigma* essays] reflect a much deeper problem of a distortion of the structure
> and value-system of society itself. Achievement, productivity, vigour, health and
> youth are admired to an extreme. Incapacity, unproductiveness, slowness and
> old age are implicitly if not explicitly deplored. Such a system of values moulds
> and reinforces an elaborate social hierarchy. The disabled are as much the
> inevitable victims of this system as the young professional and managerial
> groups are its inevitable beneficiaries. The question that is therefore raised is not
> a straightforward one. It is complicated and immense. Is it possible to secure real
> gains for those who are disabled without calling for a reconstruction of society
> and schooling new attitudes in the entire population? ...
>
> ... [The authors of these essays] disentangle themselves from conventional
> expressions of gratitude for services rendered and propose introducing new pat-
> terns of rights into a situation which has traditionally been dominated by con-
> descension and patronage on the one hand and inferiority or deference on the
> other. By insisting on these rights they are saving many from a benevolent but
> indifferent superiority and laying the basis for a general pattern of more equal
> and less discriminatory social relationships. Some new and important steps have
> been taken to establish a common humanity. (Townsend, in ibid.: vii–viii)

Townsend's perspective – written in the 'radical' 1960s, at a time when conflict theories were on the rise in sociology – certainly contrasts with what
developed (and remains dominant) in 1980s medical sociology in the UK:
the interpretative *sociology of chronic illness and disability* (see Chapter 2). As
such, his writings on disability belong to what I have termed the nascent,
never developed, *sociology of disability*.

Episode 2 – In Whose Interests? Debates about Disability and Social Policy in the Early 1990s

In 1990, a seminar on *The needs and resources of disabled people* was held at
the Policy Studies Institute in London, funded by the Department of
Social Security. This was at a time when the Conservative government of
the day was actively pursuing its reform of the welfare state and had
published three major policy documents of relevance to disabled people.[9]
The influential Griffiths Report entitled *Community Care: Agenda for
Action* had appeared shortly before in 1988. Papers presented at the sem-
inar were later published in *Disability and Social Policy* under Gillian
Dalley's (1991a) editorship, half of which were written by well-known
social policy academics. Authors of other papers were are follows:
Michael Oliver (disability studies academic and activist, see Chapter 3,
this volume), Richard Wood (then Director of the *British Council of
Organisations of Disabled People* (BCODP)), Peter Large (listed as
'Disablement Income Group and Hon. Parliamentary Advisor'), Jill
Pitkeathley (*Director of the Carers National Association*), Ian Bruce
(Director-General of the *Royal National Institute for the Blind*) and Brian
McGinnis (Director of *Mencap* – a charitable organisation *for* people with
learning difficulties and their families).

Brought together, therefore, were people with perspectives known to be
in opposition on questions of disability, need, dependency and care. That
this 1990 seminar should assemble such a mixed group is, in my view, an
interesting reflection on a number of developments: growing recognition of
the disabled people's movement; the presence of 'disability studies' on the
academic radar; and the acknowledgement among health and social care
academics that their monopoly of this intellectual terrain in the social
sciences was under challenge.

In her introductory chapter, Dalley (1991b) notes, though rather
understating the case, that there was 'a lack of consensus' at the seminar.
Papers articulating arguments from a disability movement perspective –
especially those by Richard Wood and Michael Oliver – were indeed sharp
and polemical, rejecting any common starting point with social policy
academics. Wood left no room for doubt about the response of BCODP to

the community care policy agenda:

> ... the government's proposals amount to 'more of the same' as far as we are concerned. Significantly, the White Paper [*Caring for People*] ignored the call from disabled people for self-empowerment, and concentrated instead on the re-hashing of existing inappropriate services and devising new roles for yet another new breed of professionals who will have more control over our lives than we have ourselves.
>
> The fundamental problem with these proposals stems from the notion that disabled people want care. Disabled people have never demanded or asked for care! (1991: 199)

Wood went on to argue that disabled people had sought to maximise independence and control over their lives through independent living arrangements, and had thrown off the 'medical model' interpretation of their dependency needs.

Oliver rejected the Government's care policies and proposals on similar grounds, but advanced a more generalised critique: in short: 'The welfare state has failed disabled people' (ibid.: 156) and had consolidated their dependency. He asserted that the real beneficiaries of health, social care, education, housing and employment services were the professionals and workers employed by these services – the 'denizens of the disability industry' (K. Davis, 1990): they secure salaries and wages, career structures, interesting working lives, and much more. Oliver called for a radical restructuring of state welfare so that welfare services *really* served disabled people – by maximising their independence; anti-discrimination legislation was a parallel necessity.

In my view, Dalley's (1991b) reflections on these outright rejections of Government policy and normative (lay and academic) assumptions about disabled people and their dependency are illustrative of the opening up of a tension in the academy. On the one hand she recognised the value and legitimacy of views expressed by disabled people and their academic representatives, and wanted to acknowledge these in full, but on the other hand she thought the 'radical' wing of these constituencies took matters too far. Dalley distinguished between 'radicals' and 'reformers' *within* the disability movement. The radicals held the (social model) view that society rather than impairment causes 'disability', the reformers were 'more ready to accept that such impairments may be problems in their own right (although society compounds them) ...'(Dalley, 1991b: 3). She favoured the latter view: that impairment results in varying degrees of 'disability' (functional limitation). Some limitations can be accommodated with technical aids, some cannot: more serious impairment *'creates degrees of dependency* on other people to a greater of lesser degree ...' (ibid.: 3, my emphasis). Indeed, drawing on her own research, Dalley (ibid.: 3–4) insists that:

> Although some disabled people, notably the radicals, may declare they do not want care ... others disagree. The population of those with impairments is heterogeneous; very elderly people (many of whom have severe functional limitations) may accept a reduced level of social and economic activity, while positively wishing for care and services of the sort rejected by others [...]. Similarly, those unable to articulate their aspirations themselves may have to depend on advocates to do so for them. Their requirement or need for care (care being the partner of dependency) rather than [personal assistance] may be overwhelming ...
>
> Is the term 'dependency' useful, or is it too imbued with the normative assumptions which able-bodied people hold about those with disabilities? But while a young disabled person who seeks to function in society on the same terms as a young able-bodied person demands personal support and rejects notions of dependency, an infirm elderly person recognising his or her dependency calls out for care.

Thus, Dalley refuses to reject the traditional meaning of 'disability' and sounds a note of apparent 'realism'. The radical voices of individuals (with impairments) in the disabled people's movement and disability studies are positioned as holders of a 'minority view' – a view that loses validity, in her mind, because it downplays differences among disabled people, particularly those associated with age. Her argument was reiterated by medical sociologists in later debates – see *Episode* 4 below and *Episode* 5 in Chapter 6.

The papers written by the other social policy academics in Dalley's collection illustrate what these academics think they do best: provide detailed empirical accounts and systematic analyses of disability legislation, social security benefits, formal and informal care services, and disability and employment. While the shortcomings of state provision were spelt out, the analyses do not engage with a deeper critique of the fundamental principles informing the legislative and service system. That is, the normative assumptions concerning disabled people's needs, dependency status and care requirements are not questioned. Alan Walker and Lucy Walker (1991), for example, restrict their paper to a thorough review of disability benefits, concluding that evidence shows disability to be associated with poverty, that there is a close relationship between 'severity of disability' and financial need, that disability brings 'extra costs', and that a radical overhaul of the benefits system is required. However, a telling commentary on the times, in my view, is that these authors end with the following statement: 'It is not our place, as researchers, to choose between the different income schemes on offer; that must be a task for people with disabilities themselves' (ibid.: 53).

In earlier years they may well have said that the making of such choices should be left up to politicians and policy makers.

Episode 3 – Sisterhood Under Strain: Feminism, Gender and Community Care

We now move to a clash of perspective among feminist writers on matters of care and dependency, one that started in the pages of journal papers in the 1990s rather than in face-to-face meetings. This *episode* begins when disabled feminist writers took issue with mainstream feminist theorising and research on 'community care': they saw the latter's work as echoing and compounding society's normative assumptions – that disabled people are supposedly needy, weak, passive and dependent on care.

This clash is a very British affair. By way of contrast, the Icelandic disability studies' scholar, Rannveig Traustadóttir, was able to undertake feminist research on women's care work with disabled people in such a way that disablist assumptions and outcomes were avoided. The independent interests and needs of disabled people were at the forefront of Traustadóttir's thinking, as was reciprocity between 'carers' and 'cared for' (see the account in Traustadóttir, 2004; see also Traustadóttir and Johnson, 2000).

The Background

Gathering interest in 'care' and 'carers' among British feminist social policy writers and sociologists occurred in the 1980s. This interest was stimulated by the Conservative Government's legislative programme (noted above) which, in feminists' minds, was designed to shift 'the burden' of care (read 'costs' of care) from the institutional sector to women in the informal care sector. Social policy feminists argued that euphemistic policy statements extolling 'care in the community' actually meant unpaid familial care by women in the home – care by mothers, daughters, wives. In short, the state was relieved of financing the care of dependants – 'the disabled' and 'the old' – by taking advantage of women's traditional role as family carers (Finch and Groves, 1983; Finch, 1987; Dalley, 1988; Graham, 1991). New care responsibilities would tie women even more firmly to the kitchen sink and to hours of domestic drudgery, reinforcing women's oppression:

> We are clear about what we want to reject: we reject so-called community care policies which depend on the substantial and consistent input of women's unpaid labour in the home, whilst at the same time effectively excluding them

from the labour market and reinforcing their economic and personal dependence upon men. (Finch, 1984: 16)

But what did mainstream feminists think were the alternatives to community care 'for dependants'? Janet Finch (1984) reluctantly concluded that residential care for such people was the only realistic alternative, though the quality of care in residential settings would need to be much improved. In her view, schemes to *pay* informal carers in community settings would simply result in more low waged, unskilled and undervalued jobs for women workers.

In her book *Ideologies of Caring* (1988), Gillian Dalley – whom we know from *Episode* 2 above – concluded that community care was against the interests of *both* female carers and 'dependants' in receipt of care. She acknowledged that some organisations of disabled people were demanding to live in community settings in independent living arrangements, but dismissed such demands as unrepresentative of 'dependent people' as a whole; she opted to take the side of the 'silenced majority'. Dalley's strongly articulated preference was for the introduction of what she presented as innovative forms of *residential care*, forms that displayed a new 'collective ethos'.

The Response

Disabled feminist writers, most notably Jenny Morris (1991, 1995) and Lois Keith (1992, see, also, Walmsley, 1993), objected strongly to much of the substance in this feminist critique of community care – whilst appreciating the need to highlight the relationship between caring and women's subordination. Their objections can be summarised as follows.

First, Finch, Dalley and others, were criticised for separating non-disabled from disabled and elderly women, so setting up a conflict of interest between communities of women in the guise of 'the carers' and the 'cared for' (Morris, 1991: 28). That many, indeed most, of those referred to as 'dependants' were *women* had no apparent relevance; that is, these were not the women with whom social policy feminist writers identified or included in their 'we' or 'women' categories (read again, for example, Finch's statement above). In other words, disabled and elderly women were 'Othered' in the debate about community care, as they were in feminist analyses more generally (see Chapter 3, this volume). Moreover, in her own research with disabled women, Morris (1989, 1995) had found that *reciprocity* in caring relationships was common, and that disabled women often had substantial caring responsibilities of their own – for children, partners and others; the complexity of caring relationships could not be captured in any simple carer/cared for dichotomy.

Second, mainstream feminists were taken to task for buying into constructions of disabled people as passive and dependent burdens; normative assumptions were simply not questioned. Third, and related to the first two points, feminist researchers were criticised for not involving the 'recipients of care' in their empirical research: their research did not seek to record the voices and subjective experiences of 'the cared for', only those of carers.

For these reasons, mainstream feminists' endorsements of residential care solutions, however dressed up or reformed, found no favour whatever with disabled feminists. Independent living options, allowing disabled people to live in a home of their own, were the only acceptable solutions from the latter's point of view. In Morris' words:

> Given non-disabled feminists' inability to identify with the subjective experience of ['dependants'], perhaps they should be wary of prescribing the kind of care that would be best for disabled and older people. Dalley, however, is not inhibited by this. Dismissing the demands of the Independent Living Movement, she advocates new forms of collective provision on the grounds that it is only by removing caring and servicing functions from a family setting that the sexual division of labour (in both the private and public sphere) will be fundamentally undermined. A sceptical disabled feminist may comment that if communal living is such a liberating force for women, then perhaps non-disabled women should try it first before imposing it on disabled and older women whose lack of social, economic and political power makes them all too easy a target for enthusiasms and fashions in social policy. (1991: 33)

In response to this counter-critique by Morris and other disabled feminists – together with criticisms from other sources on grounds of 'race', class and the lack of recognition of male carers – some feminists in sociology and social policy became self-critical, and revised aspects of their thinking (see Graham, 1991). This occurred as feminism diversified into 'feminisms' in line with the acknowledgement and celebration of 'difference' (see Chapter 3). One important effect has been that more recent work on care by medical sociologists and social policy analysts is marked by greater sensitivity to silenced voices. For example, Julia Twigg's book *Bathing – the Body and Community Care*, published in 2000, considers what she refers to as 'the power dynamics of care' and explores 'bodywork' 'from the perspectives of both the recipients of help and care providers' (Twigg, 2000: ix). Twigg makes reference to the disability movement, the social model of disability, and debates within disability studies on impairment and the body. Gillian Parker, a stalwart of research on care and caring, is another example of a writer who now pays careful and sympathetic attention to positions adopted in the disabled people's movement and disability studies (see Parker, 1993; Parker and Clarke, 2002).

Recent Debate

Notwithstanding these changes, mainstream feminists who acknowledge and appreciate the gains made by disabled people did not necessarily escape criticism in subsequent years. A good example of this is associated with Clare Ungerson's research on care, which moved onto the terrain of direct payments and personal assistance in the late 1990s, in response to the changing social policy landscape (Ungerson, 1997b, 1999, 2000, 2004). Ungerson included personal assistance in what she termed hybrid forms of 'work' and 'care' bound up with new systems of 'commodified care' in the UK and other countries. While she accepted that disabled people were empowered because direct payments had 'underwritten their control of the quality, timing and responsiveness of the social support they receive' (2004: 190), she also drew attention to the negative effects that direct payments and related schemes could have on care-workers, the care labour market, and the nature of care-work. The effects Ungerson documents include the creation of marginalised groups of unregulated workers, lacking formal credentials, who are frequently denied employment rights and benefits. The vast majority of these care-workers are women: thus, the 'gender and care' relationship that marked the informal care debate has reformed in connection with *new systems* of paid care-work. Moreover, taking a life course view, Ungerson (2000) warns that the conditions of employment of these women were laying down the foundations for their disadvantage in old age. That is, on retirement, some of these women would find themselves chronically ill and disabled *and in need of care* – but unable to pay for it because they lack savings or pension rights. For these reasons, Ungerson argues that direct payment arrangements are bound up with a system of care that exacerbates social inequality, along both gender and class axes.

In a paper published in 1997, *Care or Empowerment? A Disability Rights Perspective*, Jenny Morris, objected strongly to Ungerson's analyses, once again taking up the cudgels against mainstream feminist research on care. Morris (1997b: 54) was uncompromising in her rejection of Ungerson's conflation of personal assistance with 'care', stating that: 'One cannot, therefore, have care *and* empowerment, for it is the ideology and the practice of caring which has led to the perception of disabled people as powerless'. Ungerson is accused of failing to appreciate the work and activities of the independent living movement and its struggle for personal assistance in place of 'care'. Morris (1997b: 60) adds that:

> ... social researchers have a moral responsibility to collaborate with this movement in any work which they develop on issues which are not of mere academic interest but which concern people's rights to choice and control in their lives.

Despite such mutual intransigence, evidence is to be found, in other quarters, of a drawing together of 'care' or 'independence' themes in disability studies and the sociology of health and social care – marking the increasing influence of disability studies in the academy. I refer to recent to papers on 'care' published by a team combining academics in disability studies and mainstream feminist research (see, Watson *et al.*, 2004; Hughes *et al.*, 2005). However, the work of this team marks a quite complicated twist in the 'care and dependency' story because the authors associated with disability studies – Nick Watson and Bill Hughes – are among those most critical of the social model of disability *within* disability studies (see Chapter 3, this volume). And, unlike Jenny Morris, Watson and Hughes are willing to raise questions about the drive towards independent living in disability politics.

Let us briefly consider a paper produced by this team, entitled (Inter)Dependence, Needs and Care: The Potential for Disability and Feminist Theorists to Develop an Emancipatory Model (Watson *et al.*, 2004) – published, tellingly in my view, in *Sociology* – the house journal of the British Sociological Association. Written at a time when direct payments legislation made independent living a potential reality for increasing numbers of disabled people, the paper outlines the 'tensions' alluded to in its title as follows (my summary):

1. *Feminists* have long theorised the way that 'care work' is profoundly gendered and combines emotional and practical labour. These features of care are found, to varying degrees, in all forms of unpaid and paid care work – including those that carry the title 'Personal Assistant' in independent living schemes. Female care work sustains women's disadvantaged social position because it is poorly paid or unpaid, and low status in character.
2. *Disability studies* and its activist base wish to break the link between care and dependency by championing independent living schemes and the provision of 'support' services to individual disabled people by *personal assistants* (PAs). To distance 'personal assistance' from 'care', the support supplied by PAs is presented in 'mechanical' and 'instrumental' terms: the potential for emotional links between employer and employee in the 'support' relationship is not addressed.

The tension between these two positions *appears* to be irreconcilable: the emancipatory interests of disabled people and women 'care workers' (i.e. PAs) are diametrically opposed. However, Watson *et al.* (2004) go on to suggest a possible way out of this impasse. In part, this would mean encouraging disability studies to find a way to acknowledge two things: first, that reciprocity and emotional investment may well be invested in the relationship between a PA and a disabled person; second, that women who work as PAs are open to, and must be protected from, exploitation (ibid.: 338). Watson *et al.* see the key to a resolution as involving the building of what is referred to as a 'discursive bridge' to mediate between these two positions. This would involve finding common ground by mounting an ideological challenge to prevailing and deep-rooted cultural assumptions about dependency and need (of the sort outlined at the start of this chapter), and their replacement with a discourse of 'interdependency', making use of concepts such as 'caringscapes' and 'needscapes'. This discourse bridge would be woven around the idea that *everyone* is interdependent and 'in need' at some time in their lives – drawing on ideas developed by feminist philosophers concerning 'a feminist ethics of care' – as opposed to a purportedly patriarchal 'ethic of rights' (Fraser, 1989; Tronto, 1993; Sevenhuijsen, 1998; F. Williams, 2001; Fraser and Gordon, 2002; see also Shakespeare, 2000; Lloyd, 2001).

Is this 'discursive solution' likely to find favour in disability studies or among sociologists of health and social care? Its emphasis on achieving social change through changing meaning and language may appeal to some poststructuralist thinkers, but I think it unlikely to find favour with others – particularly realist thinkers who wish to push ahead with independent living options. For those inclined towards the achievement of social justice through re-distributive means, a more obvious solution to the impasse might be to suggest that disabled people join with women PAs (and other care workers) in a common campaign to increase the monetary value of direct payments, so that PAs can earn much higher hourly wages (for a related argument, see Parker and Clarke, 2002). Such a solution is not considered by Watson and his co-writers, perhaps because it has purported passé 'class struggle' overtones.

Episode 4 – Individualism versus Collectivism

The final episode revolves around the politics of independent living. The significance of the argument between individuals recounted here lies not so much in the original dispute as in the persistence and contemporary relevance of the themes raised about state welfare *versus* individualised market-driven provision. A key role in this episode is played by the sociologist, Gareth Williams, whose interpretative research on chronic illness and 'narrative reconstruction' is highly regarded within medical sociology (G. Williams, 1984a, see also Chapters 2 and 6, this volume). As a UK medical sociologist, Williams is unusual in also having a long-standing interest in, and appreciation of, disability politics and the social oppression paradigm in disability studies. Indeed, this is clearly expressed in a recent publication:

> It seems to me that the oppressive quality of everyday life for many disabled people is indubitable, and the origins of much of this oppression lie in the hostile environments and disabling barriers that society (politicians, architects, social workers, doctors, and others) erects. (G. Williams, 2001: 135)

However, in the early 1980s, Williams published what proved to be a controversial critique of independent living movements (ILMs) (G. Williams, 1984b, see, also, G. Williams, 1991). As a consequence of this critique, Williams became something of a bête-noire in disability studies for some years. His argument, and the antipathy it excited, can be summarised in what follows.

Williams' Argument

Writing in the decade during which Margaret Thatcher's 'New Right' Conservative government in the UK was busy dismantling the post-war welfare consensus by 'rolling back the frontiers of the state', Williams launched what he later characterised as a broadly socialist critique of the independent living movements in the UK and US. In his view, the ILMs played into the hands of right-wing anti-welfarist forces. In the UK, an ILM would assist in the destruction of a system of state welfare that, no matter how imperfect, was the product of decades of working-class struggle. The ILM's approach in the US, in particular, celebrated an individualised, consumerist, free-market means of obtaining personal assistance – a stance that sat comfortably with US governments' liberal individualist ideology. In Williams' view, this held danger if applied in the UK – not least because market mechanisms always favour the most advantaged in *any* community – typically people who are middle class, male, and white. That is, those who are particularly vulnerable (politically and economically) and heavily reliant on state services would be placed in peril. For these reasons, the confluence of interests between the radical disability movement and New Right governments was much to be regretted:

> At a time when governments of the New Right are looking for any chance to cut and chop their health and social security budgets, one might suspect that this is not going to do the vast majority of disabled people much good at all. (G. Williams, 1991: 521).

Looking at Williams' argument afresh, it is clear that his left-leaning critique displayed his medical sociological supposition that disabled people are necessarily dependent on professionally run health and social services. Although he was far from uncritical of the ways in which professionals dealt with disabled people, the *reform* of these services was thought to be the best option: 'Professions, local authorities, and families, for all their oppressive qualities as institutions, also provide resources through which autonomy can be realised' (G. Williams, 1991: 522). It is of note that, in retrospect, Williams has revised his thinking and gone so far as to say that the socially normative stance adopted by medical sociology on disabled people's dependency is one means by which that discipline has made a contribution to the social oppression of disabled people (see G. Williams, 2001: 135).

The Response

Ken Davis (1984), a leading activist in the campaign that founded the *Derbyshire Centre for Integrated Living* (DCIL) was among disability activists and writers who responded to Williams' 1980s arguments with extreme hostility. Here, it seemed, was a non-disabled person, a medical sociologist outside the movement, arguing against disabled people's hard-fought struggle to throw off both the yoke of professional control and patronage and the ever present threat of institutional incarceration. Williams' position was branded reactionary by a number of influential figures (Oliver, 1996a: 155); he was portrayed as an academic in cahoots with the disablist establishment. In the 1980s and early 1990s this played no small part in fuelling perceptions, on all sides, that a 'major divide' existed between medical sociology and disability studies.

  In retrospect, the vitriolic reaction to Williams can be seen as a sign of the times. From the point of view of disabled activists and their supporters, there was a desperate need to champion independent living, and it is no surprise that academics in disability studies presented defensive accounts of CILs and other schemes for independent living. One effect was that achievements in securing independent living were sometimes attributed entirely to the tenacity of disabled people. As disability studies writer, Mark Priestley (1999), suggests, this underplayed the facilitative role played by Conservative administrations in the 1980s and early 1990s in their pursuit of pro-consumerist, individualistic, and market-oriented solutions to 'the problem of welfare' and, one must add, by 'New Labour' administrations since 1997 (see, also, Morris, 1993a).[10]

  In his analysis, Priestley (1999) discusses the reluctance of social service departments in traditional Labour Local Authorities to introduce user-managed disability services and direct payments, and the contrasting enthusiasm for such arrangements in Conservative governed Local Authorities – most famously in Hampshire, where the Authority's promotion of consumer markets and individualised 'choice' made it more amenable to the individualised 'cash for care' arrangements pioneered by the Hampshire CIL in the 1980s. Priestley (1999: 117) observed that 'Within this uneven political landscape, organisations committed to independent/integrated living tread a fine line between competing ideologies of welfare'. As a consequence, independent living organisations have taken different paths. Some have accommodated to individualised *laissez-faire* models of welfare provision, others, like the Derbyshire CIL, have held to collectivist or 'communitarian' arrangements accountable to representative organisations of disabled people (ibid.: 119).

Thus, with the benefit of hindsight, it is clear that the relationship between political ideology and independent living arrangements has proved to be much more complex than Williams' 1983 critique anticipated; and this policy landscape continues to develop in its complexity, year-by-year. A wide variety of independent living schemes are securely embedded in today's pluralistic modes of service organisation. The passage of the *Direct Payments Act* in 1996, and the strengthening of this legislation by successive Labour Governments, is testimony both to the ILM's success in the UK *and* to the now normative character of 'mixed economies of welfare'.

This means that while arrangements for independent living continue to be strongly promoted and protected within disability studies (Barnes, 2002), critical questioning from diverse theoretical stances is now more in evidence. In short, there is room for 'warts and all' examinations of independent living and direct payments (see, for example, Shakespeare, 2000; Pearson, 2004; Watson *et al.*, 2004; Askheim, 2005; Riddell *et al.*, 2005). In such a climate, I think it unlikely that papers produced by 'outsiders' such as Williams would spark as much antagonism as did his 1983 critique. This suggests that the time may be ripe for academics in disability studies and the sociology of health and social care to engage in more productive and beneficial exchanges when they examine independent living and the spectrum of other 'support services for living'.

What Do These Episodes Tell Us?

The four dialogic *episodes* have cast an illuminating light on the contours of the disciplinary divide, and have also drawn attention to the divide's dynamic and contextual character. Such a close-up examination has revealed major disagreements on the themes of care and dependency, but has also shown that debates have not been fixed or static. Although initial engagements across the divide were often heated and suggestive of entrenched stances, there are signs that, as a consequence, ideas at a disciplinary level have shifted and changed over time, if not in fundamentals then in small but incremental details. We have seen that positions and boundaries, at both individual and disciplinary levels, may be solidified, may be almost imperceptibly redrawn or may undergo a marked reworking.

To summarise: the exchange between UPIAS and Peter Townsend (for TDA) in *Episode* 1 is an example of the construction and solidifying of boundaries. The policy exchange in *Episode* 2 revolved around an attempt to bring representatives of an emergent disciplinary divide to the table – to air, clarify, and evaluate sharply contrasting perspectives; this too had a solidifying effect, but also laid the foundations for the recognition of difference and future debate. *Episode* 3 told a story of the clash of ideas and political stances among feminists on 'care' that did, eventually, lead to some rethinking and redrawing of boundaries among some mainstream feminists, and, more recently, to some re-thinking on care among some academics in disability studies. The decades covered in *Episode* 4 saw remarkable changes in policy and practice – in the wake of the independent living movement and successive Governments' encouragement of a mixed economy of welfare. Evidence of a wide disciplinary divide in the early 1980s was palpable: a medical sociologist's critique of independent living movements received a hostile 'keep out' response. But by the late 1990s and 2000s, independent living had become an established policy reality, and this created space for critical thinking in both disability studies *and* the sociology of health and social care (especially in social policy).

Summary: Care and Dependency

The review of ideas about care and dependency to be found in disability studies and medical sociology, the later broadened in this chapter to include aspects of social policy, has revealed a significant disciplinary divide. This divide was thrown into particularly sharp relief by opening the chapter with reflections on 'care' and 'dependency' at a higher level of abstraction; this helped to 'make strange' and socially situate these concepts. Starting in this way served to highlight the tendency among sociologists of health and social care to unquestioningly adopt and utilise deeply rooted cultural understandings of the care and dependency needs of 'chronically ill and disabled people'. The contrasting positions adopted by disability studies writers and activists could then be described: that is, their refusal to use the language of care and dependency, a position that flowed from their analysis of the social oppression of disabled people by, and within, the care system.

We have seen that the critical faculties of medical sociologists and social policy analysts have been directed towards *social responses* to the assumed care and dependency needs of disabled people (by medicine, welfare services, professional practices and informal care systems), informed by the overarching *social deviance* paradigm of illness and disability. A substantial, rich and specialised body of work now exists on the nature and effects of these responses. The diversity of theoretical traditions in medical sociology has generated markedly different interpretations and treatments of the response themes, resulting in contrasting moral and political standpoints on medicine, patienthood and welfare dependency. Critiques of medicine vary between the benign and the damning.

In contrast, the discussion has shown that the critical thought applied by writers in disability studies to medical, state welfare, charitable, and other organisational responses to disabled people has been otherwise motivated: to uncover the social mechanisms and practices that have secured disabled people's social dependency – that is, their social oppression in the name of 'care'. Disability studies has devoted a considerable amount of intellectual and empirical endeavour to examining and encouraging non-disablist forms of social support for disabled people: schemes for independent living, direct payments and personal assistance.

The second half of the chapter outlined four documented clashes of disciplinary perspective on care and dependency. These *episodes* have illustrated moments of sharp disagreement between representatives of disability studies and the sociology of health and social care, and have also revealed the 'live' and contextual (economic, political, cultural, historic) nature of these disciplines and perspectives. Overall, the *episodes* have thrown light on the dynamic nature of the inter-disciplinary relationships; by grappling with the themes of care and dependency in academic and policy arenas, each discipline has played a direct and indirect role in shaping the development of aspects of the other.

Overall, this chapter has shown that the disciplinary divide remains wide and deep on questions of care and dependency: the social oppression and social deviance paradigms clash irreconcilably.

5

The Body: Lost and Found

Introduction

Twenty-first century sociologists have lived with several decades of disciplinary excitement about 'the body', and much scholarly energy has been invested in the elaboration of a 'sociology of the body' (Turner, 1984, 1992; Shilling, 1993, 2005). This has involved an extensive re-examination of the sociological 'corpus' – to turn up, rediscover or re-invent 'the missing body'. British medical sociologists have certainly played their part in this, but disability studies theorists have been notable by their absence. The contrast is stark: medical sociologists helped to define the sociology of the body while influential disability studies theorists have given it a wide berth. The latter's avoidance reflects the setting aside of 'impairment' by disability movement pioneers in the UK, and the refusal of leading social modellists to get entangled with either the corporeality or emotionality of disabled people's lives.

The absence of disability studies writers from mainstream sociological debate about the body does not mean that silence has reigned *within* the discipline on 'the impaired body'. On the contrary, discussion within the social oppression paradigm has been persistent, heated and uncompromising. The first part of this chapter sketches out the contours of this discussion, setting competing ideas about impairment – some from North America – side by side; and I take the opportunity to outline my own thoughts on the concept 'impairment effects'. The chapter then moves on to examine a selection of ideas about 'the body' advanced by medical and mainstream sociologists. The discussion offers a *selective review* of the mass of literature that has been produced on the body – readers are referred to excellent overviews elsewhere (see, for example, Williams and Bendelow, 1998a; Howson and Inglis, 2001; Crossley, 2001a; S. Williams, 2003; Shilling, 2005). Here, the focus is on the treatment of 'chronically ill and disabled bodies' in the 'body work' of medical sociologists; interpretative analyses of the

120

xperience of living with chronic illness and disability are discussed in
hapter 6. In this chapter's final section, I reflect on how disability studies
ight make use of some of the insights on theorising bodies available in
edical and mainstream sociology.

)isability Studies: The Absent Body?

iven the *apparent* centrality of 'the body' to both impairment and disability,
utside observers might think it odd that disability studies writers did not
articipate in the rise to prominence of theorisations of embodiment in soci-
ogy and cultural studies. The explanation is, in fact, straightforward.
isability studies made its way into the academy on the basis of its opposition
> the idea, deeply rooted both within and outside social science disciplines,
aat 'disability' and 'being disabled' is *all about* the body and its defects.
s we learnt in Chapter 3, pioneer thinkers in what became disability stud-
s strove to expose this way of thinking as itself a feature of disablism. It
as argued that the systematic social exclusion of people with impairments
ad, for too long, been disguised by the attribution of their 'limitations' to
ie 'tragedy' of physical, sensory or intellectual deficits (Finkelstein, 1980;
liver, 1990, 1996a; Barnes, 1991). From this perspective, any focus on
npairment or 'the body' conceded ground to the biological reductionism
aat had been orchestrated and sustained by doctors and other health and
>cial care professionals for more than two centuries, a reductionism that
ves on in discourses and practices in all social institutions. The time had
>me to rethink 'disability', to break the thought chain that linked it to the
ievitable' restrictions imposed by defective bodies and biological fate, to
>-conceptualise 'being disabled' from a *social oppression* perspective. In this
>ntext it was deemed diversionary and wasteful of resources to spend
sciplinary time and energy examining the impaired body. The main task
as to undertake academic work that supported people who lived with
npairment in their struggle against social barriers and exclusionary
ractices.

Materialist Objections

is the influential materialist wing of disability studies that has taken the
ardest line on this question. In their attempts to develop a radically new
nderstanding of disability using a social oppression paradigm, Paul Hunt,
ic Finkelstein and other members of UPIAS broke the causal link between
npairment and disability (see Chapter 3). This summarily dismissed
npairment, and thus 'the body', from the stage. Michael Oliver went so far

as to suggest that 'disablement is nothing to do with the body' (Olive 1996a: 42). The systematic *social* disadvantaging of people with impairmer became the only legitimate focus for theory and politics.

However, one would be mistaken to take this to mean that the difficu ties and limitations directly connected with chronic illnesses and othe impairments were thought to be of no significance in shaping disabled pec ple's quality of life. This is an important point, one lost in superfici; engagements with the thinking that informed the development of disabili studies. Rather, such matters were pushed to the margins for three reasor (Oliver, 1996a, 2004): first, it was thought diversionary to dwell on impairmen second, illness and impairment were believed to be poor foci for politic; organisation and campaigning – better to transcend impairment difference so as to make common cause against disablism; and third, illness, impai ment and their emotional sequelae were deemed by leading male materia ists to belong to the 'personal and private' domain. Reflecting on the UPIA years, Finkelstein summed these points up as follows:

> The agreed UPIAS interpretation was that, although it may be a tragedy to ha\ an impairment, it is oppression that characterises the way our society is orga ised so that we are prevented from functioning. In other words, at the person level we may talk about acquiring an impairment as a personal tragedy, but the social level we should talk about [how] the restrictions that we face are, ar should be interpreted as, a crime. (Finkelstein, 2001b: 2)

Moreover, in the 1990s, Finkelstein (1996, 2001b) objected to any form introspective dwelling on *personal experiences* of either impairment or di ability (encountering barriers), and to the dragging of such concerns int the public arena: this diverted disabled people's energies away from tł struggle to change society. Colin Barnes (1998) has similarly warned of tł dangers of 'sentimental autobiography'.

Widening Debate on the Impaired Body in Disability Studies

In recent years, materialist minded writers such as Abberley (1987, 199 2002), Gleeson (1999) and myself (Thomas, 1999) have attempted to find place for 'the impaired body' in the materialist heartland of UK disabili studies. These attempts are now rather overshadowed by more vigorou poststructuralist and phenomenological endeavours to legitimise schola ship on impairment and the body within the discipline. Overall, calls 'bring the body back in' reflect the diversification of theoretical perspectiv in UK disability studies (see Chapter 3). But why and how this should t done has become a matter of debate and disagreement.

Writers have approached the impairment question from a number of angles, as we shall see in the following sub-sections. Differentially motivated discussions are now diverse and complex. In summary:

. A group of writers, including Abberley and Gleeson, have argued that impairment must be theorised because the *social theorisation of disability and disablism* – a perquisite of effective disability politics – is compromised without it. That is, aspects of disablism are obscured if 'being impaired' or 'impairment experiences' are not addressed or are naturalised. My work on 'impairment effects', discussed later in this chapter, is in agreement with this argument.

. Feminists have argued that the inclusion of 'impairment experiences' in disability studies is necessary on political grounds, because disability/disablism cannot be effectively challenged without account being taken of the *subjective experience* of 'living with impairment'; among other things, this throws a valuable light on the *differences* among disabled people associated with gender, 'race', sexuality, age, class – and impairment type.

. Poststructuralist arguments, led by feminist thinkers, have centred on the purported fallacy of splitting 'impairment' from 'disability'. From an anti-foundationalist perspective, the *deconstruction of the impairment/disability dualism* should be the principal focus. Somewhat surprisingly, its is only recently that researchers have exploited the obvious potential to develop Foucualdian-inspired historical and contemporary analyses of the regulation and disciplining of 'disabled' bodies through the exercise of bio-power in institutional and community settings (e.g. see McFarlane, 2004 and Tremain, 2005).

n response to these and other calls to address impairment, Michael Oliver 1996a: 42) eventually conceded that 'an adequate social theory of disability nust contain a theory of impairment', and that the social model of disabil-:y might be usefully twinned with 'a social model of impairment'. Nevertheless, Oliver left this to others to pursue, and always viewed it as a ubordinate theme: *disability* (in the social oppression sense) remained the rimary business of disability studies.

Materialist Voices: Impairment Must Be Theorised

'icking up argument (1) above, there are influential writers in the materialist amp who have been unwilling to relegate the impaired body and its effects ɔ the margins, most notably, Paul Abberley (1996, 1997, 2002). As discussed in Chapter 3, Abberley suggested that the theorisation of impairment would show that inclusion in the labour force was neither possible nor desirable *for everyone* who lived with impairment, and could not, therefore offer a universal liberatory solution to everyone – something that the social model of disability appeared to promise. In his view, theorising impairment would suggest new ways to tackle disablism – offering liberatory prospects of a different order.

Like Abberley, Brendan Gleeson (1999), whose historical materialist geography of disability was briefly reviewed in Chapter 3, also insisted on the importance of an 'embodied' approach. Gleeson found the ingredients for a nascent theory of social embodiment in Marx's political economy and view of nature; these, he suggested, would allow the body to take its place in a developed theorisation of the *social* origins and nature of disability building on the ideas of Finkelstein (1980) and Oliver (1990). Gleeson suggested that the emergence of a form of social oppression based on impairment was bound up with a complex and historically uneven 'repression of certain forms of embodiment', and that this had been a core dynamic of capitalism's development. From his perspective, the inability of people with impaired bodies to sell their labour-power to industrial capitalists signalled the development of an economic system resting on the calibration of the body for its capacity to labour. That is, each human being was viewed as a unique incarceration of employable capacities and in/abilities. As a consequence – and in particular times and spaces – the embodied particularities of individuals may disqualify their claims to social legitimacy and fuel the social construction of their 'abnormality'. In this way, Gleeson asserted that he could renounce the *naturalisation of disability* while insisting upon the *natural basis of disability*.

Feminists' Insistence on the Inclusion of Impairment Experiences

Picking up argument (2) above, feminist writers active in the disabled people's movement were among the first to disturb the equilibrium that was forming in the late 1980s and early 1990s around the social model's refusal to engage with impairment (see Chapter 3). Jenny Morris expressed the challenge as follows:

> There was a concern amongst some disabled women that the way our experience was being politicised didn't leave much room for acknowledging our experience of our bodies; that too often there wasn't room for talking about the experience of impairment, that a lot of us feel pressurised into just focusing on disability, just focusing on social barriers. (1996: 13)

Drawing on the earlier feminist movement's insistence that the personal is political, Morris argued that disability studies should embrace the physical and emotional realities entailed in living with impaired bodies, including pain, fear of dying, and coping with physical change and chronic uncertainty (see, also, Wendell, 1996; Garland-Thomson, 1997b; Meekosha, 1998). Morris (1989, 1996) and other feminists insisted on publishing research-based and biographical material detailing personal struggles with *both* impairment and disablism. This connected with matters of identity, agency and politics. Liz Crow underlined the political necessity of this:

> What we need is to find a way to integrate impairment into our whole experience and sense of ourselves for the sake of our own physical and emotional well-being, and subsequently for our individual and collective capacity to work against disability. (1996: 59)

Such views on the dangers of failing to find space for the articulation of impairment experiences found favour with other feminists in disability studies but met with an unsympathetic response from leading proponents of the social model. Oliver (1996a) and Finkelstein (1996) were not prepared to give ground to arguments that, in their view, threatened to breath new life into individual or medical models of disability, that is, to revive the 'personal tragedy' perspective. Finkelstein (1996: 34) stated that any inward contemplation of the subjective experience of living with either impairment or disabling social barriers was a 'discredited and sterile approach to understanding and changing the world'. As noted above, Oliver did eventually concede that a social theory of impairment might be an option – but not one that held any interest for him.

Constructed Corporeality: the Critique of the Impairment/Disability Dualism in Disability Studies

Turning to argument (3): the rejection of social modellist's sidelining of impairment was taken in other directions by feminist and other scholars influenced by poststructuralist and related anti-foundationalist perspectives. Echoes of wider debates about 'the body' in sociology and cultural studies are much in evidence in their writing. As discussed in Chapter 3, poststructuralists view the impairment/disability distinction as a classic illustration of modernist binary divides – as a dualism badly in need of deconstruction and transcendence. Bill Hughes and Kevin Paterson (1997: 329), captured these concerns as follows:

> With respect to the body and impairment, the social model makes no concession
> to constructionism or epistemological relativism: it posits a body devoid of history.
> It also posits a body devoid of meaning, a dysfunctional, anatomical, corporeal
> mass obdurate in its resistance to signification and phenomenologically dead
> without intentionality or agency … . [T]here is a powerful convergence between
> biomedicine and the social model of disability with respect to the body. Both
> treat it as a pre-social, inert, physical object, as discrete, palpable and separate
> from the self. The definitional separation of impairment and disability which is
> now a semantic convention for the social model follows the traditional
> Cartesian, western meta-narrative of human constitution.

From this position, Hughes and Paterson acknowledged that the social model has played an important role in enabling a disabled people's movement to organise and make vitally important political gains, but insisted that it concedes the body to medicine and leaves it prey to essentialist discourses.

The North American feminist scholar, Shelly Tremain (2002, 2005), picks up this 'concession to medicine' and purported essentialism in her assertion that the British social model fails to observe that '… impairment and its materiality are naturalized effects of disciplinary knowledge/power' (Tremain, 2002: 34). Drawing on the writings of Foucault, she suggests that the category 'impairment' is a post-Enlightenment discursive object. In her view, the impairment/disability (nature/social) distinction should be deconstructed in the same way that Judith Butler (1993) dismantled the sex/gender dualism: both are products of systems of bio-power. The 'impaired subject' is produced, disciplined and governed (via direct regulation and self-regulation) by technologies of power, especially those wielded by medicine.

> Disciplinary practices in which the subject is inducted and divided from others
> produce the illusion of impairment as their 'prediscursive' antecedent in order
> to multiply, divide and expand their regulatory effects. (Tremain, 2002: 42)

This thoroughgoing constructionist approach therefore rejects any notion that there is an 'essential' body that could be said to be a 'normal' body – so setting the criteria for an 'impaired' body. Moreover, Tremain points out that by basing itself upon, and thus replicating, the biological/social binary divide, the social model inadvertently *extends* the relations of power that thrive on such dualisms – a serious charge indeed.

But how might the impairment/disability dualism be transcended? Poststructuralists have sought to dissolve it in different ways. Janet Price and Margrit Shildrick (1998, 2002) share Tremain's understanding that the 'impaired body' is socially constructed through medical regulatory practice

1d related systems of bio-power. Their approach to the dissolution of dual-
tic thinking is based on the idea that there is 'permeability between bodies
1d between embodied subjects' (Price and Shildrick, 2002: 62, see also
1ildrick and Price, 1996; Price and Shildrick, 1998). One only becomes
isabled' through the operation of discursive practices, and through an
1going process of 'becoming in the world of others'. That is, being impaired
· disabled are not pre-given or fixed social states. The 'self' and self-identity
·e effects of socially constitutive relationships, and the distinctions between
·lf and other are never fixed or final. Nevertheless, Price and Shildrick
ssert, rather unconvincingly in my view, that their theoretical perspective
oes *not* deny the 'distressing corporeality of disablement' (2002: 66).

Mairian Corker's desire to transcend the impairment/disability dualism
as a persistent theme in her writings (Corker, 1998; Corker and French,
!99a; Corker and Shakespeare, 2002). With Sally French, she explored
·hat was characterised as the discursive territory 'in between' impairment
1d disability (Corker and French, 1998a). This, they suggested, was the ter-
tory in which their experiences as women with a hearing impairment
:orker) and visual impairment (French) resided. These experiences were
·ntred on language and communication, and involved – *in a fused fashion* –
imensions of their embodied 'difference' (so-called impairment) *and*
imensions of the non-disabled world's reactions to them (so-called disability).
1 Corker's view, the social model's focus on social and economic barriers
f a material kind ignored the features of disablism that operate in linguis-
: and communicative cultural domains, with the effect that people with
·rtain types of impairment are excluded:

> … there is no doubt in my mind that deaf people, whatever their social, linguistic
> or cultural affiliations, have been marginalized or excluded from the development
> of social model theory and dialogues, because of the diminished role of language
> and discourse in social model theory, and the mind–body split inherent in some
> social model thinking. (Corker, 1998: 38)

1e expressed much confidence in the capacity of ideas derived from
·errida (1978) and other poststructuralists to overcome modernist binary
ivides and thus to offer disability studies a theoretical alternative to the
ominance of what, in her view, was a fatally flawed materialism.

It is useful to note, at this point, that Tom Shakespeare and Nick Watson
ive adopted an apparently more straightforward (rather than fully
·dged poststructuralist) means of overcoming the impairment/disability
ualism – by suggesting a 'continuum' conceptualisation:

> Impairment and disability are not dichotomous, but describe different places on
> a continuum, or different aspects of a single experience. It is difficult to determine

where impairment ends and disability starts, but such vagueness need not [debilitating. Disability is a complex dialectic of biological, psychological, cultur and socio-political factors, which cannot be extricated except with imprecisio (Shakespeare and Watson, 2001: 22)

I have critically discussed the merits of this continuum approach elsewhei (Thomas, 2004b).

Disability Studies: The Stubbornness of the 'Real' Body

Poststructuralist objections and proposed solutions to the impairment disability dualism has certainly prompted a counter-critique from hard-lir social modellists, but has also stirred up disquiet in far more sympathet quarters. Some anti-foundationalist thinkers recognise that problems aris when impairment is presented as entirely discursively constituted, as cultural artefact. That is, difficulties are posed by the evaporation of th materiality of the body – by making the 'impaired body' a fiction, a repr sentation, only discursively constituted as embodying 'real' difference through medical categorisation. Reflecting on this disappearance of corp real materiality, Mark Jeffreys (2002), an English Professor in the U reminds us that bodies have 'surprisingly stubborn resistance to reinventio (2002: 13). He suggests that the constructionist epistemology that has powere disability studies in the Humanities in North America should be criticall reassessed; indeed:

> Outright hostility to biology and to the natural history of our flesh all too easi
> plays into mind–body, theory–matter dualism and may turn out to be ju
> another effort at erasure of the body by culture. (ibid.: 13)

In my view, observations such as Jeffrey's convey a strong sense of 'the and back again'. First, the naturalisation of impairment in post-Enlightenmei epistemologies is exposed, and 'bodily abnormalities' are revealed to t cultural constructs, but this repositioning of impairment and disability i the *cultural* domain then throws up the charge of socio-cultural essentialis and the recognition that poststructuralism re-inscribes the very nature/cultu dualism it had sought to overcome. Jeffreys goes on to say:

> Just as society needs to learn how to accommodate rather than stigmatize tho
> of us with unusual and extraordinary bodies, so too humanist cultural theo
> needs to learn how to accommodate rather than demonize the study of th
> biological aspects of our bodies. (2002: 39)

Disability Studies: Phenomenological Solutions?

Hughes and Paterson (1997), cited above, have also argued that poststructuralism replaces biological essentialism with discursive essentialism (see, also, Paterson and Hughes, 1999; Hughes 2002, 2005). Their own solution to the social model's impairment/disability dualism is to turn to phenomenology (see Chapters 2 and 3). Although these authors share with poststructuralists the conviction that a post-Cartesian philosophy is required in disability studies, they cannot accept poststructuralism's annihilation of the body as palpable material object, nor its denial of disabled people's agency; indeed, Hughes has written a number of critiques of Foucauldian perspectives in recent years (see, especially, Hughes, 2005).

Phenomenology, Hughes and Paterson suggest (1997), offers a non-dualistic means of combining a refusal to concede the impaired body to medicine with a resistance to the erasure of 'the body'. Phenomenology is thought to have the capacity – especially in the version outlined by Merleau-Ponty (1962) and interpreted by the sociologist Nick Crossley (2001a, see below) – to understand 'lived experience' as at one and the same time *embodied* (the body with mindful agency) and *social*. This means that the lived-experience of impairment is *both* physical and social, as is the lived experience disablism, so dissolving the Cartesian impairment/disability dualism:

> Impairment (as physicality) cannot escape either cultural meanings and beliefs or its embeddedness in social structure. On the other hand, oppression and prejudice, not only belong to the political body, but become embodied as pain and 'suffering'. The political and the physical both belong to the body in a sentient way, and yet both belong to the social as both discourse and material/spatial location. (Hughes and Paterson, 1997: 336)

This, they argue, opens up new ways of thinking about disability and disablism: 'disability is embodied and impairment is social' (ibid.: 336). I would add that this could also offer *another* opportunity to collapse the distinction that Oliver (1996a) makes between private troubles (being in pain) and public issues (being discriminated against), a distinction discussed in Chapter 3.

Somewhat curiously, given their desire to transcend dualisms, Hughes and Paterson present this line of thinking as a route to developing a *social model (or sociology) of impairment* rather than as a route to building a unified or integrated theorisation of impairment and disability/disablism. Nevertheless, their motivation is to strengthen disability studies by these means, and, by so doing, to add weight to the political struggle against disablism.

Disability Studies: Learning Difficulty

The stubborn resistance that the material body puts up to epistemologica
erasure is perhaps at its most obdurate when impairments of the intellec
are considered. Such impairments carry a variety of names in the UK, the
most common being 'learning difficulty', 'learning disability' and 'intellectual impairment'. Physicians, psychiatrists and clinical psychologists
would all assert that people who carry such labels have real organic intellectual deficits, albeit hugely variable, that place them at one end of any
statistical bell curve plotting measurements of intellectual capacity. The
idea that such impairments have been entirely socially constructed, having
no underlying 'reality', would be rejected as nonsensical. The vast majority
of lay people would no doubt agree, as, indeed, would many in the disabled
people's movement and disability studies. For example, Simone Apsis, an
activist in *People First*[1] acknowledges that 'learning difficulty' involves 'real
impairment, and targets her critique at the disability movement's
purported failure to address the social barriers that present themselves to
people like herself:

> We are always asked to talk about advocacy and our impairments as though our
> barriers aren't disabling in the same way as disabled people without learning
> disabilities. We want concentration on our access needs in the mainstream
> disability movement. (Apsis, quoted in Campbell and Oliver, 1996: 97)

However, there are disability studies scholars and activists in this field
notably Dan Goodley in the UK (2000, see, also, Goodley, 2001; Goodley
and Rapley, 2002), who have argued that so-called learning difficulties
constitute socio-cultural and political constructs – with no biological basis
Using poststructuralist perspectives, Goodley (2000, 2001) argues that
'learning difficulty' is itself a category of social and political disablement
and that social modellists who naturalise intellectual 'difference' are complici
in bringing these exclusionary consequences into being.

Goodley has summarised some of the ways in which the social construction
of learning difficulties can be uncovered as follows (see also Walmsley
1991; Skrtic, 1995; Stalker, 1998; Swain and French, 1999). First, intelligence
(IQ) testing can be deconstructed to reveal the social origins of criteria used
by branches of medicine and psychology to construct categories of 'low
intelligence'. Second, sociological labelling theory (see Chapter 2, this volume
can be used to expose the creation of dependency and the reinforcement o
'abnormal behaviour' among people labelled and 'treated' by professionals
as learning disabled (analogous to 'secondary deviance'). Third, in some
circumstances so-called challenging and maladaptive behaviours are functionally adaptive responses to excluding environments or medical abuse

Emerson, 1995), and, therefore, as have their origins in cultural, social and political structures. Fourth, once people are constructed as 'mentally deficient', behaviours that they engage in that would otherwise be considered 'normal' in children and adults are readily interpreted by professionals as further signs of pathology.

This leads Goodley (2000) to suggest that 'a sociology of learning difficulties' should be developed, to train the spotlight on the cultural, social and political forces that construct 'learning difficulties'. Alongside a more 'inclusive' social model of disability, this would present a stronger challenge to the extreme marginalisation of people so labelled.

Disability Studies: 'Mental Illness'

The analysis of the social construction of 'mental illness' has a long history in sociological thinking – most vigorously pursued by twentieth-century labelling theorists and other writers associated with the 1960s' anti-psychiatry movement (see Chapter 2). The existence of that tradition might suggest that poststructuralists within disability studies could have deconstructed the social and cultural processes involved in medicine's discursive construction of 'mental illness' with relative ease. But few have done so to date (for one example in social geography, see Parr, 1999). This is surprising given that biomedical and psychiatric beliefs in the bodily causes of mental illness have become more deeply entrenched in the wake of recent developments in the neurosciences, pharmacology and genetics.

This relative silence is not so surprising, however, when we remember that disability studies has concentrated, in a now contested fashion, on the disablist social barriers that *physically* impaired people confront. The growth in interest in 'difference' and 'the impaired body' has only just begun to turn disability studies writers' attention to the workings of 'the mind'. As noted in Chapter 3, there are ongoing debates among 'psychiatric system survivors' about whether they can and will identify as 'disabled' and link with the disabled people's movement (Beresford, 2000, 2002; Beresford *et al.*, 2002). Members of the 'users' and survivors movement are in the midst of developing their own understanding on the nature of 'mental illness', in opposition to medical interpretations. Peter Beresford (2002) advocates the development of a 'social model of madness and distress', making use of theories in disability studies on the social oppression of people with impairments. It is as yet unclear what place, if any, 'the mindful body' might occupy in such a perspective.

As debate within the survivors movement unfolds, one can anticipate that some will favour an 'embodied approach', though opinions on 'the reality' of biological-based psychological impairment will no doubt vary enormously. Greater consensus on the attribution of physical impairments to the damaging effects of drug and other psychiatric 'treatments' can be predicted with greater certainty.

Disability Studies: Body Aesthetics

Another approach to impairment in disability studies – sometimes pursued as a route to a better understanding of disablism – involves the analysis of body aesthetics. This draws on a number of theoretical perspectives, including psychoanalysis (Marks, 1999). Body aesthetics is a strong theme in North American feminist and poststructuralist accounts of disability (Wendell, 1989, 1996; Garland-Thomson, 1996, 1997a,b; L. Davis, 2002; Snyder *et al.*, 2002; Zitzelberger, 2005), and has been of interest to a growing number of writers in UK disability studies (Hevey, 1992; Paterson and Hughes, 1997; Shakespeare, 1997; Hughes, 2000, 2002; Corker and Shakespeare, 2002; Wilde, 2004).

In part, developments in this area reflect the centrality of *representations* in body studies in sociology and cultural studies – linked with contemporary interest in poststructuralist theory and themes such as consumerism, risk, the quest for 'bodily perfection', and hyperreality (Shilling, 2005). However, it is the 'normal' body, or 'bodies like mine', that non-disabled academics almost invariably have in mind when they examine body representations in the media and other cultural arenas. In contrast, writers in disability studies have focused on 'the impaired body' and its purported freakery (Garland-Thomson, 1996, 1997a), and tested the capacity of mainstream work to inform thinking in these areas. This has involved the examination of cultural narrativisations of both normal and abnormal bodies, and explorations of the effects that living with the strong presence of these discourses has on disabled people's subjectivities and identities. It has also involved observation of, and support for, the growth of a counter-culture in the form of 'disability arts' associated with disabled people's movements (for a disabled artist's personal account, see Lapper and Feldman, 2005).

Explorations of cultural constructions of the 'disabled body', including those used by twentieth-century Charities in fund-raising endeavours, reveal such bodies to be territories of despised and uncontrolled physicality; the 'disabled mind' is similarly associated with detested and unpredictable bodily behaviours and appearances (Hevey, 1992; Garland-Thomson, 1996, 1997a,b). Chapter 3 briefly reviewed ideas about the effects that these constructions have in reaffirming *non-disabled* people's sense of their own 'normality' and relative 'beauty', thus sustaining their own psychological well-being and existential security.[2] Analyses have shown that the gulf between impaired bodies and the idealised and relentlessly promoted

body beautiful' is vast, and continues to widen as processes of aesthetici-
ation gather pace – a gulf that has always been wider than it is for bodies
hat approximate cultural understandings of 'normal' or 'average'.

Given the social premium placed on how women 'look', feminist writers
ave argued that disabled women are particularly vulnerable to the psy-
hological and emotional damage that can result from discursive represen-
ations of the idealised female body – a consequence of the intermeshing of
lisability and gender discourses (Wendell, 1996; Meekosha, 1998; Wilde,
:004). The objectification of the 'disabled body' renders a woman simulta-
ieously seen and unseen (Zitzelsberger, 2005: 399).

In a parallel fashion, disabled men, like all men, are exposed to
nasculinist narratives that celebrate height, strength and sporting
rowess. Andrew Sparkes and Brett Smith (2002) and Steve Robertson
2004) have argued that disabled men's psychological and emotional
vell-being hinges, in part, on their capacity to resist or accommodate to
he negative self-assessments that hegemonic gender discourses promote
nd encourage.

In the same way that cultural representations of 'impaired bodies' can
onfirm non-disabled people's sense of embodied normality, it has been
uggested that being 'too close' to disabled individuals often stirs up deep-
ooted fears of 'suffering', ugliness, frailty and death among 'the normal',
·specially when chronic and terminal illnesses are involved (Marks, 1999).
'om Shakespeare (1997a) and Susan Wendell (1996), among others, believe
his to be at the root of commonplace shunning and avoidance behaviours
mong the non-disabled. Wendell (1996: 93) suggests that this operates in
cademic circles too, not least within the feminist community.

From another angle, Bill Hughes (1999, 2000, 2002) argues that medicine
ias played a role of fundamental importance in shaping and sustaining
liscrediting cultural imagery of impaired bodies: 'Invalidation is shot
hrough with connotations of negativity and this negativity itself is derived
rom the cultural hegemony of medical meanings' (2000: 558). This link is
nost obvious in 'prosthetic medicine' which:

> ... is dedicated to physical normalisation and is devoted to the artificial alteration
> of both function and appearance, but it enters the realm of biopolitics because it
> uses the 'normal' body as its tribunal and blueprint for action, and treats the
> impaired body as a spoilt entity that must be hidden and corrected. (Hughes,
> 2000: 561)

The advent of medical genetics, and its application in procedures such as
renatal genetic testing, has, Hughes suggests, taken this in new and
rofoundly disablist directions; the myth of bodily perfection is fuelled by
n apparent but spurious scientific credibility, encouraging aesthetic

discrimination and what Synnott (1993) has termed 'body fascism'. This
takes us to other engagements with the geneticised body in disability studies

Codes of Life: The Genetic Body

From a disability studies perspective, the arrival of 'the new genetics', most
publicly flagged by the Human Genome Project (HGP), has underlined the
profoundly political nature of the terrain occupied by 'impaired bodies' in
disability studies. The spectre of 'the elimination of disabled people' raises
its head in the wake of scientific hype about the prospects for eliminating
disease and disability, as it did in the heyday of twentieth-century eugenics –
in fascist, other totalitarian and liberal democratic states (Burleigh, 1995;
Kerr and Shakespeare, 2002).

Tom Shakespeare's response to these developments has been to study the
social processes bound up with geneticisation, and to immerse himself in
the complexities of contemporary bioethics – though not without criticism
from some sections of the disabled people's movement (Shakespeare, 1999;
2003; Shakespeare and Erikson, 2000; Kerr and Shakespeare, 2002). This
move has meant that Shakespeare has rejected attempts within disability
studies either to sideline the impaired body or to sustain the social modellist
divide between disability and impairment. In his view, disability studies
and disability politics must take geneticised social responses to impairment –
current and future – extremely seriously, and recognise that a 're-biologization
of disability' is underway (Shakespeare, 2003: 201).

Writing with Anne Kerr, Shakespeare details the profound significance of
genetic medicine and politics for *everyone*, at every life-stage, on a global
scale (Kerr and Shakespeare, 2002). It is within this context, he argues, that
the consequences for disabled people should be understood. At present
these are most evident in the realm of reproductive medicine, with stem
cell research, gene therapy and 'biotechnical solutions to social problems'
following some distance behind in the scientific race. The expansion of
prenatal screening and foetal diagnostic testing has implications and
consequences for both disabled and non-disabled adults who wish to have
children, but the impact is felt especially keenly by adults carrying genetically
inheritable conditions. Such adults, Shakespeare suggests, bear the brunt of
medical imperatives to prevent the birth of 'congenitally impaired babies'
or 'wrongful lives'. Shakespeare, like others, has wrestled with the ethics of
selective abortion in this brave new world. For many disability studies
writers and activists, adherence to the feminist commitment to allow abortion in the name of 'a woman's right to chose' has always sat uncomfortably
alongside the reality of legal abortions on the grounds of impairment. This
and other tensions have been exacerbated by geneticisation and the

growing social commitment to 'consumer choice' (see, also, Asch, 2000, 2001; Priestley, 2003).

Shakespeare argues that while genetic medicine appears to threaten a 'wipe-out' of disabled people, and in so doing to intensify disablist responses to those that do survive, the opposite will actually result. This is because geneticisation: 'expands the disability category, and de-stabilizes the identity of non-disabled people' (Shakespeare, 2003: 206). The HGP has revealed that there is no perfect human genome. That is, everyone can be found to be impaired and 'abnormal' in some way or other: 'The dividing line between the minority of people that society defines as disabled or impaired and the non-disabled majority is of degree, not of kind (ibid.: 207). Moreover, generic testing of a *predictive* character has shown that people who appear healthy and 'normal' are 'at risk' of developing diseases as they grow older (genetic testing in connection with breast cancer is best known). Predictive genetics is set to expand enormously, and this can only unsettle non-disabled people's sense of self and make them vulnerable, like 'the disabled', to discrimination by employers and insurance companies. Shakespeare's reflections on these and related matters point to the profoundly *bio-social* nature of impairment.

Impairment Effects

Having reviewed the positions taken by materialists, feminists and post-structuralists on the question of the impaired body, I shall close this part of the chapter with an extended outline of a concept first introduced in *Female Forms: Experiencing and Understanding Disability* (1999): impairment effects. My hope had been that this concept, informed by a materialist feminist perspective, could make a contribution to the development of *a non-reductionist materialist ontology of the body*, in the interests of enriching theorisations of disability and disablism. Many writers in disability studies have made use of the impairment effects idea, not least because it has provided a means by which academics signed up to the social model of disability can acknowledge the *direct* or *immediate* impact that 'being impaired' can and does have in the daily lives of disabled people. That is, it allows impairment and its effects to be acknowledged without undermining the importance and centrality of disablism.

In my mind, a non-reductionist materialist ontology of the body should neither deny the 'realness' of bodies and their flesh-bound variations nor concede ground to the idea that any acknowledgement of the material reality of 'the body' is tantamount to naturalising, medicalising or biologising it. It should be possible to understand 'the impaired body' as simultaneously biological, material and social – in short, as *bio-social* in character – and in more ways than one. Put at its simplest, impairment effects refer to those restrictions of bodily activity and behaviour that are *directly attributable* to bodily variations designated 'impairments' rather than to those *imposed upon* people *because* they have designated impairments (disablism). However, as will become clearer below, this simple formulation does not convey the subtleties of the bio-social processes and factors involved.

To develop the illustration[3] used in *Female Forms*: consider a young woman missing a hand. Her absent hand is a 'real' phenomenon, representing a marked variation in human morphology – in *any* time or place. In *contemporary* society, she cannot hold a boiled kettle in one hand while lifting a jug or saucepan in the other to receive the boiled water. This restriction of activity is an immediate *impairment effect*. If, however, other people in positions of power or authority (parents, doctors, social workers) were to decide that she is unfit to be a paid care worker, or to become a parent, *because* she cannot pour boiling water from a kettle into a hand-held container – or perform other commonplace 'two-handed' actions – then the restrictions of activity that follow (becoming a parent, obtaining employment in the care sector, and so forth), premised on the impairment effect, constitute disablism. In such circumstances an impairment effect intermeshes with the effects of disablism to shape lived experience.

However, this briefly sketched scenario involving the interaction of 'the biological' (missing a hand since birth), and 'the social' (being prevented from taking up social activities and roles because of the impairment and its effects) is more complex than it may at first appear. Delving beneath the surface soon demonstrates that the biological/social dualism cannot be sustained, for at least three reasons.

First, the impairment and its effect are at one and the same time *of the body* or *embodied* (an absent hand that limits manual activity) and *socially contingent* in a materialist sense. That is, in Western societies today, it is an expectation that most people live in dwellings with kitchens containing standard appliances, and that pouring boiling water from an electric kettle into hand-held domestic containers is an everyday activity. That is, the bodily action involved is *itself* a socially contingent one: the embodied act is thus bio-social.

Second, the impairment itself – the missing hand – is an attribute of the body that is determined, in a profound way, by social factors and circumstances. That is, bodies with only one hand have become extremely uncommon phenomena in advanced industrial societies, not least because 'modern' medicine has attempted, by various means, to minimise 'birth defects' (though it can cause them too) and to contain diseases that can result in limb loss; moreover, state legislation and official agencies seek to prevent the accidental or non-accidental loss of limbs. Today, the vast majority of people have two hands, albeit with varying degrees of age-related physical functioning. Once again, the missing hand should be understood to be a bio-social phenomenon, as should all other 'impairments'. For this and the first reason, neither the impairments themselves nor their immediate effects can be reduced to biological matter (corporeal, physiological, morphological): they are in and of themselves complex bio-social phenomena. Put another way, bodily impairments and their impairment effects are profoundly social in nature, in a material or 'real' sense. Impairment effects then become the foci for social responses that exclude the bearers of impairment from full social participation and citizenship. That is, these bio-social phenomena become the substratum or medium for disablism.

Third, bodily variations only carry the 'impairment' label in particular socio-cultural times and places. This takes us into the constructionist territory discussed in Chapter 3 and above. In capitalist society, a missing hand at birth is constructed by medicine as a biological 'abnormality', an impairment, and medical meanings carry tremendous weight in society. Disablism thus rests on what is constituted as bodily abnormality, and this, in the wider view, is socially variable and conditional. In previous eras, and in some contemporary non-Western cultures, a missing hand at birth may be explained and responded to through spiritual or other cosmologies. Again, the bio-material intersects with the socio-cultural.

In summary: in any 'real' social setting, impairments, impairment effects and disablism are thoroughly intermeshed with the social conditions that bring them into being and give them meaning. The materiality of the body is in a dynamic interrelationship with the social and cultural context in which it is lived. Moreover, the impaired body is changing and dynamic: whether or not the impairment is 'fixed' (chronic illnesses, for example, are usually marked by flux and change), the body is constantly ageing. The distinctions made between impairment and disability (disablism) cannot, therefore, be mapped onto familiar biological/social or natural/cultural dualisms, nor should impairment be sidelined as an irrelevant category. In my view, this demands of disability studies that it engages in the full theorisation of 'the impaired body' and its relationship with disablism.

Medical Sociology: Resolutions to the Body Problem

Bringing the Body Back In

We have seen that ideas about the impaired body in disability studies developed in response to a deliberate initial sidelining or 'leaving out' of impairment and other bodily concerns by pioneering social modellists. This instigated challenges from a variety of theoretical and political standpoints, leading to a focus on how to theorise the impaired body without conceding ground to biologically determinist models of disability.

In both mainstream sociology *and* medical sociology, debate about the body was also instigated by a growing realisation that its social actors were strangely disembodied. This was not because the 'founding fathers' of long ago had purposively left the body out, but, it has been argued, because their reference points in Western philosophy 'marginalized the importance of the body, by suggesting that it was the *mind* that made us truly human' (Shilling, 2005: 7). This encouraged the dichotomising of mind and body and the under-determination of the body in favour of the mindful (male) social actor – clearly evident in twentieth-century sociology, including medical sociology (Frank, 1991). Although medical sociology has illness and thus 'ill bodies' at the heart of its concerns, it has been preoccupied with the *meanings* attached to illness by both 'sufferers' and those that deal with them either professionally of personally (see Chapters 2 and 6), and with the nature of collective *social responses* to the social deviance represented by illness (see Chapters 2 and 4). As in the early days of disability studies, thinking on body matters *per se* was seen as territory belonging to medicine and biology. The body remained shadowy even in research on chronic illness (Kelly and Field, 2004).

Calls to bring the body back into sociology were stimulated by diverse intellectual projects in the 1980s, and gave rise to a wide range of *'why?'* and *'how to?'* theoretical responses in the academy, with all participants anxious to avoid opening any door to biological reductionism and sociobiology. In medical sociology, how to theorise the *creation and application of medical knowledge of the body* became the preoccupying topic (Nettleton and Gustavsson, 2002: 14).

Body Theory

Chris Shilling (2005: 6) has noted that 'the body' is now one of the most contested concepts in the social sciences, and that:

> its analysis has produced an intellectual battleground over which the respective claims of post-structuralism and post-modernism, phenomenology, feminism, socio-biology, sociology and cultural studies have fought.

Shilling (2001, 2005) and Nick Crossley (2001a,b) have advocated a key role for phenomenological perspectives on the lived body, especially the writings of Merleau-Ponty (see Chapter 2, this volume). These perspectives give ontological primacy to social action (rather than social order), and start from the living, feeling and perceiving body. However, Shilling and Crossley are cautious about treading singular theoretical pathways because these almost invariably fail to offer solutions to the central conceptual problem in sociology, that is, how to theorise the *interface* between social structure and social agency. Whilst acknowledged to be of great utility, Merleau-Ponty's (1962) phenomenological 'being-in-the-world' approach is viewed as placing too much emphasis upon human agency, and as failing to take sufficient account of the ways in which social structures *shape*, rather than *determine*, social action. In their different ways, Shilling and Crossley, have sought solutions by revisiting sociological classics in an attempt to assemble the building blocks necessary to produce theorisations of the body that attend to both agency and structure – without slipping into biological reductionism: Crossley's (2001a,b) answer involves integrating Merleau-Ponty's insights with Bourdieu's and those of other thinkers; Shilling's 'corporeal realism' (2001, 2005) grew out of detailed engagements with Durkheim, Simmel and Merleau-Ponty.

Feminist body theorists like Elizabeth Grosz (1994) have also grappled with the need to assemble ideas from diverse theoretical sources to develop an understanding of the body that can take account of the corporeality and culturally constructed qualities of 'sexed' bodies. However, Grosz threw her net beyond the sociological classics and phenomenology, drawing additional insight from psychoanalysis, neurophysiology and Nietzsche's philosophy. Her intention was to overcome mainstream feminism's 'somatophobia', that is, its resistance to engagements with 'the body' fuelled by male thinkers' historical tendency to 'link women's subjectivities and social positions to the specificities of their bodies' (1994: x). Her approach to developing a theoretical perspective that served the feminist intellectual and political project centred on adapting the Mobius strip[4] idea: '[the Mobius model] has the advantage of showing the inflection of mind into body and body into mind, the ways in which, through a kind of twisting or inversion, one side becomes another' (ibid.: xii). By undertaking a detailed analysis of a wide range of disciplines and authors, Grosz concluded that segments of thought can be woven together to support her Mobius strip conceptualisation of bodies in their cultural, sexual and racial distinctiveness. However, despite her insistence that bodies are to be understood in their *specificity*, it is notable that 'the disabled body' is missing from Grosz's bodies of interest.

Indeed, like many social theorists and philosophers, when Grosz does briefly touch upon bodily impairment and disability it is to cite theorists and researchers who seek to prove *the rule* ('the normal') by wheeling in *the exception* ('the ill and disabled'). That is, the exceptionality of clinically observed 'abnormal bodies' is used as case study material for the sole purpose of illustrating and illuminating 'normality', 'the standard' and the 'taken for granted'. The effect is that the social deviance, 'otherness' and 'freakishness' of impaired bodies is reinforced. Thus, although Grosz, like many other feminists, uncovers and objects to the historical practice of presenting male bodies as illustrative of 'the norm' against which women's bodies are judged and found wanting, it does not seem to have occurred to her to apply the same logic to the 'non-disabled/healthy' versus 'disabled/chronically ill' bodily dichotomy. Put another way, feminism's exposure of the gendered, sexed and racialised nature of what are culturally normative 'universal' categories ('human', 'the body') rarely extends to recognising social specificities or 'differences' associated with impairment (an exception is found in Shildrick, 1997, see below).

Body Sociology in Medical Sociology

Medical sociologists often resist anti-foundationalist flights of fancy about the 'discursively constructed' body because their studies testify to 'the reality' of illness and health-related 'suffering' (see Fox, 1993, for a poststructuralist exception). We know from Chapter 2 that medical sociologists' intellectual tradition has attuned many of its practitioners to the difficult life experiences that follow when illness and disability render a body 'deviant' and 'stigmatised'. Moreover, the need for realism has also stemmed from reminders that 'health inequalities' persist, and that social factors play a crucially important role in the determination and social distribution of diseased bodies (Graham, 2001, 2002).

    Such reality checks have drawn some medical sociologists away from 'oversocialised' poststructuralist approaches that deny the materiality of bodies, and towards philosophical and theoretical perspectives that allow for 'lived experience'. This notwithstanding, Kelly and Field's observation retains its relevance:

> In most types of sociological narrative about chronic illness, the body remains theoretically elusive. Its existence is seldom explicitly denied, but its presence has a kind of ethereal quality forever gliding out of analytic view. (Kelly and Field, 2004: 257, first published in 1996)

This elusiveness is commented upon in Bryan Turner's recent sketch of a *potential* theoretical framework to apply to 'the disabled body' (Turner, 2001 – his chapter in Albrecht *et al.*'s *Handbook of Disability Studies*, 2001). As a leading body analyst, Turner notes the paucity of theoretical work on disability *per se* in both mainstream sociology and medical sociology (see Chapter 2, this volume). Informed by sociological perspectives that approach illness and disability through the social deviance lens (Turner, 1987), Turner goes on to suggest that 'the sociology of the body can make important contributions to the study of impairment and disability' (2001: 253). He recommends the synchronised use of two apparently antithetical approaches: first, an engagement with the subjectivity of 'the lived body' in the Merleau-Ponty phenomenological tradition, and second, an application of Foucauldian thinking to the social construction of 'disability' through an examination of the 'external social and political structures that regulate, produce, and govern bodies and populations' (ibid.: 253). In Turner's view, Foucaldian thinking is crucial but cannot suffice:

> The paradox of the social constructionist position is that the specific character of embodiment in the everyday lives of people who are regarded as disabled disappears because the 'body' appears as only a phantasm that is produced by the discourses and practices of 'ablement'. (ibid.: 254)

As in the body writings of Crossley, Shilling and Grosz – Turner concludes that it is necessary and possible to *combine* what he terms ontological foundationalism with cultural constructionism. He argues that the foundational *embodiment* of the self, the social actor, must be taken account of, as must the historico-cultural setting that supplies the context for subjective experiences of embodied day-to-day living. Indeed, Turner observes that contemporary cultural contexts make living with a disabled or chronically ill embodied *self* particularly problematic because body projects (to remain 'active', 'slim', 'youthful' and 'independent') are so pivotal to the regulation of bodies and the formation of valued social selves (ibid.: 259) (see also Nettleton and Watson, 1998, and Bunton and Petersen, 2005). Clearly, such observations link with the body aesthetics theme in disability studies, discussed earlier.

The Lived Body

Turner's theoretical pluralism resonates with Simon Williams' and Gillian Bendelow's (1998a) approach in The Lived Body: Sociological Themes, Embodied Issues; they call for a synthesis of a foundationalist ontology (in the realist tradition) with a social constructionist (relativist) epistemology. Their ideas on how to develop a sociology of the body that could serve medical sociology and contribute to theoretical debate in the parent discipline involves the creation of a 'corporeal notion of the "mindful" body' (ibid.: 126), an approach that also encompasses human emotions. This, they suggest, would avoid the poststructuralist dissolution of the body's presocial 'materiality' and 'real' emotionality. Moreover, it would assist in overcoming both mind/body and other dualist legacies of the past and sociology's ongoing structure–agency problematic. Grosz's (1994) Mobius strip idea is viewed as helpful in this regard.

One point made by Williams and Bendelow is that a fully *embodied sociology* is required, rather than simply a 'sociology of the body'. An embodied sociology would take 'the embodiment of its practitioners as well as its subjects seriously, rooted as it is in the 'lived' body' (1998a: 24). This is an interesting suggestion and one that seems to me to hold potential for understanding some of the differences in ideas and priorities found in medical sociology and disability studies: the former being populated at any one time (though by no means exclusively) by people with relatively 'normal' non-disabled bodies, the latter attracting significant numbers of social scientists living with impairments that mark them out as 'different'. Rather disappointingly, however, Williams and Bendelow fail to use this insight in a reflexive fashion, or indeed to take it very far at all.

Given their credentials in medical sociology, it is perhaps surprising that the nearest Williams and Bendelow come to the specificities of 'chronically ill and disabled bodies' in *The Lived Body* is in a chapter on pain; a rather 'universal' (though sometimes gendered) body occupies most pages of their book. Biomedical constructions of pain and its effects are critiqued, but when dealing with the problematic body in pain, it becomes clear that their reference point is actually the 'normal body'. That is, it is 'the normal' body type that informs their own 'embodied sociology':

> *our relationship to our bodies*, in the normal course of events, remains largely unproblematic and taken-for-granted; bodies are only marginally present, giving us the freedom to be and to act. (ibid.: 159, my emphasis)

On the living with pain theme, Williams and Bendelow describe how sickness and pain betrays the body. Consciousness is awakened to the body's *presence* in a negative fashion, with profoundly disruptive consequences: 'Suddenly, the body becomes a central aspect of experience, albeit in an alien, dysfunctional sense' (ibid.: 159). Reference is then made to interactionists' analyses of the 'biographical disruption' that occurs (see Chapters 2 and 6, this volume):

> Not only do individuals have to suffer the physically debilitating effects of their condition, but also the profound sense of loneliness, isolation, stigmatisation and dependence that frequently follows in its wake. Loss of self, therefore, becomes a fundamental form of suffering in (chronic) pain and illness. (Chamaz, 1983, cited in Williams and Bendelow, 1998a: 161)

Williams and Bendelow believe their overall theoretical project is well served by this analysis of 'the body in pain': such bodies highlight the need for a corporeal notion of the 'mindful' body, one that pays heed to subjective experience. That is, the topic illustrates the necessity of combining: 'the physical, affective and cultural dimensions of human suffering in a seamless web of lived experience. Pain, in other words, is located at the intersection of mind, body and culture' (1998a: 168).

Getting 'Real' about the Chronically Ill and Disabled Body in Medical Sociology

In a paper published in 1999, Simon Williams fleshes out his foundationalist ontology of the body in the shape of a *critical realist* analysis (see also Scambler and Scambler, 2003). The paper is of particular interest here because it takes issue with the social model of disability, reflecting, in my view, his acknowledgement of the growing significance of disability studies (see also S. Williams, 2000).

Williams' interest in what he calls 'the disability debate' centres on the social model's refusal to accept that disability is caused by impairment, by 'the body'. He makes use of several critiques of the social model *within* disability studies on this question, especially arguments by Hughes and Paterson (1997) and Crow (1996) (see above) to support his own view that the body cannot be 'written out'. Indeed, Williams (1999: 804) goes so far as to claim that interest in bringing the body back in, on all sides, indicates that: 'signs of rapprochement between medical sociologists and disability theorists are now beginning to appear, including an opening up of questions surrounding impairment itself'.

The nub of Williams' argument is that the social model's denial of what, in his view, is the crucial and obvious role played by the impaired body in *causing* disability (restricted activity), represents a good example of a more generalised failure among social scientists to engage with the body and biology. On this basis, he goes on to bracket (materialist) social model advocates together with anti-foundationalist postmodernist sociologists on the grounds that both groups deny 'the reality' of the material body: both attempt to explain phenomena in purely socio-cultural terms.

In counter-position, Williams asserts that:

> The body ... diseased or otherwise, is a real entity, no matter what we call it or how we observe it. It also, like all other social and natural domains, has its own mind-independent generative structures and causal mechanisms. (1999: 806)

His claim is that a critical realist perspective – the theoretical home of the terms 'generative structures' and 'causal mechanisms' (see Chapter 2, this volume) – can allow for the theorisation of *the real* impact of bodily impairment (illness, pathology, injury) on disability (restricted activity) *without* descending into biological reductionism *or* denying the importance of the *additional* social restrictions imposed upon disabled people. That is, critical realism allows bodily biology to operate as a pre-discursive causative force. By these means, Williams (ibid.: 810) offers an updated and 'embodied' rationale in support of the standard medical sociological view that 'disability' is restricted activity caused mainly by impairment (see Chapters 1 and 2, this volume):

> Disability … is an emergent property, located, temporally speaking, in terms of the interplay between the biological reality of physiological impairment, structural conditioning (i.e. enablements/constraints), and socio-cultural interaction/ elaboration. (ibid.: 810)

Indeed, I would suggest that if the critical realist overlay in Williams' argument is left aside, his position as far as disability is concerned is identical to that adopted by Michael Bury (1996b, 1997) in earlier arguments concerning the 'over-socialised' and 'unidimensional' character of Michael Oliver's social model of disability.

Bury's own realist position remains uncompromising on 'the cause' of disability:

> The denial of any causal relationship between illness, changes in the body, and disability comes up against the daily realities experienced by the chronically sick and those who care for them, whether in the community or in health care systems … . The point needs to be stressed … that in any overview of disability in modern society, chronic illness remains its most significant cause. (2000: 179)

It follows that: 'Just as the prevalence of chronic illness rises with age, so too does disability' (ibid.: 179). Like Simon Williams, Bury does not deny that *some* restrictions of activity have social and cultural causes, but much greater causal weight is attributed to the body.

In my view, these arguments by Simon William and Michael Bury demonstrate that their engagements with ideas in disability studies remain superficial. They persist in conflating, and rejecting, 'disability theory' with a narrow range of writings on the social model of disability. A closer acquaintance with the content and history of ideas about disability and impairment in disability studies – in the social oppression paradigm – would surely give William's cause to doubt the wisdom of suggesting that materialist thinkers in disability studies deny 'the reality' of the impaired or chronically ill body. As we know from the first half of this chapter (and Chapter 3), the debate in the discipline is complex and nuanced. Only a serious engagement by medical sociologists with the subtleties of arguments in disability studies would actually further the disciplinary 'rapprochement' that Williams mentions.

Finally, given their understanding of disability and its causation, and of the importance of microbiology and genetics in the contemporary medical agenda, it is not surprising that Williams and Bury also agree on the need for sociologists to take biology more seriously (see especially Williams *et al.*, 2003; Bury, 2005). Indeed, Williams has aligned himself with sociologists who have called for a fresh dialogic orientation to 'biology' (both the subject matter and the scientific discipline). Such an approach, he suggests, would be appreciative of biology's relevance, and reflexive about sociology's historical antipathy to biological matters. However, it goes without saying that in making any kind of 'biological turn', Williams has no desire to reinvent or reinforce nature/social dualisms or sociobiology – quite the contrary.

Feminist Accounts of Ill and Disabled Bodies

Given the legacy of feminist 'somatophobia' (Grosz, 1994), it is not surprising that there are very few feminist accounts of 'the body' in its chronically ill or 'disabled' state in medical sociology; Bendelow's work on bodies in pain, mentioned above, counts as one example (Bendelow, 1993; Williams and Bendelow, 2001). Throwing the net beyond medical sociology, this section briefly considers two contrasting feminist approaches to disabled and chronically ill bodies. The first is found in Leaky Bodies and Boundaries (1997) by the feminist poststructuralist philosopher, Margrit Shildrick, the second is Women, Body, Illness (2003) by Pamela Moss and Isabel Dyck – two Canada-based feminist social geographers who make much use of sociological theorisations of the body. Shildrick's work with the disabled feminist writer, Janet Price, was touched upon in the earlier discussion of feminist poststructuralist work within disability studies. She would no doubt be gratified by the repetition of her name here because it suggests success in the transgression of boundaries – disciplinary or otherwise – something much favoured by social constructionists (see, also, Price and Shildrick, 1998, 1999).

Shildrick's *Leaky Bodies* relies entirely on what she refers to as 'postmodernist' scholarship, but, unusually for work in that genre, features 'the disabled body' as a means of illustrating the 'fabricated' nature of *all* bodies and the marginalised character of particular bodies. Indeed, she views disability as an important theme because it: 'imbricates conceptually with the wider issue of the existentialist disablement of the female body in Western society' (1997: 40). Shildrick is not at all troubled by what other body theorists see as poststructuralism's limitations: that is, social reductionism and the denial of the materiality of the body. On the contrary, in Shildrick's view, 'feminist postmodernism' is alone in its capacity to avoid conceptual fixity and essentialism (hence the attraction of 'leaky') and to develop a feminist ethics that can displace the mechanisms by which women's bodies are 'othered' and devalued – by biomedicine and other patriarchal discursive systems of authority. With this in mind, she applies Foucault's ideas about disciplinary 'practices of the body' to an analysis of biomedical and state welfarist constructions of 'disabled' bodies. Interestingly, her focus involves the prosaic trials associated with obtaining a welfare benefit: the Disability Living Allowance (DLA) (see Chapter 4, this volume). To be considered for this benefit, applicants had to submit themselves to 'extraordinary procedures', that is, to comply with an application process involving detailed questioning and demands for a thorough self-analysis of personal behaviour. Answers were demanded on everyday activities such as washing, dressing, cooking, and toileting, demanding that the claimant 'freely confess to her own bodily inadequacy' (ibid.: 53).

In Shildrick's view, this amounts to an impressive display of power/knowledge, in the Foucauldian sense (ibid.: 53); 'disability' is constituted through processes of state denial or attribution:

> the claimant is inserted into patterns of normalisation which grossly restrict individuality. Ultimately, what the technologies of the body effect, while appearing to incite the singular, is a set of co-ordinated and managed differences. (Shildrick, 1997: 51)

Readers may have noted that this Foucaldian theorisation of the construction of 'disability' through the disciplinary regulation and self-regulation of 'disabled' bodies has some resonance with Deborah Stone's and Gary Albrecht's analyses of the social construction of disability by the state, business and professional practices, discussed in Chapter 2. Shildrick's analysis also provides support for Turner's (2001) contention that the application of Foucauldian thinking to 'the social construction of disability' can make an important (though *partial*, in his view) contribution.

In their book-length engagement with chronic illness in women's lives, based on empirical research in Canada,[5] Moss and Dyck suggest that poststructuralist perspectives on the body are necessary, but insufficient on their own. In contrast to Shildrick, their preference is to 'work from women's experiences of body rather than from a theory of discourse' (2003: 34) – taking care to avoid treating 'experience' as an unproblematic given. This leads them to advocate a spatially informed 'radical body politics' that: (a) involves reference to 'a material base' and 'subjectivity' (ibid.: 17–18), but (b) sits alongside analyses of discursive practices and constructionism:

> We locate our project at the intersection of poststructuralist conceptions of power, feminist theory, critical social geography, and women's experiences of chronic illness ... *[to] understand women's bodies as simultaneously discursive and material entities* and space as both social and physical ... (ibid.: 18, my emphasis)

From this perspective, theoretical pluralism is demanded if sense is to be made of 'real' lives and identities shaped by living with embodied change, fluctuation and unpredictability. These authors' claim that reading bodies through corporeal sensations, combined with acknowledging the discursive inscriptions imposed upon bodies, can avoid both the dismissal and devaluing of bodily sensations and the failure to place illness in 'social, political, economic and structural contexts' (ibid.: 35). In this spirit, a number of their chapters are devoted to the interpretation of women's experiential accounts:

> Materially, our bodies circumscribe our existences. In this sense we are sensual beings, ones that are tactile, emotional, and sensorial. With chronic illness, women feel pain, fatigue, disorientation, fear, malaise, frustration, alienation, isolation, anxiety, and excitement. At the same time, our bodies carry cultural markers that tag us as aged, raced, sexed, classed, sexualized, disabled, and ill. (ibid.: 67)

Moss and Dyck fully acknowledge that their approach does not shatter dualisms (discursive/material, biology/society); they make only a 'modest claim' for the 'destabilisation' of such dualisms (ibid.: 26).

In summary, it is evident from the theoretical position adopted by Moss and Dyck – and by the positions taken by Turner, Williams, Bendelow, Shilling, Crossley and Grosz, discussed above – that getting close to real bodies, especially ill bodies, leads to a refusal to pursue a singular social constructionist (poststructuralist) line of thought. Margrit Shidrick's approach is the exception in this regard.

Further Thoughts on Mindful Bodies: The Storied Body and 'Mental Illness' in Medical Sociology

This final section on 'body work' in medical and mainstream sociology turns to Arthur Frank's *The Wounded Storyteller: Body, Illness and Ethics* (1995) – an influential embodied sociology informed by the author's personal experience of living with life threatening illness, in North America. Like Moss and Dyck, Frank uses more than one theoretical perspective and expresses optimism about the capacity of chronically ill people to regain some control in their lives by reclaiming their bodies from medicine (see also Frank, 1991a).

Frank considers how, in 'postmodern times', individuals tell illness stories *through* their diseased and problem bodies, reflecting his interest in social action orientations to the body (Frank, 1991b): the body is conscious of itself, and autobiography is embodied. His phenomenological approach leads to the identification of three narrative types that find expression at different times in individuals' illness journeys: the restitution narrative ('tomorrow I'll be healthy again'), the chaos narrative ('all is lost') and the quest narrative ('I'll use this illness to seek to improve myself, and others'). In Frank's view, these narrative types guide action in the face of suffering – and build on his earlier suggestion (1991b) that there are four ideal types or styles of 'body usage': the disciplined body, the dominating body, the mirroring body, and the communicative body.[6]

Noted for his capacity to draw phenomenological, Foucauldian, and other theoretical insights into close dialogue, a number of medical sociologists concerned with chronic illness and disability have been influenced by the Frankian embodied perspective. Bury (2000, 2005), for example, finds appeal in Frank's understanding of patient agency: embodied illness narratives enable long-standing illness to be integrated into everyday life – though Bury (2005) adds that this varies by age and socio-economic status. He also makes use of Frank's (1995) observation that narratives of suffering demand an 'ethics of the body' among 'witnessing' disciplines like sociology and medicine.

Frank's 'holistic' approach to health, illness, body and mind leads us, finally, to the place of 'mental illness' in medical sociologies of the body. Building on Foucault's (1967) study of 'madness', poststructuralists understand 'mental illnesses' to be discursively constructed categories. In the poststructuralist view, contemporary biomedicine looks to neuroscience, genetics, and pharmacology for contemporary expertise on types of 'abnormalities of the mind', and, in so doing, deepens its regulatory control of persons and societies through drug regimens and other 'treatment orders'. In this view, institutional means of confinement and control (the asylums) have been replaced by more subtle disciplinary mechanisms, often administered 'in the community' (Busfield, 1988, 2001; Rose, 1990; Pilgrim and Rogers, 1999).

But is 'mental illness' entirely socially constructed? Is it without any 'real' or 'material' embodied foundation? Such questions pick up on much longer standing debates on the nature of mental distress and disorder in sociology, particularly those initiated by labelling theorists (discussed in Chapter 2). Joan Busfield (2001), a leading figure in the British sociology of 'mental illness', favours the development of a multidimensional approach in twenty-first-century sociology – echoing much of the 'plural' theoretical directionality favoured by 'body theorists', summarised above. Such an approach, she suggests, can certainly recognise and theorise the power that biomedicine wields in the construction and control of 'mental illness', but also finds room, first, for the identification of *other* social mechanisms that *create* (embodied) mental distress (for example, traumatic life events or poverty) and, second, for the acknowledgement of 'the pain, difficulty and suffering involved in mental disorder' (ibid.: 6), that is, the experiential. Also required, in her view, are studies that use a range of theoretical approaches and empirical methods to uncover the character and ideological underpinnings of professional practice in the mental health services (ibid.: 12).

Summary and Reflections on Border Crossings

This chapter has ranged far and wide over disciplinary engagements with 'the body'. I shall take the opportunity in this final section to set out a few thoughts on how disability studies might be enriched by taking up *some* of the insights on theorising bodies available in medical sociology and sociology more generally. First, a summary of the ground covered is required.

The first half of the chapter demonstrated that debates on 'the impaired body' among and between materialists, feminists, poststructuralists and phenomenologists in disability studies have moved far beyond initial considerations on whether impairment should or should not be addressed at all. Indeed, it would be crass to characterise British disability studies as a discipline that continues to ignore body matters; the body began to make its way 'back in' almost from the start. Discussion is now plentiful and rich on how to theorise impairment *per se*, and on the relationship between the impaired body, disability and disablism. Today, few would deny the theoretical or political necessity of debate on these matters. In addition, feminist scholars and phenomenologists have won growing acceptance for their insistence that the discipline must find space for the *lived experience* of impaired bodies, alongside the personal experience of disablism (see Chapters 3 and 6).

The review of debates about impairment has also uncovered the crystallisation of theoretical disagreement along contour lines defined by an old philosophical divide: whether one is for or against realist and foundational premises. Disability studies scholars whose theoretical points of departure are materialist, realist or phenomenological have not been able to accept the poststructuralist proposition (however varied in its presentation) that impaired bodies are nothing other than discursive constructions; rather, bodies are thought to have *real* or *mind-independent* ('pre-social') material qualities, and to possess agency. On the other side, those whose reference points include the constructionist writings of Foucault and Derrida demand the reformulation of 'impairment' in purely socio-cultural terms. Only by these means, it is argued, can the Cartesian nature/society dualism embedded in the modernist social model of disability (and wider discourses) be transcended. Foucault's later writings are invoked to insist that subjects' 'resistance' to bio-power is possible. However, *all* agree that biological reductionism is to be avoided at all costs.

The second half of the chapter revealed that the same theoretical tension is found at the heart of longer-standing debates on the body in sociology and its medical sub-discipline, though this tension has intersected more explicitly with ongoing sociological deliberations on theorising social structure (order) and social agency (action). However, and somewhat in contrast to disability studies as the younger discipline, we have seen that leading sociologists of the body have sought to develop theoretical frameworks that bridge theoretical divides, by one means or another. In reaction to the strong 'cultural turn' in the latter part of the twentieth century, writers as theoretically disparate as Bryan Turner, Chris Shilling, Nick Crossley, Elizabeth Grosz, Simon Williams, Gillian Bendelow and Arthur Frank have refused to pursue *singular* lines of thought on the body, though their own solutions to the body puzzle vary markedly.

This acceptance of theoretical plurality or multiplicity is certainly evident in the work of most sociologists who have turned their attention to 'chronically ill and disabled' bodies, but so too is an inclination towards theoretical perspectives that accept the materiality or corporeality of bodies and 'minds' – without descending into biologism. Simon Williams' advocacy of a critical realist approach is perhaps the clearest expression of this: the body 'has its own mind-independent generative structures and causal mechanisms' (Williams, 1999: 806). Indeed, my reading suggests that, as a general rule, there is an *inverse relationship* between (1) how close medical sociologists get in their research to the realities of living with chronic illness and disability, and (2) the strength of their theoretical preference for strong constructionist interpretations of the body. This does not mean that representational or constructionist sociological perspectives are thought to have no part to play. On the contrary, Foucauldian and other poststructuralist interpretations are believed to be of considerable importance; indeed, as Turner puts it, an essential contribution is made by constructionist perspectives that examine the 'external social and political structures that regulate, produce, and govern bodies and populations' (2001: 253).

Theorising Impairment in Disability Studies: Does the Work of Medical Sociologists Have Any Relevance?

These observations lead to my first suggestion for future developments: that theorists in disability studies could learn something of value from attempts made in medical and mainstream sociology to overcome the limitations imposed by single track theorisations of 'the body'. That is, theoretical plurality or multiplicity on questions of impairment and embodiment should be encouraged in disability studies – a discipline that I would

ıggest (alongside others) is poised to make important moves in the develop-
ıent of its own *sociology of impairment*. Let me be clear: I am not suggesting
ıat disability studies take on board the *outcomes* of medical sociologists'
ınalyses of 'the chronically ill or disabled body'. Rather, disability studies
ıould treat the *epistemological strategies* employed by medical sociologists
ınd other body theorists as a valuable resource for its own theorisations of
ımbodiment, impairment, disability and disablism.

At one level, this is to make the obvious point that disability studies, a
ılatively new discipline, requires a rich palate of theoretical options at its
ısposal if it is to tackle the further complexities of 'the impaired body'.
ıciology has already done a great deal of the spade-work on the substance
ınd diversity of body theories – albeit with 'normal' bodies at the forefront
f its thinking, and with impaired bodies often used as the 'exceptions that
rove the rule': a corpus of literature has been produced that disability
:udies would be foolish to ignore. At another level, it is to suggest that the-
rists in disability studies could learn from the tried and tested 'models'
ıat sociologists have developed for *combining* theoretical threads and tradi-
ons, or at least for bringing these into productive *dialogue* (good examples
re offered by Shilling, Crossley, Turner, Grosz, Williams and Bendelow,
ınd Moss and Dyck).

At present, writers in disability studies who have addressed the impairment
ıuestion, including myself and other feminists, tend to single-mindedly
ırsue *either* materialist *or* poststructuralist lines of argument, and to reject
ıe positions and preoccupations found in the opposite camp. The time has
ɔme, in my mind, for disability scholars to undertake a more measured
ıssessment of the strengths, weaknesses and limitations of *all* theoretical
:hools of thought on body matters; a well-informed dialogue across theo-
ıtical boundaries is to be encouraged, and would be to the benefit of all.
his does *not* mean that we should all aspire to be theoretical pluralists or
:lectics, and certainly not to the revelry in theory as an end in itself. It
ıeans, rather, that intellectual journeys – in the service of strengthening the
ıallenge to disablism – should pay closer attention to the full range of
rguments and analyses available, and especially to ideas that originate in
ıeoretical traditions other than our own.

This might best be illustrated if I reflect on my own journey on the
npairment question in disability studies. In *Female Forms* (1999) I stated
ıy preference for the development of a non-reductionist materialist ontology
f the body. This has not changed in its fundamentals, but reading sociolog-
:al writings on 'the body' has extended my thinking about the theoretical
genda. Three illustrations must suffice.

First, I have become more appreciative of the importance of theoretical
erspectives that can diversify understanding of *cultural representations* of
ıe impaired body – for example, scholarship on body aesthetics and on the

social construction of new medical diagnostic categories. The same can b said for theorisations that uncover the historical and contemporary mecha nisms involved in the *disciplining* and *regulation* of bodies. I can see tha Foucauldian and other poststructuralist perspectives have a valuable rol to play in this regard, and that there are helpful examples of the use of sucl approaches in medical sociology (Peterson and Bunton, 1997; Nettleton an Watson, 1998; Scambler and Higgs, 1998). The relatively recent appearanc of Foucualdian-inspired scholarship in disability studies on the historica and contemporary exercise of bio-power in health and social care institu tions, and in 'special schools', is much to be welcomed and encourage (McFarlane, 2004; Tremain, 2005). However, I do not accept that Foucaul and neo-Foucauldians have, or should be granted, a monopoly on question of *power*. On the contrary: Marxist, materialist, feminist, critical realist an other perspectives on the nature and exercise of power are not to be can celled out or superseded by so-called post-Enlightenment thinking. In m view, the former retain legitimacy and have the potential to make furthe important contributions to theorisations of the representation and socia control of bodies.

The second illustration concerns *psycho-emotional disablism*, discussed i Chapter 3. In this closing section, I wish to acknowledge that my thinkin on this question to date has been insufficiently *embodied* (Thomas, 1999 That is, I have come to recognise that psycho-emotional disablism – both it enactment and its effects – should be thought about as fully embodied. Thi form of disablism should not be treated as one that operates simply at th level of mind or consciousness. This new thinking has been influenced b scholars (to be found in medical sociology, in sociology more broadly *and* i disability studies) who use Merleau-Ponty's phenomenology to understand the embodied nature of 'lived experience', and by the ongoing work b feminists on embodied experience. The ideas discussed by Hughes an Paterson (on the phenomenology of impairment), Williams and Bendelov (on emotions and the lived body), Frank (on the storied body), Crossley (o linking Merleau-Ponty with Bourdieu) and Moss and Dyck (on women' experience of body) have all excited my interest. The following observatio by Hughes and Paterson is particularly helpful:

> … oppression and prejudice, not only belong to the political body, but becom embodied as pain and 'suffering'. The political and the physical both belong t the body in a sentient way, and yet both belong to the social as both discours and material/spatial location. (1997: 336)

The final illustration involves the concept impairment effects. As indicate earlier, this concept remains key to my thinking about the potential for th development of a non-reductionist materialist ontology of the body – in th ervice of a sociology of disablism. In this case, sociological literature of a *ealist* persuasion on how social scientists might engage creatively and *ympathetically* with biology and 'the biological' (Shakespeare, 2003; Villiams *et al.*, 2003) has drawn my attention to the need for a more ophisticated understanding of the 'bio-social' relationships embedded in mpairment effects. The section on impairment effects in the first half of this hapter represents an attempt to move in this direction. To restate the key bservation set out there: in any 'real' social setting, impairments and mpairment effects are thoroughly intermeshed with the social conditions hat bring them into being and give them meaning, as is disablism. The naturality of the body is in a dynamic interrelationship with the social and ultural context in which it is lived.

These illustrations give just a flavour of themes that could be taken up in theoretically diverse and conceptually sophisticated sociology of impairment nd impairment effects in disability studies. No doubt, future debate on mbodiment and 'the biological' in medical sociology will provide further ood for thought, as will growing interest in critical realist perspectives on the body' more generally. Indeed, I would welcome the development of *ritical realist thinking in disability studies* – engaged with all topics of interest. rom another angle, this call for realist analyses of impairment also suggests hat Abberley's (1987, 1997, 2002) work on the *social production* (as opposed o 'construction') of impairment should be developed further and, in my iew, linked with the 'health inequalities' debate in medical sociology (see Chapter 2), as should Gleeson's (1999) *embodied* materialist geography of lisability. Overall, disability studies can use body theories and embodied hinking on many fronts in its sociology of disability.

6

Experiencing Disability, Chronic Illness and Other Impairments

Introduction

Sociologies of lived experience play a central role in a number of theoretical traditions in both disability studies and medical sociology. Importance is attached to uncovering the first-hand experiences of people for whom impairment, including chronic illness, is woven into life's warp and weft. This shared interest in the experiential has not, however, served the same ends, and the focus has been on different dimensions of lived experience. Contrasting purposes have been at work, and we know from foregoing chapters that different analytical frameworks have been applied.

Working with the social oppression paradigm, researchers in disability studies have documented the lived experiences of individuals and groups in order to understand and expose the social mechanisms that create, sustain and reinforce disablism – an approach that goes back as far as Paul Hunt's (1966) collection of autobiographical accounts of institutional life in *Stigma: The Experience of Disability* (see, also, Campling, 1981; Oliver *et al.*, 1988; Morris, 1989; Barnes, 1990). In medical sociology, research on 'living with' disability and chronic illness'– on the part of 'sufferers' and their families – has been rooted in interpretative perspectives informed by the illness as social deviance paradigm; the legacy of Goffman's (1968) thinking on stigma is much in evidence in studies on illness experiences in micro-social context.

This chapter explores these differential disciplinary engagements with lived experience, building on discussions in earlier chapters – especially the review of medical sociology's interactionist and phenomenological theoretical traditions in Chapters 2 and 5, and the discussion of theoretical debates in disability studies in Chapters 3–5. It also reviews debates about how disability should be researched. An important theme in the latter part of the chapter concerns recent shifts and changes on questions of the experiential: movement can be observed in both disciplines, but what are the directions of travel? Use is made of extracts from research papers that allow 'the voices' of lay people living with disability and impairment to be expressed.

We start with a fifth *episode* of disciplinary debate, adding to the discussion of *Episodes* 1–4 in Chapter 4.

Episode 5: Disciplinary Debate on the Lived Experience of Disability and Chronic Illness

This *episode* involves debate between researchers in disability studies and medical sociology at a conference in 1995, entitled *Accounting for Illness and Disability*. The event was initiated by sociologists in the disability studies community, and conference papers were later published in a collection edited by Colin Barnes and Geoff Mercer: *Exploring the Divide: Illness and Disability* (1996). Medical sociologists who agreed to participate found themselves in the rather unusual position of having to defend their approach to illness and disability to a community of sociologists who adopted entirely different starting points. The divergence in sociological perspectives on 'disability and illness experiences' was illuminated sharply, and light was also thrown on intra-disciplinary debates.

Among other things, the papers in *Exploring the Divide* by the medical sociologists – Michael Bury, Michael Kelly, Ruth Pinder and Gareth Williams – support the case for empirical research and theorising informed by the interactionist and phenomenological traditions. We know from Chapter 2 that the key themes in these traditions include: exploring individuals' own accounts of living with long-term illness and disablement; the impact of symptoms on daily life and everyday social relationships; the personal and social mechanisms involved in maintaining a sense of order, self-identity and meaningful social interaction in the face of unwelcome bodily change and loss of 'self'; adjustment to, and coping with, symptoms and limitations on activity; sense-making and the attribution of meaning to illness, challenging life-events, and 'biographical disruption'; regaining a sense of control over life's trajectory; and the illness trajectory and change over time.

Kelly's (1996) paper on the consequences of radical abdominal surgery associated with ulcerative colitis on 'negative attributes of self' articulates many of these themes, and typifies the large volume of research that has been published by medical sociologists on the lived experience of a wide range of chronic illnesses and 'disabilities'. As such, it is helpful to summarise the paper's research method and analytical emphasis.

Kelly reports on semi-structured interviews – 'guided conversations' – undertaken with 45 people who had experienced surgery, in which respondents were encouraged to talk about their lives, post-surgery. He states that the analysis of interview data generated 'a great variety of themes' but selects the 'self and identity' theme for special attention.

> What is of particular interest ... is the impact on self and identity of illness and surgery, and the attempts to present self and the processes of legitimation which then come into play. When someone has an illness or a condition that actually or potentially cuts across interaction a new dynamic is established in that interaction (ibid.: 79)

Of the many interview extracts presented by Kelly (1996: 82–3), one features 'Frances's' experience:

> *Frances*: I can't really face telling anyone about it. [Health care professionals ... kept saying it's nothing to be ashamed of. But I just don't feel ready to tell anyone about it. So no one actually knows apart from my family. I don't want to tell anyone just now. I think that's probably a bad thing in a way as well, cos I'm kinda keeping it all in. But I just don't want to. I think its going to be quite hard going, going back to work as well.

This woman's account is used, with the others, to illustrate the experiential inter-personal territory traversed by people with a medically diagnosed condition resulting in faecal incontinence and the need to wear appliances on the abdomen – territory marked by embarrassment, strategies of concealment, and dread of exposure and rejection. Kelly (1996: 90–91) reflects on individuals' struggle to retain or re-form an acceptable sense of self in such circumstances:

> At the level of self, the individual will not only have to confront the daily graft of managing the illness and the post-operative sequelae, but also have to manage all the other aspects of their lifeworld too ... . They anticipate that others, who do not have their inner knowledge, will respond according to broad cultural stereotypes. In part, their task is breaking through the stereotype, of rendering it irrelevant, so that they can reveal their true self and develop a social identity in which more important aspects of themselves are given precedence over the illness or surgery. (ibid.: 90–1)

In response to medical sociological research of this type, disability theorists Colin Barnes and Geof Mercer insist that this preoccupation with what they refer to as *the subjective experiences of impairment* is unhelpful – both to disabled individuals and to those attempting to ιderstand the nature of disability:

> The portrayal of chronic illness by medical sociologists has [] been criticised by disabled people as all too often a one-dimensional catalogue of negative conse- quences and meanings – the stigma, 'loss of self' and dependence – and the generally defensive coping strategies and manoeuvring. Studies which suggest a more diverse experience, or which report a positive sense of self and creative involvement in the lives of disabled people are far less in evidence. At the same time, medical sociology has tended to investigate all impairments, including stable or hearing impairments, from an illness perspective.
>
> The impact and dominance of the interpretative approach in the studies of chronic illness is a further source of disagreement. It is a matter of debate within medical sociology whether such research gives undue weight to subjective meanings and too little attention to wider structural forces. (1996: 5–6)

ιese authors argue that it is 'the impact of disabling barriers and hostile ιcial environments' (ibid.: 7) that should constitute the focus for research ιd theorising, and that this requires both the exploration of individuals' ιperience *of disablism* together with the examination of social structures ιd institutional and cultural practices that produce and sustain this form ˙ discrimination and social oppression.

Disability studies scholar, Michael Oliver, adds to these concerns in his ∨n contribution to the debate:

> … the language used in much medical discourse including medical sociology is replete with words and meanings which many disabled people find offensive or feel that it distorts their experiences. In particular the term chronic illness is for many people an unnecessarily negative term, and discussions of suffering in many studies have the effect of casting disabled people in the role of victim. (1996b: 43)

ke Barnes and Mercer, Oliver argues that if 'the experiences' of disabled ɛople are to be explored then the investigator should avoid seeking out ιd interpreting only 'the negative' and, more importantly, should use such ιperiential research as a vehicle for exposing the workings of disablist ˙actices in employment, health and welfare services, the built environment ιd other social domains.

In defence of medical sociology, Ruth Pinder (1996) goes onto the offen- ∨e by using two 'illness experience' case studies to highlight what she sees the key weakness of the social model of disability: its exclusive focus on e social environment, on external social factors. On the one hand, Pinder ˙cepts that disabled people face exclusionary barriers in employment, ιucation and other social arenas, and that these must be exposed through

research and campaigning; on the other, she contends that living wit
chronic illness and disability has profoundly individual and person:
dimensions that must be acknowledged:

> The reification of 'disabling environments' is as partial as the previous exclusiv
> concentration on bodies-to-be-rehabilitated neglected the social structure. Whil
> focusing on those common external structures which deny access to disable
> people has proved to be a powerful unifying political force, such a focus represen
> only part of a much more complex, multi-layered picture. (ibid.: 137)

Pinder calls for a more 'holistic' approach, and illustrates this through th
employment and 'sickness absence' experiences narrated by two peop:
with arthritis in her own research. In her view, simply examining disablin
barriers in the workplace would generate a far from adequate account c
these individuals' experiences, and would blank-out important difference
between them. The exploration of their illness experiences reveals the *variab*
ways in which their bodies live, articulate their sense of self and identit
and attach meaning to features of their worlds. These insights, Pinde
argues, should be tied in with 'a wider web of economic, social and cultur:
relationships' (ibid.: 153).

In his contribution to the debate, Michael Bury – whom we know fro:
Chapter 2 to be an architect of the sociology of chronic illness and disability i
the UK – affirms the value of the interpretative approach in medical sociolog:

> … sociological work on specific disabling illnesses [has] been undertaken, doc:
> menting both the problems people face and the active steps they take to overcon
> them. The emphasis on meaning in this work has revealed, in more depth, tł
> issues that people find most difficult in adapting to in disabling illness. (Bur
> 1996: 23)

In a bid to refute the idea that UK research on disability has *only* focusse
on the intricacies of subjective meaning, Bury goes on to claim that parall
studies in the social sciences have also 'highlighted the constraints of soc
etal responses and the availability or the lack of resources needed to tack
[the problems]' (ibid.: 23). Cited in this connection are Mildred Blaxter
book *The Meaning of Disability* (1976), discussed in Chapter 2 (this volume
and Strauss and Glaser's work in the US, particularly their book *Chron*
Illness and the Quality of Life (1975). Indeed, Bury devotes a large proportic
of his paper to outlining an earlier policy and practice oriented body (
'socio-medical' research in the UK with which some medical sociologis
had collaborated. He cites both impairment-specific and national disabili
prevalence studies, including those carried out by the Office of Populatio
Censuses and Surveys (OPCS) (Harris *et al.*, 1971a,b; Martin *et al.*, 1988), ar

evelopmental work on the WHO's ICIDH. In a publication that appeared oon after, Bury characterised the social model of disability as 'over-ocialised', socially reductionist, unidimensional and over-politicised Bury, 1997: 137–8).

Despite this attempt by Bury to broaden the 'social' provenance of med-:al sociological research on chronic illness and disability, Gareth Williams 1996b: 202), another medical sociologist with an interpretative pedigree, oncedes in his contribution to the debate that:

> In the end, however, the danger in much of this [medical sociological] work is that it loses sight altogether of the structures which make the experience [of chronic illness and disability] take the shape it does. History and even biography are dissolved in ever deeper phenomenological penetration into the interstices of self and world. What started out as a sociological analysis becomes part of a quasi-religious or spiritual quest for the truth which illness is supposed to reveal.

his preoccupation with 'illness and the human condition' in medical soci-logy is of interest to Williams, but only up to a point (see, also, G. Williams, :001). Though his own influential research on the lived experience of hronic illness centred on what he termed the *narrative reconstruction* of self G. Williams, 1984a), Williams' statement, above, reflects his supportive tance towards materialist perspectives and conflict theory. This is partly xplained by his admiration for the work of Irving Zola, the disabled \merican sociologist who drew on his own lived experience of impairment nd disability to inform his scholarship and activism in US disability studies see Chapter 2, this volume). Williams (1996a: 117–18) celebrates Zola's dual nsistence on the exploration of personal experience of disability and mpairment, including 'suffering', *and* the structurally oriented pursuit of nti-oppression policy and politics:

> During the 1980s, Zola recognised that while his politics had to be unwavering in the articulation of demands for independence and an end to discrimination, [he thought] there was more to a sociological analysis of disabled people's oppression than an empirical identification of environmental barriers conjoined with a conspiracy theory regarding the interests of professionals engaged in rehabilitation … . Zola recognised that the oppression experienced by people with disabilities was a complex matter.

This support for Zola's insistence on the examination of the subjective xperience of impairment and disability finds an echo in an internal debate n disability studies, discussed in Liz Crow's chapter in *Exploring the Divide* 1996). Expressing the views of a growing number of feminist disability activists, Crow challenged the refusal of leading male disability theorists to engage with the 'subjective experiences of impairment' – a challenge I report in Chapters 3 and 5, Crow argues forcibly for attention to be paid to disabled people's personal experiences of living with both the realities of the impaired body and the effects of disablism. A failure to do so, she and other feminists assert, does both political and epistemological damage to the disability movement and its intellectual resources. Crow (1996) expressed her desire to see disability studies move into the territory monopolised by medical sociologists and psychologists: the lived experience of impairment. Addressing her fellow disability activists she states:

> The experience of impairment is not always irrelevant, neutral or positive. How can it be when it is the very reason used to justify the oppression we are battling against? How can it be when pain, fatigue, depression and chronic illness are constant facts of life for many of us? (Crow, 1996: 58)

She went on to insist that impairment experiences must be integrated into disability activism and consciousness if both individual and collective *resistance* to disablism is to be sustained, and made a case for developing new ways of interpreting 'our experience of our bodies' (ibid.: 60):

> We need a new approach which acknowledges that people apply their own meanings to their own experiences of impairment. This self-interpretation adds a whole new layer of personal, subjective interpretations to the objective concept of impairment ... the experiences and history of our impairments become a part of our autobiography. (ibid.: 61)

Taken together, the contributions sketched out in this *Episode* reveal that the 1995 *Accounting for Illness and Disability* conference tapped into a deep disciplinary 'divide' on the significance and treatment of subjective experiences, though disagreements *within* disability studies and medical sociology are also evident.

The Experiential: Research in Disability Studies and Medical Sociology

This section attempts to flesh out these disciplinary differences on experiential matters by selecting, for closer scrutiny, a number of published research papers that are broadly representative of disciplinary approaches. We must start, however, with a discussion of research practices and methods.

Doing Research on Disability

The practice and ethics of social science research on disability, whether it has an experiential or any other focus, are topics of great importance in both disability studies and medical sociology, but disability studies' concerns about the *politics of research* in the 1990s placed research activities centre stage (Abberley, 1992; Oliver, 1992; Zarb, 1992).

At stake, from a disability studies perspective, are answers to questions such as: whose interests are served by the proposed research? Whose side is the researcher on? For whom were classificatory schemas for use in research *on* disability developed – most notably, the WHO's ICIDH and ICF? Disability studies writers argued that research activity 'on disabled people' in sociology and other disciplines is just another arena in which disablism can flourish, in a number of ways. Whether or not it does hinges on many things, including: the expectations and conditions tied to research funding; the framing of research questions and project designs; researchers' values and the way that they relate to and treat disabled people in research projects; the appropriateness of data collection methods (e.g. when working with people with learning difficulty); the theory (and prejudices) behind the interpretation of data and the generation of new knowledge; and the presentation and use made of research findings.

A famous and oft-cited 'case' of *disablist research* concerns research undertaken on living conditions at the Le Court Cheshire Home (and other institutions) in England in the 1960s by social scientists from the Tavistock Institute, Eric Miller and Geraldine Gwynne (1972) (funded by the Department of Health and Social Security). Disabled residents in Le Court, including Paul Hunt, initially supported the entry of these researchers onto the premises so that the realities of disabled people's institutionalised lives could be uncovered. But Hunt and others were horrified by the study's outcome. Miller and Gwynne reported on the inevitability of the 'social death' experienced by 'the crippled' in institutional settings, and failed to condemn the institutional regime; they identified with Le Court's management and staff rather than with the interests of residents (see Hunt, 1981; Finkelstein, 1991). In his account of this episode, Vic Finkelstein (1991) describes how Miller and Gwynne brought prevailing cultural attitudes about disability and dependency with them into the research setting, and failed to think beyond their prejudices.

Together with such 'real life' experiences, the theoretical innovations in disability studies in the 1980s and early 1990s, reviewed in Chapter 3, led to the development and advocacy of *emancipatory research* (Oliver, 1992; Barnes *et al.*, 1999). The principles of the emancipatory research approach are as follows: adherence to the social model of disability (i.e. the rejection of individual/medical/personal tragedy models); adoption of a partisan research approach (so denying researcher objectivity and neutrality) in order to facilitate the political struggles of disabled people; rejection of the traditional researcher–researched hierarchy and the adoption of an equalised set of research relationships; and pluralism in choice of method-ologies and methods (adapted from Mercer, 2002: 233). The emancipatory approach does not centre on the use of particular tried and tested qualitative or quantitative research methods and techniques *per se*, but on the features and qualities of the *relationships* between researchers and those researched (Zarb, 1992), together with the theoretical underpinnings and purpose of any research. In short, 'The emancipatory mode is geared to praxis-oriented research that exposes social oppression and facilitates political action to transform society' (Mercer, 2002: 233).

Much has been written on these and related themes within disability studies – readers are referred elsewhere for detailed discussion (see Finkelstein, 1991; Abberley, 1992; Oliver, 1992, 1997; Zarb, 1992; Rioux and Bach, 1994; Barnes and Mercer, 1997; Shakespeare, 1997b; M. Moore *et al.*, 1998; Thomas, 1999; Goodley and Moore, 2000; Truman *et al.*, 2001; Mercer, 2002; Walmsley, 2002; Barnes, 2003; Swain *et al.*, 2003). One related theme has been the role and responsibility of non-disabled researchers in disability research (Stone and Priestley, 1996; Priestley, 1999). It is of note that Michael Oliver, an architect of emancipatory research, later came to question the possibility of implementing it *in full* (Oliver, 1997). Others have argued that a great deal of valuable research has been undertaken that aspires, or comes close, to meeting the requirements of the emancipatory approach, even if reference to it is only implicit (Barnes, 2003).

Medical sociologists, comfortable with their own research ethics, practices and methods, have not shared in the enthusiasm for 'emancipatory research' on disability or chronic illness. While researchers in the interac-tionist and conflict theory traditions have sought to uncover the plight of those deemed socially deviant and socially disadvantaged, and have cham-pioned the interests of patients in clinical and public health arenas, most would refuse to call their approach partisan or emancipatory. The aspira-tion to be seen as 'objective' and 'balanced' retains a powerful disciplinary hold. Moreover, ethical standards and 'independence' are believed to be held in check by UK Research Council guidelines, professional codes of practise and academic peer review processes. Nevertheless, feminist researchers in the social sciences have long sought to develop and defend anti-oppressive research practices in the gender domain (Maynard and Purvis, 1994; Mertens *et al.*, 2000).

Mike Bury is one of the few medical sociologists to comment on the research challenges posed by writers in disability studies. His response has been to defend both 'academic freedom' and the research tradition in his own and related academic disciplines (Bury, 1996a,b, 1997); indeed,

e asserts that 'official' research such as the OPCS disability study
Martin *et al.*, 1988) resulted in important policy-related gains for dis-
bled people. In his view, there is no evidence that medical sociological
esearch has alienated or harmed disabled people, though he conceded in
ne late 1990s that:

> In the future it seems clear that (funded) research projects will need to take
> account of the political agendas of specific groups of the chronically sick and
> disabled more than they have in the past. The active involvement of 'client
> groups' in research design and conduct is rapidly growing. One benefit of the
> current debate is the view that medical sociologists might have held earlier, that
> they were providing a voice for the voiceless, will need to be more carefully
> considered in the future. (Bury, 1997: 140)

Finally, many researchers in both medical sociology and disability stud-
es today have been influenced by feminist and constructionist thinking on
ne epistemological status of experiential accounts. This has highlighted the
ocially constructed and 'positioned' (or 'located') character of *all* knowledge,
ncluding the knowledge embedded in the narratives shared by intervie-
vees in research contexts and, of course, in the analytical accounts written
p and published by researchers. The need for researcher *reflexivity* is
nderlined, and the 'mediated' character of interview data accepted: that is,
is known that researchers cannot straightforwardly access or recount 'the
eality' of lived experience. This is not at all to imply that interviewees'
eliberately fabricate their accounts, though it is well known that intervie-
vees may tell researchers what they think the researcher wishes to hear.
ather, the contention, now widely accepted, is that we all construct our
tories and truths in the process of communicating them to others and
urselves, and that everybody makes continuous use of social discourses or
ublic narratives in 'telling' and 'interpreting'.
  Debate in disability studies and medical sociology on the 'doing
esearch' themes outlined here have had an impact on the research papers
nat feature in the following two sections, and have influenced published
esearch in these disciplines more generally.

)isability Studies: Examples of Experiential Research

)espite the international reputation that UK disability studies has for a social
nodellist preoccupation with research at the macro-social scale on disabling
ocial barriers, a great deal of micro-sociological experiential research has been
onducted by British-based academics and activists; earlier chapters carry
nany references to this work. In the main, this research has focused on the

subjective experience of *coming up against* disabling social barriers – physical, organisational, attitudinal, and cultural – in a range of social settings and contexts. Whatever the theoretical perspective employed, the research is characterised not so much by a concentration on analysing how this made disabled people *feel about themselves*, though this may be set out, but on what they communicate about the limitations imposed upon their *social action*. That is, the guiding question in the minds of most researchers is: what barriers are perceived to exist, and what are disabled people prevented from *doing*, or from *accessing*, by the presence of these barriers?

This can be illustrated by selecting – almost at random – three research papers as exemplars from the journal *Disability & Society*. The first is a paper on the experiences of women with learning disabilities by Katrina Scior (2003).[1] Scior reports on repeat in-depth interviews with five women in contact with services for people with learning disabilities. After discussing her personal research ethics in a field acknowledged to be wide-open to oppressive research practices (Goodley, 1996, 2000; Warmsley, 2001), Scior presents many interview extracts, including the following:

> *Interviewer*: What sort of things do you do in the daytime?
> *Jenny*: I stay here today. I stay here all the time doing things around the house, like cleaning, washing, washing up, ironing, peeling potatoes, shopping. I'm good at making coffee, right? I'm good at making coffee and tea. Good at packing dishwasher, wiping tables and hoovering and dusting. Really! (Scior, 2003: 784)

The gendered character of Jenny's daily life is obvious in her account, as in the accounts of the other four women. Scior's 'discourse analysis' approach to her data uncovers a range of other themes that, together, throw light on the experiences of gendered disablism: exploitation, social exclusion and abuse. Moreover, she suggests that her data show how: 'individuals with learning disabilities use linguistic representations developed by the majority group to justify the oppressive treatment of people with learning disabilities'. In this way, Scior links individual biographies to the broader disablist social landscape.

The second example, Jenny Harris' (2003) paper on the experiences of 3 disabled refugees and asylum seekers in the UK (from Somali, Vietnamese, Sonali (Kurdish) and Tamil communities – 15 women, 23 men), also connects personal stories with macro-sociological themes. Harris uncovers 'the constellation of oppressions' (ibid.: 395) experienced by people whose lives are already marked deeply by personal danger, physical and psychological trauma, and serious medical needs. One respondent's account gives a flavour of these people's desperate personal histories in home countries:

> In 1987, the government bombed my house in [location]. Also in 1994, they bombed my [new] house. I lost my one eye ... I came alone ... my family are in

[location]. After I left [location] I do not know their details. Because of that I am mentally upset. I do not know what is happening with my family. (ibid.: 402)

Harris chooses not to analyse either the existential consequences of these dimensions of experience or impairment experiences *per se* – as medical sociologists might well have done. Rather, her interest lies in disabled refugees access to social and welfare services in the UK, as disabled people. The interview data tell of the many barriers that the refugees and asylum seekers encountered when attempting to access services, grouped together under the headings: health barriers, safety barriers, social service barriers, barriers to the benefit system and barriers to social contact. Here is just one interview extract:

Doctor gave me medical certificate; I received Invalidity Benefit for 12 months. After 12 months I was examined by the benefits doctor. I got 13 points. I needed 15 points in order to receive Invalidity Benefit. I was told to go to the job centre to sign on. Job centre said I cannot work I have to get Invalidity Benefit. The benefit department said I did not have enough points to receive Invalidity Benefit, I have to sign on at unemployment centre. (ibid.: 406)

Harris concludes that, taken a whole, the respondents' accounts:

… depict a landscape of barriers to the basic necessities of life. Arguably, many of these barriers also continue to affect British disabled people who are not refugees and asylum seekers … . However, the respondents in this study are far more likely to be confronting all of these barriers simultaneously. (ibid.: 408)

The third example of experiential research is a paper that focuses, once again, on personal experiences of encounters with statutory services. In this case, it is education services that are in the frame, and it concerns the experiences of parents rather than disabled children or young adults themselves. Barbara Cole (2005) reports on six in-depth interviews with 'mother-teachers' about the educational trajectories of their own children with a range of impairments and what the services term *special educational needs* (SEN). In a UK policy climate that purports to support the inclusion of disabled children in mainstream schools, Cole formulates her key question as follows:

How can we, as teachers, parents and members of a caring society find effective ways of supporting potentially vulnerable children within an education system which, both explicitly and implicitly, through people, processes and procedures, encourages and values the development and contribution of all its members? (ibid.: 331–2)

Influenced by what she refers to as the growth of feminist and auto/biographical research, and the acknowledged importance of researcher reflexivity, Cole includes a pen-portrait of her own story as a 'mother-teacher' and presents extracts from the narrative accounts of her respondents. One mother-teacher, tells of the process that led up to the exclusion of her son from a mainstream school:

> Although [the Head] said yes, she meant no. She dillied and dallied an um'd and ah'd and things weren't right, and we lost. It took about a year before she had the courage to say no, we don't want James in our school! ... . We got another placement but it would have been nice for him to go there, as that was where all the other local children went. (ibid.: 333)

On the basis of the narratives offered by the women, some recounting more positive experiences with the educational system and its staff, Cole (2005: 342) concludes that there are many risks involved in the education of children with special needs:

> The children can face isolation if they travel to special school miles away from home; if they attend mainstream schools they may risk bullying and isolation. Inclusion can be a risk for schools if performance indicators are to be the overriding concern; and there is always the risk that other parents may choose to take their children elsewhere. There is a financial risk in that, under the present system, money may have to go to support children in both special and mainstream schools to meet the needs of all children. Committing education to 'real' inclusion for all children could even be a critical risk for governments. (ibid.: 342)

Thus, like Scior and Harris, Cole links personal biographies to socio-structural matters of policy, politics and finance, with a view to laying bare the difficulties and barriers to the achievement of the full educational inclusion of disabled children.

A fourth and final example comes from another source: Tracey Bignall and Jabeer Butt's (2000) research about young black disabled people's experiences of independent living. Their research places emphasis on enabling 'the voices' of especially marginalised groups in the disabled community to find expression (see also Begum and Stevens, 1994). Based on interviews with 44 young disabled people with a range of impairments (Asian, African and Afro-Caribbean in origin), Bignall and Butts explore both access to resources for independent living (including education, employment, and social care support) *and* features the way the young people see themselves and their circumstances; they draw attention to multiple oppressions, illustrated by one respondent as follows:

> ... because I'm a woman and I'm Asian and I'm deaf, I ... you know, feel I'm limited and it's difficult. For example, in the Asian community women are not allowed

to go out at night so that's been a real problem for me. I feel that there's a lot of discrimination ... . A lot of people think that I can't do a job because I'm deaf so I get discriminated against on all three counts. (Bignall and Butt, 2000: 20)

One of Bignall and Butt's (ibid.: 49) many conclusions is that the ambitions of young black disabled people are frequently frustrated or ignored, sometimes by their own families, and often by the education sector and other social institutions.

All four of the examples discussed illuminate dimensions of the social oppression, exclusion and marginalisation experienced by disabled people. The disablism uncovered includes what I would call psycho-emotional disablism, and bears witness to the presence of Iris MarionYoung's (1990) five faces of oppression, discussed in Chapter 3. The expansion of scholarship in this mode, with a contemporary or historical focus, has been quite remarkable in recent decades. The focus on barriers to social action, to *doing and having*, is paramount. Experiential research that addresses aspects of *being* – matters of ontology and existential status – is less common, though of interest to some feminist researchers and the phenomenologically minded. However, one *being* research foci that has been of importance is whether people with impairments identify as 'disabled', a theme touched upon in Chapter 3 (see, Shakespeare, 1996; Swain and French, 2000; Reeve, 2002; Watson, 2002; Swain *et al.*, 2003).

Medical Sociology: Examples of Experiential Research

The core themes to be found in medical sociologists' research on chronic illness and disability – outlined in the earlier discussion of *Episode* 5 and Kelly's (1996) paper on radical surgery and the lifeworld – have informed a great many studies on the lived experience of chronic illnesses and 'disabilities'. Indeed, the longevity of these interactionist and phenomenological themes in medical sociology is remarkable. Let's compare, for example, a 'classic' paper published in the early 1980s in a British journal by the North American writer, Kathy Charmaz, *Loss of Self: a Fundamental Form of Suffering in the Chronically Ill* (1983), with a paper published in the early 2000s by Bie Nio Ong and colleagues, *Establishing Self and Meaning in Low Back Pain* (2004).

Based on interviews with 57 people with a range of chronic diseases, Charmaz reports on 'restricted lives', 'social isolation', 'being discredited' and 'burdening others'. Of the many interview extracts presented, one young man with renal failure talks of his restricted life as follows:

I used to be very stubborn, and I'd always stick with relationships and stay with them to the bitter end and work things out, and now I find I don't have as much energy for doing that, and it frustrates me at times because I don't want to lose those friendships, but yet they want more from me that I am able to give, and so I can't. And I know that when I feel miserable from dialysis, it is a hundred times harder for me to relate to people in a full way. And I slough off, and I don't throw all my energy into dealing with things that are going on in the relationship and that frustrates other people, frustrates me. (1983: 178)

Charmaz is interested in the 'loss of self' and personal dignity involved here, not with the failure of friends to accommodate to this person's changed circumstances. This is also illustrated by extracts from respondents newly dependent on others for their personal care needs, such as this woman whose mother-in-law, a nurse, stepped into the caring role:

She wanted to *bathe* me. I told my husband, 'But she's my mother-in-law.' My husband was getting awfully angry with me – he would say, 'But she's a nurse and knows how to take care of you,' which was true … It was heartbreak to me – my mother-in-law! … . I didn't want [her] to see me nude … When a nurse comes through your door, that's one thing, but to have your mother-in-law cleaning you up after you and bathing you, that's another – it is just too much to take. (ibid.: 186)

Charmaz's many observations on the 'miseries of life' with chronic illness leads her to conclude that one of the most significant sources of suffering involves 'the inability to control one's self and life in ways that had been hoped for, anticipated, or assumed' (ibid.: 187). Life is now disrupted, unpredictable, and fragile; valued self-images from the past crumble and are lost, often irrevocably, and suffering is exacerbated by strained relationships of dependency upon family members. However, Charmaz does acknowledge, in her closing lines, that some respondents 'had improved' and no longer suffered as greatly as they had in the past. Indeed, these individuals were more likely to see their earlier suffering as a path to new knowledge and self-discovery' (ibid.: 191). As discussed in Chapter 2 (this volume) this 'reconstruction' of self has been taken up as an important theme by other researchers.

Charmaz's approach served as a model for many sociological studies on the lived experience of chronic illness and disability in subsequent years. It is echoed some 30 years later in Ong *et al.*'s (2004) account of lives blighted by low back pain. This is not to say that Ong *et al.* replicate Charmaz's precise foci or analytical categories, but that they similarly explore the micro-social existential terrain. These authors consider how 16 respondents describe their pain and the way they claim to present their 'unseen' problem to clinicians. The sociological lens is trained on respondents' attempts to sustain their moral status and social legitimacy. The language of 'narratives' is used to refer to the biographically contextualised 'illness stories' that people tell. Indeed, Ong *et al.* note that the interviews themselves 'can be viewed as social encounters in which [respondents] construct themselves as believable narrators of their own pain experiences'(ibid.: 547). This is something that back pain sufferers must replicate in clinical dialogues with doctors and other therapists. Here are three short interview extracts:

> I mean, I have been to the point where you have to crawl in a bed ... crawl into bed at night, and erm ... sort of crawl out again in the morning and you can't even ... I've struggled to fill a kettle at the sink, 'cos holding anything in front of you kills you, you know. It really, it's sort of so sharp, but luckily I haven't had it as much as I used to get it, lately. (Ian) (ibid.: 542)

> Of course, there are times when I just weep and all the rest of it, with the pain. But I get angry, most of the time I just try to set myself targets of things to achieve. (Carolyn) (ibid.: 544)

> But, there again, sometimes you can be 'right as nine-pence', you can just go. Pick something up. It's strange, and then you can, like, suffer a few days and then you can move in a certain direction and it just goes, just like that. It's strange. (Graham) (ibid.: 543)

Central to respondents' accounts, in Ong *et al.*'s interpretation, is the use of cultural reference points to establish the authenticity and legitimacy of the suffering self: to make it evident that the pain 'really' exists. Individuals' moral character is at stake (ibid.: 547).

These papers by Charmaz and Ong *et al.* are broadly typical of a great deal of experiential research in the sociology of chronic illness and disability. Such studies focus on *being* in illness rather than *doing* in the face of disablism. Although implicit or explicit reference may be made to systems of cultural meaning, there is little or no attempt to make an explanatory link between personal illness biographies and the social structures and mechanisms that serve to exclude or oppress. Moreover, it is the commonality among adults or children wrought by sharing a particular type of chronic illness or impairment that generally determines their selection for a research study, rather than their gender, 'race', class or sexuality. Indeed, there are relatively few studies that look at the gendered or 'race' experience of chronic illness or disability.

However, some interpretative researchers in this tradition do pay attention to *practical* difficulties faced by individuals and their 'carers' in daily life (undertaking domestic or paid work, for example), and to coping and illness management strategies. These are viewed, primarily, as difficulties that are caused by having a chronic illness or other impairment (Anderson and Bury, 1988, see the review in Lawton, 2003). And studies frequently consider the impact upon *other* people in 'sufferers' immediate social networks – especially spouses or partners, and children. Localised criticisms of health and social care services and some professional staff may come into play, though the critical examination of entitlement to, and receipt of, welfare benefits and social care services is generally left to social policy researchers. Another recent theme of research interest has been the development of 'expert patients'; this theme examines the ways in which patients with chronic conditions become expert – sometimes more expert than health professionals – in the therapeutic management of their conditions (Bury, 2005).

Recent Signs of Disciplinary Change: Straws in the Wind

Thus far, this chapter has reviewed the deeply entrenched disciplinary divide between disability studies and medical sociology on the question of the experiential dimensions of illness and disability. We now move on to consider some recent signs of movement in ideas and 'loosening up' of disciplinary profiles, starting with medical sociology.

Medical Sociology: Signs of Change

One of the most notable and significant examples of this, in my view, is found in a recent paper published by a leading British medical sociologist, Graham Scambler, tellingly entitled, *Re-framing Stigma: Felt and Enacted Stigma and Challenges to the Sociology of Chronic and Disabling Conditions* (2004).[2] I shall consider this in some detail because Scambler's interpretative research on epilepsy in the 1980s – utilising Goffman's analysis of social stigma (see Chapter 2, this volume) – was influential in shaping 'the sociology of chronic illness and disability', and is continues to be widely cited (Scambler, 1984, 1989; Scambler and Hopkins, 1986).

In *Re-framing Stigma* (2004), Scambler undertakes a refreshingly critical review of both his own 'hidden distress model of epilepsy' and the broader interpretative research tradition in which it sits. He summarises the three propositions at the core of the hidden distress model of epilepsy as follows:

(a) when a doctor passes on the diagnosis of epilepsy, recipients quickly learn to regard the status of 'epileptic' as a liability, largely because the special view of the world they accommodate to privileges a fear of enacted stigma;

(b) this special view of the world predisposes people to conceal their condition and the diagnosis from others, to attempt to 'pass as normal': the fear of enacted stigma promotes a policy of non-disclosure that remains viable as long as people are discreditable rather than discredited;

(c) the policy of strict concealment reduces the opportunities for enacted stigma, one important consequence of which is that felt stigma is typically more disruptive of the lives of people with epilepsy than enacted stigma. (ibid.: 33)

Scambler now believes this model retains credibility only *as far as it goes*. He notes that it became subject to three important criticisms:

[T]hat the model [1] takes as given the epistemic authority of the biomedical perspective; [2] presumes epilepsy to be a 'personal tragedy'; and [3] intimates a form of fateful passivity conventionally associated with 'victimhood'. (ibid.: 34)

A significant part of Scambler's detailed discussion of these criticisms involves an examination of the shortcomings of interpretative medical sociology from the point of view of disability studies theorists. Scambler concedes that his work, like that of many others in the interpretative tradition, lacks an appreciation of, first, structures of social *power* involved in the designation and social treatment of 'epileptics', and, second, the possibility (and means) of resistance to, and escape from, victimhood. He notes that 'it is conflict theory that is most conspicuous by its absence' (ibid.: 36), and concludes that: ' The hidden distress model of epilepsy was at best *partial*, at worst *deficient*, in its failure to address sociologically a series of theoretical questions' (ibid.: 37). Scambler formulates new questions, as follows:

How and why did the institutional order and symbolic framework emergent in modernity in nation-states like Britain come to incorporate cultural norms of identity or being that denounced and oppressed people with epilepsy as *imperfect*? To what extent were these norms the intended or unintended consequences of the system imperatives of the economy and state? Do they bear the taint of ideology? When people with epilepsy were interred in 'epileptic colonies', a practice not long abandoned, did this process represent also a 'colonization of the lifeworld'? What social relations other than the class relations of the economy and the command relations of the state have had a significant impact on the definition and control of those with epilepsy … . And, of course, how paradigmatic of stigma is epilepsy in these respects? The posing of questions such as these provides a number of pointers towards a long overdue re-framing of stigma. (ibid.)

One can almost hear a chorus of 'at last!' going up amongst disability studies scholars, both materialist and poststructuralist, in response to the posing of such questions, and for Scambler's telling use of the word 'oppression'. We know from Chapters 3–5 in this book that these are precisely the kinds of questions that have been posed *and answered* by theorists and activists in disability studies.

Scambler does not turn, however, to the disability studies literature for answers. He looks for new approaches *within* medical sociology itself. He turns, for example, to Parker and Aggleton's (2003) work on HIV and AIDS-related stigma, failing to note that scholars in disability studies in the UK (or in North America, the Nordic countries or Australasia) might well have written the following passage by Parker and Aggleton:

> ... stigma and stigmatization function, quite literally, at the point of intersection between *culture, power* and *difference* – and it is only by exploring these different categories that it becomes possible to understand stigma and stigmatization not merely as isolated phenomenon, or expressions of individual attitudes or of cultural values, but as central to the constitution of the social order. (2003: 5, cited in Scambler, 2004: 38)

Moreover, in his re-framing of stigma, Scambler does not abandon or reject the medical sociological tradition of viewing illness through the *social deviance* lens. On the contrary, he suggests that the deviance perspective should be strengthened through broader theorising.

Scambler proposes a 'new' research agenda based on four claims. The claims are, first:

> Any appreciation of why and how epilepsy persists as a stigmatizing condition must be articulated against the background of the logics of capitalist accumulation (of the economy) and mode of regulation (of the state) and their respective relations of class and command. (Scambler, 2004: 42)

Second: 'the logic of shame and its relations of stigma have become more volatile with the switch from organized to disorganized capitalism' (ibid.: 43). Third: 'our more fluid or volatile postmodern culture, more permissive of – if not necessarily tolerant of – "difference," facilitates forms of "identity politics" ' (ibid.: 43). Fourth: 'the effectiveness of identity politics in relation to epilepsy – measured in terms of the removal of "oppression" via enacted and felt stigma – depends primarily on the nature of the prevailing nexus of structural antecedents of stigma' (ibid.: 43–4).

Once again, in my view, writers in disability studies would be justified in asserting that much research and theorising in this vein has *already* been undertaken in their discipline (see, especially, Chapters 3 and 5, this volume).

Lesser but nonetheless significant signs of change are to be found in the writings of another leading UK medical sociologist, Michael Bury. As we know from *episode 5* above, Bury was one of the few medical sociologists willing to engage in debate with influential figures in disability studies in the 1990s. At that time, he was willing to acknowledge that 'some aspects of disability are clearly a function of social expectations and the impact of social structure' (Bury, 1997: 137) but rejected the social model of disability on the grounds that it was 'over-socialised', socially reductionist, unidimensional, and over-politicised (ibid.: 137–8). However, a more conciliatory tone is now evident (Bury, 2000, 2005), perhaps in recognition of the significant impact that advocates of the social model have had on wider social policy and sociological thinking about disability.

In a paper published in 2000, for example, Bury proposes 'a sociology of disability' in the Irving Zola tradition (see, also, Bury, 2005). This would draw, on the one hand, upon Arthur Frank's (1995) attention to ill people's capacity to construct new selves and life trajectories through illness narratives, and, on the other, on some features of the social model of disability: 'The mid-range, between a wounded storyteller and an overly politicised conception would, as Zola suggests, seem to offer the best way forward' (Bury, 2000: 182). This is an interesting shift. In Bury's mind, Frank's approach 'helps to overcome the tendency to rely only on documenting the negative experiences of patients' (Bury, 2005: 71), while debates *within* disability studies help to overcome the social model's 'over-socialisation' (ibid.: 74–5). Both trends are, in his view, to be encouraged:

> In this way, self-identity, body and society are best seen … as a set of dynamic processes. The demands of the 'outside' social environment and the nature of the distribution of resources are clearly of importance here. (ibid.: 78)

Unlike Scambler, Bury makes little explicit reference to the 'illness as social deviance' paradigm that strongly underpins the interactionist tradition upon which he and many others draw. 'Deviance' barely gets a mention in Bury's writing from the late 1990s. This may be another sign of disciplinary change: perhaps the sheer presence of disability studies and the disabled people's movement makes it unacceptable to refer to chronically ill and disabled people as 'deviants'. Bury alludes to this when he states:

> There is now a propensity for at least some of those living with a chronic illness or disability to challenge their erstwhile 'deviant status'. As a result, there is a growing insistence on 'difference', reproducing and acting as a critical example of a more general process of relativising the boundaries between normality and abnormality, pathology and health. (1997: 133–4)

In contrast, the use of the term 'stigma' retains acceptability and utility for Bury and others (see Kelleher and Leavey, 2004): chronic illness and disability continue to be characterised as socially stigmatised states of being that require individual management in the interactional order.

Finally, another sign of change is the more frequent appearance of papers and book chapters written by medical sociologists that engage seriously with ideas to be found in disability studies, such as Julie Mulvany's (2000) *Disability, impairment or illness? The relevance of the social model of disability to the study of mental disorder.* Another example is Neil Small and Penny Rhodes's (2000) *Too Ill to Talk? User involvement in palliative care.*

However, changes merely in form rather than substance characterise the positions adopted by some. Simon Williams (1999, 2000), for example, has thought it necessary to *engage* with UK disability studies (to a limited degree), but interprets segments of the impairment debate found therein as symptomatic of its shift *toward medical sociology.* Williams' arguments were discussed in some detail in Chapter 5, and will not be revisited. Suffice it to say that he has persistently rejected the social model of disability on the grounds that it denies the 'disabling effects' of chronic illness and other impairment.

Disability Studies: Signs of Change

Attention now turns to disability studies: are there signs of movement and change in ideas and positioning on the question of lived experience of impairment and disablism?

As discussed at length in Chapter 5, there is certainly evidence of considerable movement on the question of impairment, and it is indisputable that the development of poststructuralist, phenomenological, and some feminist thinking on impairment has been greatly influenced by ideas developed on 'the body' in sociology and cultural studies (rather than in medical sociology *per se*). While the experiential theme is only one thread running through debates about the impaired body, it is an important and recurring one.

Meanwhile, lively discussion about the place and role of the experiential *per se* continues. Opposition to becoming embroiled in 'sentimental autobiography' (Barnes, 1998) remains strong among some materialist social modellists, for reasons outlined in Chapter 5. In the words of Barnes *et al.*:

> There remains a basic disagreement about the ways in which experience is properly integrated into a social model perspective. There is no dispute that experience is central, but writers divide on whether the focus should be restricted to disability or extend to impairment as well. Indeed, for the 'critics', the experience of impairment and disability cannot be compartmentalized. (1999: 93)

Nevertheless, illness and impairment narratives, some autobiographical, have appeared with greater frequency in disability studies publications in recent years, usually linked to the overarching debate about the relevance of impairment and impairment-related experiences. Examples, some provocative, are readily found in *Disability & Society*. One is Patricia de Wolfe's (2002) paper, *Private Tragedy in Social Context? Reflections on Disability, Illness and Suffering*. This introduces a related theme concerning *types* of impairment, and poses the question: do chronic illnesses have a place in disability studies and disability politics? De Wolfe tells something of her story as an 'ME sufferer' (ibid.: 255–6) and a person subject to discrimination and exclusion. She positions herself as someone who is 'frail, with fluctuating symptoms of tiredness and pain' (ibid.: 256), and suggests that:

> ... ambivalences towards illness within disability theory are linked to a reluctance to acknowledge, and indeed an embarrassment about acknowledging suffering as an intractable feature of the human condition. This reluctance relegates to the realm of the private, both conceptually and materially, those whose suffering cannot be relieved by either medical intervention or social change. (ibid.: 255–6)

In de Wolfe's view, the realities of living with chronic illness should be recognised and accommodated, not least because the experiences of 'the sick' give rise to particular social demands:

> By contrast with certain impairments discussed by disability activists, illness does often constitute tragedy, both for its victims and for those close to them. It can turn minuscule daily tasks into draining chores; make valued activities impossible, or ruin enjoyment in them; abort short-term and long-term plans; strain relationships to breaking point. Many of the problems result from the bodily condition of the sufferer and no amount of social accommodation can totally compensate for lost quality of life. This does not mean that social arrangements and atmosphere do not make a great difference to the experience of illness. (ibid.: 261)

By excluding such considerations, de Wolfe agues, disability studies is (unintentionally) complicit in the marginalisation and stigmatisation of 'the incurably long-term sick' because their particular social needs – for social recognition and inclusion, for material and emotional support, *and* for improved medical treatment – remain unexamined (ibid.: 262). In her conclusion, de Wolfe calls for the full and meaningful inclusion of the chronically ill in the disabled people's movement and disability studies (see, also, Wendell, 1996).

Moving on, my own ideas about the close intermeshing of the effects of disablism and impairment in the daily lives of disabled people have played a part in widening the scope of debate in UK disability studies in recent years; this is especially true of my reflections on the gendered nature of the lived experience of *psycho-emotional disablism*, discussed in Chapter 3 (Thomas, 1999; Reeve, 2002, 2006). My contribution to debate has also attracted interest among disability studies scholars in the Nordic countries, and has helped to encourage international dialogue and the fruitful exchange of ideas (Kristiansen and Traustadóttir, 2004; Thomas, 2004c). Many agree with me that research and theorising on lived experience has to be sensitive and sophisticated enough to recognise and analyse the complex social processes and forces in play. I now venture that this would benefit from analytically *embodying* experiences of disablism and impairment effects, as discussed in Chapter 5.

Another sign of a greater willingness to accommodate the experiential dimension of impairment in disability studies is the inclusion of papers in *Disability & Society* that appear, at first sight, to resemble research papers generated by sociologists of chronic illness and disability. Examples include Whitehead and William's (2001) article *Medical Treatment of Women with Lupus. The case for sharing knowledge and decision making*, Zitzelberger's (2005) *(In)visibility: accounts of embodiment of women with physical disabilities and differences*, and Smith and Sparkes' *Men, sport, and spinal cord injury: an analysis of metaphors and narrative types*. Each places the experiential accounts ('voices') of disabled people centre stage. But the authors differ from interpretative medical sociologists by making an analytical linkage between these experiences and broader socio-structural and cultural agendas. In short, what makes these authors' papers contributions *to disability studies* is the location of experiential concerns in the social oppression paradigm.

Summary

This chapter has compared the sociologies of lived experience to be found in disability studies and medical sociology, starting with *episode 5* of inter-disciplinary debate. The importance of non-oppressive and emancipatory approaches to research in disability studies was highlighted in the second section. Attention then turned to examples of published research in both disciplines. These illustrated that researchers in disability studies have worked with the social oppression paradigm to uncover and analyse the social mechanisms that create, sustain and reinforce disablism, while interpretative researchers in medical sociology have continued to explore the micro-sociology of meaning and self-identity in chronic illness and 'disablement'. The final section considered examples of work that signal interesting developments in approach in both disciplines.

There is evidence that some writers in medical sociology are showing greater appreciation of ideas and arguments articulated in disability studies, most notably, Graham Scambler (2004). I would encourage medical sociologists to take Scambler's 're-framing stigma' lead, but, in so doing, to look closely at the literature *already published* by writers in disability studies on questions of power, oppression and forms of disablism. Disability studies scholars have completed much of the intellectual groundwork in the areas that Scambler flags up. At the very least, the interpretative exploration of 'living with chronic illness and disability' should recognise the positive as well as the negative in disabled peoples' lived experience (Swain and French, 2000), and should combine a core preoccupation with meaning, coping and loss of self with a broader set of interests focused on the social structural shaping of experience.

Turning to disability studies, research on lived experience must, in my view, continue to give priority to the subjective experience of *disablism*, that is, to people's encounters with social exclusion, discrimination, and marginalisation – wherever and however these occur. Research of this kind is at the heart of the discipline in the UK, providing both ballast and directionality – and must endeavour to keep up with the fast changing scene of disability legislation and policy implementation in the 2000s. Nevertheless, the argument that I have returned to several times in this book, from different angles, is that the discipline should nurture its own sociology of impairment and impairment effects, one that includes the lived experience of chronic illness. Put another way, the discipline's social oppression paradigm is analytically incomplete without a sociology of impairment (see Chapter 5). Moreover, I suggest that it is time for disability studies to take intellectual ownership of the social 'suffering' that often accompanies impairment *and* disablism. This would include research on the ways in which disablism – especially psycho-emotional disablism – creates suffering that can *cause* or *worsen* illness and other impairment. Research in medical sociology on lived experience does, in my view, have insights to offer in this regard.

Among other things, a more inclusive or all-rounded approach to lived experience in disability studies could offer yet another means of addressing and connecting with the social experiences and interests of disabled people, especially the many people with impairments – old and young – who do not self-identify as disabled, and refuse to countenance 'disabled' signifiers in their own lives.

7

Towards a Sociology of Disability?

The purpose of this final chapter is to draw together my observations on the sociologies of disability, impairment and chronic illness to be found in disability studies and medical sociology in the UK, and to reflect on the prospects for, and desirability of, a singular *sociology of disability*.

The review of theoretical perspectives in Part One revealed that a multiplicity of sociological ideas and approaches are at work in both disciplines. These are, however, located within overarching paradigms: medical sociology makes sense of 'chronic illness and disability' through the *social deviance* lens, while disability studies has *social oppression* as its analytical signature. Within these paradigms, theoretical perspectives are varied and fluid. Medical sociology saw mid-twentieth century Parsonian functionalism succeeded by interactionism, phenomenology, conflict theories, and Foucaldian poststructuralism. As well as producing analytical diversity, this bifurcation has given rise to sharply contrasting moral and political stances on chronic illness and disability. In this way, the social deviance paradigm has come to accommodate both medico-centric and what might be termed 'social deviant-centric' positions. In disability studies, the younger discipline, materialism, poststructuralism and phenomenology – and feminist variants of these – are all in evidence today; no attempt is made to disguise an ideological commitment to challenging social oppression and exclusion in the interests of disabled people.

Despite this conceptual multiplicity, it is also clear that particular theoretical approaches have played both formative and dominant roles within each discipline in the UK. These qualities belong to materialist social modellism in disability studies, and to interpretative (interactionist and phenomenological) perspectives in medical sociology – especially in its sub-field known as *the sociology of chronic illness and disability*. Feminist thinking has played a crucial role in both disciplines, though feminists' engagement with a variety of theoretical perspectives has ensured that their contributions are also characterised by diversity.

I argued in Chapter 2 that a nascent 'sociology of disability' could be found in medical sociology, that is, a body of work from the 1960s distinguished by its concentration on disability *per se* and by the use of a number of macro-sociological perspectives, sometimes in combination with interpretative approaches. This never flourished in medical sociology in the UK. It was eclipsed first by the influence of interpretative perspectives and then by the emergence of disability studies.

The three chapters in Part Two laid bare the contours of what writers in disability studies have termed 'the divide' between their discipline and medical sociology. This divide is particularly stark and deep in the contested terrain of care and dependency (Chapter 4), but also has a clear presence in scholarship on 'the body' (Chapter 5), and in research on the experiential dimensions of living with disability and impairment (Chapter 6). However, the multiplicity of theoretical perspectives *within* disciplines in these areas is also much in evidence, and disciplinary overlaps can be discerned.

Chapter 4 commenced with a discussion of the concepts 'need', 'care' and 'dependency' at a level of abstraction that is necessary if we are to rise above commonplace assumptions. This enabled us to see that medical sociologists and social policy analysts have taken the dependency and 'care needs' of disabled people *as given*, as normative, and have concentrated their critical analytical gaze upon *social responses* to the care and dependency needs (by medicine, professional practices, welfare services, informal care systems). However, the diversity of theoretical traditions in play has generated contrasting interpretations of social response themes, and has resulted in the adoption of a range of moral and political standpoints: medical practices, for example, may be accepted without question or subject to damning critique. In contrast, disability studies writers have challenged the 'inevitability' of the dependency of disabled people in the strongest terms, have rejected the 'care' system, and have sought to uncover the social mechanisms and practices that constructed the historical and contemporary lived reality of 'care' and dependency. Taking a lead from the disabled people's movement, a great deal of intellectual endeavour in disability studies has been devoted to examining and encouraging non-disablist forms of social support for disabled people: 'independent living' arrangements and related user-determined support services.

Chapter 5 on 'the missing body' reviewed debate on 'the impaired body' in disability studies, alongside a selection of the key ideas found in 'the sociology of the body' in medical sociology. It also outlined my own reflections on how disability studies might make use of some of the ideas developed in sociological analyses of the body. The chapter demonstrated that debate in disability studies on the impaired body among and between materialists, feminists, poststructuralists and phenomenologists has moved far beyond initial considerations on whether or not impairment should be addressed *at all*: the body is no longer 'missing'. However, scholars' adherence to contrasting theoretical perspectives have taken analyses of the impaired body in different directions – mirroring earlier debate about the merits of foundationalist and anti-foundationalist interpretations of 'the body' in sociology and cultural studies more generally. The review of recent ideas on embodiment in medical and mainstream sociology suggested that this trend towards theoretical diversification on body matters has been superseded, at least in the minds of some 'body theorists', by another conceptual project: how to develop theoretical frameworks that bridge epistemological divides. That is, there is a growing consensus among body theorists that an understanding of embodiment cannot be achieved by pursuing *singular* lines of thought. In my view, disability studies might usefully take a lead from this in developing its own sociology of impairment and impairment effects: the time may have come for a measured assessment of the strengths, weaknesses and limitations of *all* schools of thought on impairment and 'the impaired body', with a view to bridging theoretical divides. My own thinking on *impairment effects* is positioned in this context. A well-informed dialogue across theoretical boundaries in disability studies could ultimately enrich theorisations of both the social character of impairment *and* the embodiment of disablism.

The sociology of lived experience was the theme explored in Chapter 6. A review of research on the experiential found that medical sociologists and disability studies scholars have pursued empirical research for different purposes. Researchers in disability studies have accessed the lived experiences of disabled individuals and groups in order to expose the social mechanisms that create, sustain and reinforce disablism. In medical sociology, research on 'living with chronic illness and disability', on the part of 'sufferers' and their families, has been rooted in interpretative perspectives informed by the social deviance paradigm; attention has focused on the micro-sociology of *meanings* that the onset of stigmatised chronic illness or other impairments has for individuals' 'sense of self' and for their patterns of coping and social interaction. However, the chapter also considered recent signs of movement in ideas on the experiential among researchers in both medical sociology and disability studies, and particular note was made of Graham Scambler's re-thinking of 'stigma' in medical sociology. I argued that disability studies should continue to prioritise research on the subjective experience *of disablism* but should also develop a sociology of the lived experience of impairment and impairment effects – including the realities of social suffering.

Chapter 4 featured four of the five disciplinary *episodes* discussed in this book; the fifth is found in Chapter 6. These episodes refer to selected occasions of direct debate between leading representatives of disability studies and medical sociology in the UK, recorded during the last 40 years. That four of these are in Chapter 4 highlights the persistence of fundamental disagreement on matters of 'care' and dependency. Each episode is marked by particularly sharp and concise expressions of view and political stance, and thus has the merit of highlighting the paradigmatic approaches in play. A 'clash' of approach is not an understatement in most cases, and the 'embodied sociology' (Williams and Bendelow, 1998a) of the protagonists is evident. By researching and writing up these episodes I came to appreciate more fully the *living*, *dynamic* and *impassioned* nature of the relationship between the two academic disciplines, having long appreciated their internal dynamism. Overall, it is clear that through recent decades – marked, of course, by important economic, political and cultural changes – each discipline has played a direct and indirect role in shaping the development of features of the other; there is a close but antagonistic historical relationship.

What of the Future?

How might disciplinary developments unfold in years to come? Will the disciplinary 'divide' persist or deepen, or will inherent disciplinary dynamism lead to a new phase of respectful dialogue across the boundaries, possibly even to collaboration and the forging of common purpose? I can only speculate on the answers to such questions, as have others (Oliver, 1996c; Barnes *et al.*, 1999, 2002; G. Williams, 2001). There are certainly indications that the weight and quality of the disability studies corpus will ensure that new generations of medical sociologists will find it necessary to educate themselves in it, alongside classic and contemporary writings in medical sociology. This might begin to dissolve disciplinary boundaries and give rise to new theoretical and empirical developments. At the very least, medical and mainstream sociologists may become interested in the recognition, re-claiming and further development of their lost 'sociology of disability'.

   It follows from my presentations and commentary in preceding chapters that I support the further development of a sociology of disability *within* the social oppression paradigm – under the multi-disciplinary disability studies umbrella. It also follows that I encourage medical sociologists interested in disability and chronic illness to critically reassess their discipline's use of the social deviance paradigm – in whatever theoretical guise – and to give careful consideration to the ideas at work in disability studies. In my view, any sociology of disability should make use of theories that engage both with social structure (order) and social agency (action), and should therefore accommodate analyses of the social relations and social forces that construct, produce, institutionalise, enact and perform disability and disablism. The *lived experience* of both disablism *and* impairment should have its place, as should social theorisations of impairment *per se* – with chronic illnesses duly represented among categories of impairment. Such a sociology must pay full attention to social 'difference': to gender, 'race', sexuality, age, social class – and socially designated 'impairment type'.

Within such a framework, I intend to pursue a sociology of disability that encompasses *a sociology of disablism*, its primary concern, and *a sociology of impairment and impairment effects*. In developing these interrelated lines of enquiry within disability studies, earlier chapters have signalled my particular interest in the following themes: the *gendered* character of disablism, *psycho-emotional disablism* and theorisations of impairment that can grasp the dynamic interrelationship between 'the social' and 'the biological', and can find a way to engage with the sociology of 'suffering'. Moreover, the nature and consequences of the *embodiment* of both disablism and impairment attract my interest, with social difference and diversity being the watchwords at every turn. There is no doubt, in my mind, that some of the ideas developed by medical sociologists have the potential to play an important role in this regard.

This book has concentrated on ideas in disability studies and medical sociology within the UK, but it is important to end on an internationalist and multi-disciplinary note. The disciplinary dialogue and developments that I recommend must also be outward-looking, prepared to engage (further) with scholars and disability activists in other parts of the world and in other disciplines, including the humanities. Today, vibrant groupings of disability studies' academics and activists are well established and flourishing in North America, the Nordic countries, and Australia, and such groupings are already present or beginning to emerge elsewhere, including in the resource-poor majority world. The best hope for the development of a body of sociological ideas that can play a part in overcoming disablist structures, systems, discourses, attitudes, practices and behaviours – wherever and however these appear – lies in the encouragement and building of global networks and the exchange of ideas across continents and disciplinary boundaries.

Notes

Chapter 2

1. Roy Bhaskar made his position clear in a lecture series that I attended in the *Institute for Advanced Studies* at Lancaster University in January 2006.
2. This point was brought home to me in personal communication with Mildred Blaxter in 2004. In my view, the later shift in medical sociology towards a 'sociology *of* medicine' diminished this desire to be 'helpful', a trend reinforced when poststructuralist perspectives became fashionable. Nevertheless, many sociologists in the UK continue to undertake research designed to contribute to policy and practice in health and social care services.

Chapter 3

1. Vic Finkelstein explained this to me in a personal communication.
2. Shortly before she died in 2004, Mairian Corker changed her name to Mairian Scott-Hill.
3. It is interesting and telling to note that the materialist, Paul Hunt, wrote powerfully about these kinds of reactions in his 1966 essay – his observations arising from personal experience (see Hunt, 1966: 155–6).

Chapter 4

1. For recent overviews relating to disability, see special editions of the journals *Policy & Politics*, 2002 and *Social Policy & Society*, 2005. See also Dalley, 1991; Drake, 1999; Priestley, 1999; Rummery, 2002; Borsay, 2005; Oliver and Sapey, 2005.
2. Nancy Fraser and Linda Gordon provide a helpful account of the contemporary meanings – all pejorative – of the word 'dependency':
    > In current usage, we find four registers in which the meanings of dependency reverberate. The first is an economic register, in which one depends on some other person(s) or institution for subsistence. In a second register, the term denotes a sociological status, the lack of a separate legal or public identity, as in the status of married women created by coverture. The third register is political: here dependency means subjection to an external ruling power and may be predicated of a colony or of a subject caste of noncitizen residents. The fourth register we call the moral/psychological; dependency in this sense is an individual character trait like lack of willpower or excessive emotional neediness. (2002: 16)

    Histories of the lives of disabled people in the last two centuries testify to the relevance of all four of these meanings, with the first and fourth being the most meaningful today.
3. Note, for example, the absence of chronic illness themes in the collection of chapters in Peterson and Bunton's, *Foucault, Health and Medicine*, 1997.
4. See, for example: Gerhardt, 1989; Bury, 1997; Annandale, 1998; Nettleton and Gustavsson, 2002; Bury and Gabe, 2004.

5. Other organised challenges to traditional 'care' systems have also been influential, mounted by people with HIV/AIDS, mental health system survivors, and members of women's and older people's movements. All of these value peer support and mutual aid.

6. The 1970 Act did not consolidate these rights by placing mandatory duties upon local authorities to provide the necessary services. A later piece of legislation, the *Disabled Persons Act*, 1986, sought to add more substance to disabled people's rights by giving them the right to have their needs assessed by their local authority – but, once again, no mandatory obligation was placed on authorities to provide the services required.

7. I am sure that I am not alone in being mistaken, initially, about the nature of this document, a document fabled in disability studies. Having read about it in other sources, I had understood the document to be a statement of the UPIAS perspective alone. When I read the original, I was fascinated to find what it actually consists of: a record of a dialogue between disability activists and disability campaigners, with Peter Townsend among the latter – published in the names of both UPIAS and The Disability Alliance. UPIAS made a detail record of the meeting 'to be available for disabled people'. The document can be accessed on the Leeds University Disability Archive: http:// www.leeds.ac.uk/ disability-studies/archiveuk/archframe.htm.

8. In their follow up 'Comments' paper, UPIAS expands, with no holds barred, on its opposition to the single issue 'incomes' approach. An incomes approach, it claimed, should more properly be called a 'pensions' strategy, and has the features of 'an academic' and narrowly parliamentary (as opposed to mass movement) world view. As such, it was thought to be very objectionable:

> 'Benefits' which are not carefully related to the struggle for integrated employment and active social participation will constantly be used to justify our dependence and expulsion from the mainstream of life – the very opposite of what is intended. This is why the Alliance's appeal to the state for legislation to implement a comprehensive, national disability incomes stream is in reality nothing so much as a programme to obtain and maintain in perpetuity the historical dependency of physically impaired people on charity. It does not even have the merit of revealing to the public it wishes to educate that its incomes policy is really a form of State Charity – that is, help which essentially entrenches our independence and active participation in the mainstream of life … . Experts begging for state charity on our behalf can do nothing but lower our status, by reinforcing out-of-date attitudes …

> Thus the Alliance logically sees the need to establish objective criteria which would enable the State's social administrators to determine the 'degree of disability' and to exclude the malingerers from benefit. A whole new generation of researchers and testers will be created to administer the incomes policy of the Alliance. The scene facing every impaired person, then, is of an army of 'experts' sitting on panels which are set up all over the country. These 'experts', armed with the latest definitions and tests for measuring, will prod and probe into the intimate details of our lives. They will bear down on us with batteries of questions, and wielding their tape measures will attempt to tie down the last remaining vestige of our privacy and dignity as human beings. To calculate the 'degree of disability' they will be forced to snoop and spy. (UPIAS statement, in UPIAS and TDA, 1996: 15–18)

In its commentary – almost certainly written by Peter Townsend (this is my presumption) – the *Alliance* defended its position, and stated the following:

> The Alliance would reply that its work is not devoted solely to income in isolation, since income is inextricably linked with education and employment opportunities, mobility, adequate accommodation, clothing, recreation, freedom from anxiety, and so on, and all of these are discussed in its research work and is emphasised in its arguments with Government representatives … . The Alliance therefore submits that the absence of income has a far greater effect on a disabled person's life than other individual aspects of his social isolation, and that in fact all of these individual aspects are crucially linked to his financial status … . The adage that money is power has some bearing here, since his lack of entitlement to a standard of living at least equal to that of the able-bodied, and his ability to buy services, reduce the status of a disabled person to

that of dependent, in which his right to free choice, action and association are curtailed in direct proportion to the degree of his disability and the extent of his financial means. The curtailment of these rights are crucial in causing the disabled person's isolation and exclusion from full participation in society, just as admission to the workhouse meant the withdrawal of all rights to emphasise society's condemnation of the individual's insolvency. (ibid.: 21–2)

9. These were the social security White Paper, *The Way Ahead: Benefits for Disabled People* (Department of Social Security, Cm.917, London: HMSO); the Employment Department's Consultative Document, *Employment and Training for People with Disabilities* (1990, Employment Department Group, London); and the Department of Health's *Caring for People: Community Care in the Next Decade and Beyond* (DoH, Cm. 849. London: HMSO). The third followed the Griffiths' Report on Community Care, and took legislative form as the *National Health Service and Community Care Act*, 1990, though the implementation of most parts relating to community care was delayed. The thrust of this Act was the separation of responsibilities for *social* care from *medical/health* care – the former was to belong to local authorities and the latter to the NHS. Local authorities were responsible for undertaking assessments of anyone seeking care, and for devising 'packages of care' as recommended. Social Service departments became the gatekeepers to care and services; a 'case' or 'care manager' had responsibility for negotiating the best care package for the individual client from a range of service providers – whether in the public, commercial ('private') or voluntary sectors. Account was also to be taken of informal care provision (Dalley, 1991b). Hence, the phrase the 'mixed economy of care'.

10. For international comparisons on 'cash for care' developments, see Askheim, 2005, and Ungerson, 2004.

Chapter 5

1. *People First* is a national self-advocacy organisation of people with 'learning difficulties'.
2. For an interesting account of the portrayal of disabled people in UK television 'soap operas', see the unpublished PhD thesis by Alison Wilde (2004).
3. This example is derived from my own personal experience, having been born without a left hand.
4. The Mobius strip is a three-dimensional model based on an inverted figure of eight in which the two sides twist into one another.
5. Data collection involved in-depth interviews with 25 women with Myalgic Encephalomyelitis (ME) and 25 with Rheumatoid Arthritis (RA). Dyck (1995) is also known for her research on women's experiences of living with Multiple Sclerosis (MS).
6. In my view, it is interesting and telling that Frank acknowledges the 'disability narratives' (my characterisation) provided by Robert Murphy (1987) and Irving Zola (1982a) (see Chapter 2, this volume) but concludes that bodies like theirs have no place in his (mainstream) sociological body typology:

> Both their stories are about in the fundamental conditions of the ill body: lack, dissociation, contingency, and monadic self-relatedness. It is not a condition that fits my [ideal types schema], thus demonstrating that any sociological body schema theory must have its residual categories. (Frank, 1991b: 87)

Chapter 6

1. 'Learning disabilities' is Scior's own term – she does not use the term preferred by the self-advocacy organisation *People First* and many in disability studies: 'learning difficulties'.
2. See also Scambler and Scambler's (2003) paper dealing with Juvenile Batten disease, and Sasha Scambler's (2005) paper, Exposing the Limitations of Disability Theory: The Case of Juvenile Batten Disease.

References

Abberley, P. (1987) The Concept of Oppression and the Development of a Social Theory of Disability, *Disability, Handicap and Society*, 2: 5–20.

Abberley, P. (1992) Counting Us Out: a Discussion of the OPCS Disability Surveys, *Disability, Handicap and Society*, 7 (2):139–55.

Abberley, P. (1993) Disabled People and 'Normality', in J. Swain, V. Finkelstein, S. French and M. Oliver (eds) *Disabling Barriers – Enabling Environments*. London: Sage.

Abberley, P. (1995) Disabling Ideology in Health and Welfare: The Case of Occupational Therapy, *Disability & Society*, 10 (2): 139–55.

Abberley, P. (1996) Work, Utopia and Impairment, in L. Barton (ed.) *Disability & Society: Emerging Issues and Insights*. London: Longman.

Abberley, P. (1997) The Limits of Classical Social Theory in the Analysis and Transformation of Disablement – (Can this really be the end; to be stuck inside of Mobile with the Memphis Blues again?), in L. Barton and M. Oliver (eds) *Disability Studies: Past, Present and Future*. Leeds: The Disability Press.

Abberley, P. (2002) Work, Disability, Disabled People and European Social Theory, in C. Barnes, M. Oliver and L. Barton (eds) *Disability Studies Today*. Cambridge: Polity.

Abu-Habib, L. (1997) *Gender and Disability. Women's Experiences in the Middle East*. Oxford: Oxfam.

Adkins L. and Skeggs, B. (eds) (2004) *Feminism after Bourdieu*. Oxford: Blackwell.

Ahmad, W.I.U. (ed.) (2000) *Ethnicity, Disability and Chronic Illness*. Buckingham: Open University Press.

Albrecht, G.L. (ed.) (1982) *The Sociology of Physical Disability and Rehabilitation*. Pittsburgh, PA: University of Pittsburgh Press.

Albrecht, G.L. (1992) *The Disability Business. Rehabilitation in America*. Newbury Park, CA, and London: Sage.

Albrecht, G.L. (2002) American Pragmatism, Sociology and the Development of Disability Studies, in C. Barnes, M. Oliver and L. Barton (eds) *Disability Studies Today*. Cambridge: Polity.

Albrecht, G.L. and Bury, M. (2001) The Political Economy of the Disability Marketplace, in G.L. Albrecht, K.D. Seelman and M. Bury (eds) *Handbook of Disability Studies*. London: Sage.

Albrecht, G.L. and Verbrugge, L.M. (2000) The Global Emergence of Disability, in G. Albrecht, R. Fitzpatrick and S. Scrimshaw (eds) *Handbook of Social Studies in Health and Medicine*. London: Sage.

Albrecht, G.L., Seelman, K.D. and Bury, M. (eds) (2001a) *Handbook of Disability Studies*. London: Sage.

Albrecht, G.L., Seelman, K.D. and Bury, M. (2001b) The Formation of Disability Studies, in G.L. Albrecht, K.D. Seelman and M. Bury (eds) *Handbook of Disability Studies*. London: Sage.

Alcock, P. (1997) *Understanding Poverty*. 2nd edn. Basingstoke: Macmillan.

Althusser, L. (1971) *Lenin and Philosophy and Other Essays*. London: New Left Books.

Althusser, L. (1984) *Essays on Ideology*. London: Verso.

Anderson, R. and Bury, M. (eds) (1988) *Living with Chronic Illness. The Experience of Patients and their Families*. London: Unwin Hyman.

Annandale, E. (1998) *The Sociology of Health and Medicine*. Cambridge: Polity Press.

Annandale, E. (2004) *Feminist Theory and the Sociology of Health and Illness*. London: Routledge.

nnandale, E., Elston, M.E. and Prior, L. (eds) (2004) *Medical Work, Medical Knowledge and Health Care*. Oxford: Blackwell.

ppleby, Y. (1994) Out in the Margins, *Disability & Society*, 9 (1): 19–32.

psis, S. (2001) Inclusive Education, Politics and the Struggle for Change, in L. Barton (ed.) *Disability Politics and The Struggle For Change*. London: David Fulton.

rber, S. and Evandrou, M. (eds) (1993) *Ageing, Independence and the Life Course*. London: Jessica Kingsley.

rcher, M. (1995) *Realist Social Theory: The Morphogenic Approach*. Cambridge: Cambridge University Press.

rmstrong, D. (1983) *Political Anatomy of the Body. Medical Knowledge in Britain in the Twentieth Century*. Cambridge: Cambridge University Press.

rmstrong, D. (1995) The Rise of Surveillance Medicine. *Sociology of Health and Illness*, 17 (3): 393–403.

rmstrong, F. and Moore, M. (2004) *Action Research for Inclusive Education: Changing Places, Changing Practices, Changing Minds*. London: Routledge Falmer.

sche, A. (2000) *Prenatal Testing and Disability Rights*. Washington DC: Georgetown University Press.

sche, A. (2001) Disability, Bioethics and Human Rights, in G.L. Albrecht, K.D. Seelman and M. Bury (eds) *Handbook of Disability Studies*. London: Sage.

skheim, O.P. (2005) Personal Assistance – Direct Payments or Alternative Public Service. Does it Matter for the Promotion of User Control?, *Disability & Society*, 20 (3): 247–60.

tkinson, P.A. (1981) *The Clinical Experience: The Construction and Reconstruction of Medical Reality*. London: Gower.

tkinson, P.A. (1995) *Medical Talk and Medical Work*. London: Sage.

arnes, C. (1990) *Cabbage Syndrome: The Social Construction of Dependency*. London: Tavistock Publications.

arnes, C. (1991) *Disabled People in Britain and Discrimination*. London: Hurst and Co.

arnes, C. (1996) Theories of Disability and the Origins of the Oppression of Disabled People in Western Society, in L. Barton (ed.) *Disability & Society: Emerging Issues and Insights*. London: Longman.

arnes, C. (1998) The Social Model of Disability: a Sociological Phenomenon Ignored by Sociologists?, in T. Shakespeare (ed.) *The Disability Reader: Social Science Perspectives*. London: Cassell.

arnes, C. (2002) Introduction: Disability, Policy and Politics. *Policy and Politics*, 30 (3): 311–18.

arnes, C. (2003) What a Difference a Decade Makes: Reflections on Doing 'Emancipatory' Disability Research. *Disability & Society*, 18(1): 3–17.

arnes, C. and Mercer, G. (eds) (1996) *Exploring the Divide: Illness and Disability*. Leeds: The Disability Press.

arnes, C. and Mercer, G. (eds) (1997) *Doing Disability Research*. Leeds: The Disability Press.

arnes, C. and Mercer, G. (2001) Disability Culture: Assimilation or Inclusion?, in G.L. Albrecht, K.D. Seelman and M. Bury (eds) *Handbook of Disability Studies*. London: Sage.

arnes, C., Mercer, G. and Morgan, H. (2000) *Creating Independent Futures: Stage 1 Report*. Leeds: The Disability Press.

arnes, C., Mercer, G. and Shakespeare, T. (1999) *Exploring Disability: A Sociological Introduction*. Cambridge: Polity Press.

arnes, C., Oliver, M. and Barton, L. (eds) (2002) *Disability Studies Today*. Cambridge, Polity.

arrett, M. (1981) *Women's Oppression Today*. London: Verso.

arton, L. (1996a) Sociology and Disability: Some Emerging Issues, in L. Barton (ed.) *Disability & Society: Emerging Issues and Insights*. London: Longman.

arton, L. (ed.) (1996b) *Disability & Society: Emerging Issues and Insights*. London: Longman.

arton, L. (ed.) (2001) *Disability Politics and the Struggle for Change*. London: David Fulton.

arton, L. and Oliver, M. (eds) (1997) *Disability Studies: Past, Present and Future*. Leeds: The Disability Press.

arton, L. and Slee. R. (1999) Competition, Selection and Inclusive Education: Some Observations, *International Journal of Inclusive Education*, 3 (1): 3–12.

ecker, H. (1963) *Outsiders: Studies in the Sociology of Deviance*. New York: Free Press.

Begum, N. (1992) Disabled Women and the Feminist Agenda, *Feminist Review*, 40: 70–84.

Begum, N., Hill, M. and Stevens, A. (eds) (1994) *Reflections: The Views of Black Disabled Peop on their Lives and Community Care*. London: CCETSW.

Bell, S.E. (2000) Experiencing Illness in/and Narrative, in C.E. Bird, P. Conrad an A.M. Fremont (eds) *Handbook of Medical Sociology*, 5th edn. Upper Saddle River, N Prentice Hall.

Bendelow, G. (1993) Pain Perceptions, Gender and Emotion. *Sociology of Health and Illnes* 15 (3): 273–94.

Bendelow, G. and Williams, S.J. (eds) (1998) *Emotions in Social Life: Critical Themes an Contemporary Issues*. London: Routledge.

Beresford, P. (2000) What Have Madness and Psychiatric System Survivors Got to Do wit Disability and Disability Studies? *Disability & Society*, 15 (1): 167–72.

Beresford, P. (2002) Thinking About 'Mental Health': Towards a Social Model, *Journal Mental Health*, 11 (6): 581–4.

Beresford, P., Gifford, G. and Harrison, C. (1996) What has Disability Got to Do with Psychiatr Survivors?, in J. Reynolds and J. Read (eds) *Speaking Our Minds: Personal Experience of Ment Distress and its Consequences*. Open University Reader for new Open University cours Mental Health: Issues, Skills and Perspectives, pp. 209–14. Basingstoke: Macmillan.

Beresford, P., Harrison, C. and Wilson, A. (2002) Mental Health Service Users and Disabilit Implications for Future Strategies. *Policy and Politics*, 30 (3): 387–96.

Best, S. and Kellner, D. (1991) *Postmodern Theory: Critical Interrogations*. Basingstok Macmillan.

Bhaskar, R. (1989) *Reclaiming Reality: A Critical Introduction to Contemporary Philosoph* London: Verso.

Bickenbach, J.E., Chatterji, S., Badley, E.M. and Ustun, T.B. (1999) Models of Disablemen Universalism and the International Classification of Impairments, Disabilities an Handicaps, *Social Science and Medicine*, 48: 1173–87.

Bignall, T. and Butt, J. (2000) *Between Ambition and Achievement: Young Black Disabled People Views and Experiences on Independent Living*. Bristol: The Policy Press.

Bird, C.E, Conrad, P. and Fremont, A.M. (2000) Medical Sociology at the Millenium, i C.E. Bird, P. Conrad and A.M. Fremont (eds) *Handbook of Medical Sociology*, 5th edn. Ne Jersey: Prentice Hall.

Blaxter, M. (1976) *The Meaning of Disability: A Sociological Study of Impairment*. London: Heineman

Blaxter, M. (2004) Life Narratives, Health and Identity, in D. Kelleher and G. Leavey (ed *Identity and Health*. London: Routledge.

Bloor, M. (1976) Professional Autonomy and Client Exclusion: A Study of ENT Clinics, i M. Wadsworth and D. Robinson (eds) *Studies in Everyday Medical Life*. Oxford: Marti Robertson.

Bloor, M. (1995) *The Sociology of HIV Transmission*. London: Sage.

Blumer, H. (1969) *SymbolicI Interactionism: Perspective and Method*. Englewood Cliffs, N Prentice Hall.

Borsay, A. (2005) *Disability and Social Policy in Britain since 1750*. Basingstoke: Palgrave Macmilla

Bourdieu, P. (1977) *Outline of a Theory of Practice*. Cambridge: Cambridge University Press.

Braddock, D.L. and Parish, S.L. (2001) An Institutional History of Disability, in G.L. Albrech K.D. Seelman and M. Bury (eds) (2001) *Handbook of Disability Studies*. London: Sage.

Breckenridge, A.A. and Volger, C. (eds) (2001) The Critical Limits of Embodiment: Reflection on Disability Criticism, Special issue of *Public Culture*, 13 (3), Fall.

Brittan, A. and Maynard, M. (1984) *Sexism, Racism and Oppression*. Oxford: Blackwell.

Brown, G.W. and Harris, T. (1978) *Social Origins of Depression*. London: Tavistock Publication

Brownworth V.A. and Raffo, S. (eds) (1999) *Restricted Access. Lesbians on Disability*. Seattl WA: Seal Press.

Bunton, R. and Petersen, A. (2005) *Genetic Governance*. London: Routledge. Bunto R., Nettleton, S. and Burrows, R. (eds) (1995) *The Sociology of Health Promotion: Critic Analyses of Consumption, Lifestyle and Risk*. London: Routledge.

Burleigh, M. (1995) *Death and Deliverance: Euthanasia in Germany c.1900–1994*, Cambridg Cambridge University Press.

Bury, M. (1982) Chronic Illness as Biographical Disruption, *Sociology of Health and Illness*, 4 (2): 167–82.

Bury, M. (1988) Meanings at Risk: the Experience of Arthritis, in R. Anderson and M. Bury (eds) *Living with Chronic Illness: the Experience of Patients and their Families*. London, Unwin Hyman.

Bury, M. (1991) The Sociology of Chronic Illness: a Review of Research and Prospects. *Sociology of Health and Illness*, 13 (4):167–82.

Bury, M. (1996a) Disability and The Myth of the Independent Researcher: a Reply, *Disability & Society*, 11 (1): 111–13.

Bury, M. (1996b) Defining and Researching Disability: Challenges and Responses, in C. Barnes and G. Mercer (eds) *Exploring the Divide: Illness and Disability*. Leeds: The Disability Press.

Bury, M. (1997) *Health and Illness in a Changing Society*. London: Routledge.

Bury, M. (2000) On Chronic Illness and Disability, in C. E. Bird, P. Conrad and A. M. Fremont (eds) *Handbook of Medical Sociology*, 5th edn. New Jersey: Prentice Hall.

Bury, M. (2005) *Health and Illness*. Cambridge: Polity.

Bury, M. and Gabe, J. (eds) (2004) *The Sociology of Health and Illness. A Reader*. London: Routledge.

Busfield, J. (1988) Mental Illness as a Social Product or Social Construct: A Contradiction in Feminists' Arguments? *Sociology of Health and Illness*, 10: 521–42.

Busfield, J. (2001) Introduction: Rethinking the Sociology of Mental Health, in J. Busfield (ed.) *Rethinking the Sociology of Mental Health*. Oxford: Blackwell.

Butler, J. (1993) *Bodies That Matter: On the Discursive Limits of Sex*. New York: Routledge.

Butler, J. (1995) Contingent Foundations: Feminism and the Question of Postmodernism, in Nicholson, L. (ed.) *Feminist Contentions: A Philosophical Exchange*. London: Routledge, pp. 35–57.

Butler, R. and Parr, H. (eds) (1999) *Mind and Body Spaces. Geographies of Illness, Impairment and Disability*. London: Routledge.

Cabinet Office (2004) *Improving the Life Chances of Disabled People*. London: The Prime Minister's Strategy Unit.

Campbell, J. and Oliver, M. (1996) *Disability Politics: Understanding Our Past, Changing Our Future*. London: Routledge.

Campling, J. (ed.) (1981) *Images of Ourselves: Women With Disabilities Talking*. London: Routledge and Kegan Paul.

Chappell, A.L. (1992) Towards a Sociological Critique of the Normalisation Principle, *Disability, Handicap and Society*, 7 (1): 35–53.

Charlton, J.I. (1998) *Nothing about Us without Us: Disability, Oppression, and Empowerme*. Berkeley, CA: University of California Press.

Charmaz, K. (1983) Loss of Self: a Fundamental Form of Suffering in the Chronically Ill, *Sociology of Health and Illness*, 5: 168–95.

Charmaz, K. (1991) *Good Days, Bad Days: The Self in Chronic Illness and Time*. New Brunswick, NJ: Rutgers University Press.

Chesler, P. (1972) *Women and Madness*. New York: Doubleday.

Chouinard, V. (1997) Making Space for Disabling Differences: Challenges Ablist Geographies. *Environment and Planning D: Society and Space*, 15: 379–87.

Cockerham, W.C. (2004) *Medical Sociology*, 9th edn. Pearson Education: London.

Connors, J.L. and Donnellan, A.M. (1993) Citizenship and Culture: the Role of Disabled People in Navajo Society, *Disability, Handicap and Society*, 8 (3): 265–80.

Cole, B.A. (2005) 'Good Faith and Effort?' Perspectives on Educational Inclusion, *Disability & Society*, 20 (2): 331–44.

Cooper, H., Arber, S., Fee, L. and Ginn, J. (1999) *The Influence of Social Support and Capital on Health*. Health Education Authority: London.

Corbett, J. (1994) A Proud Label: Exploring the Relationship Between Disability Politics and Gay Pride, *Disability and Society*, 9 (3): 343–57.

Corbett, J. (1998) *Special Educational Needs in the Twentieth Century: A Cultural Analysis*. London: Cassell.

Corker, M. (1998) *Deaf and Disabled, or Deafness Disabled?* Buckingham: Open University Press.

Corker, M. and French, S. (1999a) Reclaiming Discourse in Disability Studies, in M. Corker and S. French (eds) *Disability Discourse*. Buckingham: Open University Press.

Corker, M. and French, S. (eds) (1999b) *Disability Discourse*. Buckingham: Open University Press.

Corker, M. and Shakespeare, T. (eds) (2002a) *Disability/Postmodernity: Embodying Disability Theory*. London: Continuum.

Corker, M. and Shakespeare, T. (2002b) Mapping the Terrain, in M. Corker and T. Shakespeare (eds) *Disability/Postmodernity: Embodying Disability Theory*. London: Continuum.

Crewe, N.M., Zola, I.K. and Associates (eds) (1987) *Independent Living for Physically Disabled People*. San Francisco, CA and London: Jossey-Bass Publishers.

Crossley, N. (2001a) *The Social Body. Habit, Identity and Desire*. London: Sage.

Crossley, N. (2001b) Embodiment and social structure: a response to Howson and Inglis *The Sociological Review*, 49 (3): 318–26.

Crow, L. (1996) Including All Our Lives: Renewing the Social Model of Disability, in C. Barnes and G. Mercer (eds) *Exploring the Divide: Illness and Disability*. Leeds: The Disability Press.

Couser, G.T. (1997) *Recovering Bodies: Illness, Disability and Life Writing*. Madison, WI: University of Wisconsin Press.

Dalley, G. (1988) *Ideologies of Caring: Rethinking Community and Collectivism*. London: Macmillan.

Dalley, G. (ed.) (1991a) *Disability and Social Policy*. London: Social Policy Institute.

Dalley, G. (1991b) Disability and Social Policy, in G. Dalley (ed.) *Disability and Social Policy* London: Social Policy Institute.

Danemark, B. and Coniavitas Gellerstedt, L. (2004) Social Injustice: Redistribution and Recognition – a Non-Reductionist Perspective on Disability, *Disability & Society*, 19 (4): 339–54.

Darke, P.A. (2004) The Changing Face of Representations of Disability in the Media, in J. Swain, S. French, C. Barnes and C. Thomas (eds) *Disabling Barriers – Enabling Environment*, 2nd edn. London: Sage.

Davidson, J. (2001) A Phenomenology of Fear: Merleau-Ponty and Agoraphobic Life-worlds, in J. Busfield (ed.) *Rethinking the Sociology of Mental Health*. Oxford: Blackwell.

Davis, F. (1961) Deviance Disavowal: The Management of Strained Interaction by the Visibly Handicapped, *Social Problems*, 9: 120–32.

Davis, F. (1963) *Passage through Crisis: Polio Victims and Their Families*. Indianapolis, IN: Bobbs-Merrill.

Davis, J. and Watson, N. (2001) Where are the Children's Experiences? Analysing Social and Cultural Exclusion in 'Special' and 'Mainstream' Schools, *Disability & Society*, 16 (5): 671–87.

Davis, K. (1984) The Politics of Independent Living: Keeping the Movement Radical *Derbyshire Coalition News*, July.

Davis, K. (1990) The Crafting of Good Clients, *Coalition*, September 1990.

Davis, K. (1994) The Crafting of Good Clients, in J. Swain, V. Finkelstein, S. French and M. Oliver (eds) *Disabling Barriers – Enabling Environments*. London: Sage.

Davis, L.J. (1995) *Enforcing Normalcy: Disability, Deafness and the Body*. Verso: London.

Davis, L.J. (2002a) Bending over Backwards: *Disability, Dismodernism and Other Difficult Positions*. New York and London: New York University Press.

Davis, L.J. (2002b) Bodies of Difference: Politics, Disability, and Representation, in S.L. Snyder, B.J. Brueggeman and R. Garland Thomson (eds) (2002) *Disability Studies Enabling the Humanities*. New York: The Modern Language Association of America.

DeJong, G. (1983) Defining and Implementing the Independent Living Concept, in N.M. Crewe and I.K. Zola (eds) *Independent Living for Physically Disabled People*. San Francisco, CA: Jossey-Bass.

Derrida, J. (1978) *Writing and Difference*. Chicago, IL: University of Chicago Press.

De Wolfe, P. (2002) Private Tragedy in Social Context? Reflections on Disability, Illness and Suffering, *Disability & Society*, 17 (3): 255–67.

Dingwall, R. (2001) *Aspects of Illness*, 2nd edn. Aldershot: Ashgate.

Dowse, L. (2001) Contesting Practices, Challenging Codes: Self-advocacy, Disability Politics and the Social Model, *Disability & Society*, 16 (1): 123–42.

Doyal, L. (1979) *The Political Economy of Health*. London: Pluto Press.

Doyal, L. (1995) *What Makes Women Sick?* London: Macmillan.

Doyal, L. and Gough, I. (1991) *A Theory of Human Need*. London: Macmillan.

Drake, R.F. (1999) *Understanding Disability Policies*. London: Macmillan.

Drake, R.F. (2001) Welfare States and Disabled People, in G.L. Albrecht, K.D. Seelman and M. Bury (eds) *Handbook of Disability Studies*. London: Sage.

Durkheim, E. (1964 [1895]) *Rules of Sociological Method*. New York: Free Press.

Dyck, I. (1995) Hidden Geographies: The Changing Lifeworlds of Women with Multiple Sclerosis, *Social Science and Medicine*, 40: 307–20.

Ehrenreich, B. and English, D. (1979) *For Her Own Good: 150 Years of Experts' Advice to Women*. London: Pluto.

Ehrenreich, B. and Ehrenreich, J. (1970) *The American Health Empire: Power, Profits and Politics*. New York: Random House.

Emmerson, E. (1995) *Challenging Behaviour: Analysis and Intervention in People with Learning Disabilities*. Cambridge: Cambridge University Press.

Evans, M. and Lee, E. (eds) (2002) *Real Bodies. A Sociological Introduction*. Basingstoke: Palgrave.

Fawcett, B. (2000) *Feminist Perspectives on Disability*. London: Prentice Hall.

Featherstone, M. and Hepworth, M. (1998) Ageing, the Lifecourse and the Sociology of Embodiment, in G. Scambler and P. Higgs (eds) *Modernity, Medicine and Health. Medical Sociology Towards 2000*. London: Routledge.

Fine, M. and Asche, A. (eds) (1988) *Women With Disabilities: Essays in Psychology, Culture and Politics*. Philadelphia, PA: Temple University Press

Finch, J. and Groves, D. (eds) (1983) *A Labour of Love: Women, Work and Caring*. London: Routledge and Kegan Paul.

Finch, J. (1987) Whose responsibility? Women and the future of family care. In I. Allen, M. Wicks, J. Finch and D. Leat (eds) *Informal Care Tomorrow*. London: Policy Studies Institute.

Finkelstein, V. (1980) *Attitudes and Disabled People: Issues for Discussion*. New York; World Rehabilitation Fund.

Finkelstein, V. (1981) *Disability and Professional Attitudes*. Sevenoaks: NAIDEX Convention.

Finkelstein, V. (1991) Disability: An Administrative Challenge?, in M. Oliver (ed.) *Social Work – Disabling People and Disabling Environments*. London: Jessica Kingsley.

Finkelstein, V. (1996) Outside, 'Inside Out'. *Coalition*, April, 30–6.

Finkelstein, V. (2001a) *A Personal Journey into Disability Politics*. The Disability Studies Archive UK, Centre for Disability Studies, University of Leeds. Retrieved May 2003 from http://www.leeds.ac.uk/disability-studies/archiveuk/archframe.htm.

Finkelstein, V. (2001b) *The Social Model Repossessed*. The Disability Studies Archive UK, Centre for Disability Studies, University of Leeds. Retrieved May 2003 from http://www.leeds.ac.uk/disability-studies/archiveuk/archframe.htm.

Finkelstein, V. (2004) Modernising Services?, in J. Swain, S. French, C. Barnes and C. Thomas (eds) *Disabling Barriers – Enabling Environments*, 2nd edn. London: Sage.

Fleischer, D. and Zames, F. (2001) *The Disability Rights Movement: From Charity to Confrontation*. Philadelphia, PA: Temple University Press.

Foster, P. (1995) *Women and the Health Care Industry*. Buckingham: Open University Press.

Foucault, M. (1965) *Madness and Civilisation. The History of Insanity in the Age of Reason*. New York: Random House.

Foucault, M. (1973) *The Birth of the Clinic. An Archaeology of Medical Perception*. London: Tavistock Publications.

Foucault, M. (1977) *Discipline and Punish. The Birth of the Prison*. London: Allan Lane.

Foucault, M. (1988) 'Technologies of the Self', in L.H. Martin, H. Gutman and P.H. Hutton (eds) *Technologies of the Self. A Seminar with Michel Foucault*. London: Tavistock Publications.

Fox, N. (1993) *Postmodernism, Sociology and Health*. Milton Keynes: Open University Press.

Frank, A. (1991a) *At the Will of the Body: Reflections on Illness*. Boston, MA: Houghton Mifflin.

Frank, A.W. (1991b) For a Sociology of the Body: An Analytical Review, in M. Featherstone, M. Hepworth and B. Turner (eds) *The Body: Social Processes and Cultural Theory*. London: Sage, pp. 36–102.

Frank, A.W. (1995) *The Wounded Storyteller: Body, Illness, and Ethics*. Chicago, IL: University of Chicago Press.

Fraser, N. (1989) *Unruly Practices: Power, discourse and Gender in Contemporary Social Theory*. Cambridge: Polity Press.

Fraser, N. (1995) From Recognition to Redistribution? Dilemmas of Justice in a 'Post-Socialist' Age. *New Left Review*, 212: 68–93.

Fraser, N. (2000) Rethinking Recognition, *New Left Review*, 3: 107–20.

Fraser, N. and Gordon, L. (2002) A Geneology of *Dependency*: Tracing a Keyword of the U.S. Welfare State, in E.F. Kittay, and E.K. Feder (eds) *The Subject of Care: Feminist Perspectives on Dependency*. Lanham, MD: Rowman and Littlefield.

Freidson, E. (1966) Disability as Social Deviance, in M. Sussman (ed.) *Sociology of Disability and Rehabilitation*. Washington, DC: American Sociological Association.

Freidson, E. (1970) *Profession of Medicine*. New York: Dodd, Mead.

French, S. (1993) Disability, Impairment or Something in Between?, in J. Swain, V. Finkelstein, S. French and M. Oliver (eds) *Disabling Barriers – Enabling Environments*. London: Sage.

French, S. (ed.) (1994) *On Equal Terms: Working with Disabled People*. Oxford: Butterworth-Heinemann.

French, S. (2001) *Disabled People and Employment: A Study of the Working Lives of Visually Impaired Physiotherapists*. Aldershot: Ashgate.

French, S. and Swain, J. (2001) The Relationship between Disabled People and Health and Welfare Professionals, in G.L. Albrecht, K.D. Seelman and M. Bury (eds) *Handbook of Disability Studies*. London: Sage.

Gabel, S. (1999) Depressed and Disabled: Some Discursive Problems with Mental Illness, in M. Corker and S. French (eds) *Disability Discourse*, Buckingham: Open University Press.

Garfinkel, H. (1956) Conditions of Successful Degradation Ceremonies. *American Journal of Sociology*, 61: 420–4.

Garfinkel, H. (1967) *Studies in Ethnomethodology*. Englewood Cliffs, NJ: Prentice Hall.

Garland-Thomson, R. (ed.) (1996) *Freakery: Cultural Spectacles of the Extraordinary Body*. New York: New York University Press.

Garland-Thomson, R. (1997a) *Extraordinary Bodies: Figuring Physical Disability in American Culture and Literature*. New York: Columbia University Press.

Garland-Thomson (1997b) Feminist Theory, the Body, and the Disabled Figure, in L.J. Davis (ed.) *The Disability Studies Reader*, pp. 279–94. London: Routledge.

Garland-Thomson, R. (2005) Feminist Disability Studies, *Signs: Journal of Women in Culture and Society*, 30 (2): 155887.

Gellner, E. (1992) *Postmodernismn, Reason and Religion*. London: Routledge.

Gerhardt, U. (1989) *Ideas about Illness: An Intellectual and Political History of Medical Sociology*. London: Macmillan.

Gerschick, T.J. and Miller, S.A. (1995) Coming to Terms: Masculinity and Physical Disability, in D. Sabo and D.F. Gordon (eds) *Men's Health and Illness*. Thousand Oaks, CA: Sage, pp. 183–204.

Giddens, A. (1979) *Central Problems in Social Theory: Action, Structure and Contradiction in Social Analysis*. Cambridge: Cambridge University Press.

Giddens, A. (1991) *Modernity and Self-Identity. Self and Society in the Late Modern Age* Cambridge: Polity Press.

Gilles, S, Howie, G. and Munford, R. (eds) (2004) *Third wave Feminism: a Critical Exploration* Basingstoke: Palgrave Macmillan.

Glaser, B.G. and Strauss, A.L. (1967) *The Discovery of Grounded Theory: Strategies for Qualitative Research*. New York: Aldine De Gruyter.

Gleeson, B. (1999) *Geographies of Disability*. London: Routledge.

Goffman, E. (1961) *Asylums. Essays on the Social Situation of Mental Patients*. New York: Anchor Doubleday (first published by Penguin in 1968).

Goffman, E. (1968) *Stigma. Notes on the Management of Spoiled Identity*. Harmondsworth Penguin. (first published in 1963)

Goodley, D. (1996) Tales of Hidden Lives: a Critical Examination of Life History Research with People Who Have Learning Difficulties, *Disability & Society*, 11 (3): 333–48.

Goodley, D. (2000) *Self-advocacy in the Lives of People with Learning Difficulties*. Buckingham Open University Press.

Goodley, D. (2001) 'Learning Difficulties', the Social Model of Disability and Impairment Challenging Epistemologies. *Disability & Society*, 16 (2): 207–31.

oodley, D. and Lawthom, R. (eds) (2006) *Disability and Psychology: Critical Introductions and Reflections*. Basingstoke: Palgrave Macmillan.

oodley, D. and Moore, M. (2000) Doing Disability Research: Activist Lives and the Academy. *Disability & Society*, 15 (6): 861–82.

oodley, D. and Rapley (2002) Changing the Subject: Postmodernity and People with 'Learning Difficulties', in M. Corker and T. Shakespeare (eds) *Disability/Postmodernity: Embodying Disability Theory*. London: Continuum.

raham, H. (1991) The Concept of Caring in Feminist Research: the Case of Domestic Service, *Sociology*, 25 (1): 67–78.

raham, H (ed.) (2001) *Understanding Health Inequalities*. Buckingham: Open University Press.

raham, H. (2002) Building an Inter-disciplinary Science of Health Inequalities: the Example of Lifecourse research, *Social Science and Medicine*, 55: 2005–16.

roce, N. (1985) *Everyone Here Spoke Sign Language: Hereditary Deafness on Martha's Vineyard*. Cambridge, MA: Harvard University Press.

rosz, E. (1994) *Volatile Bodies: Toward a Corporeal Feminism*. Bloomington and Indianapolis, IN: Indiana University Press.

ustavsson, A. (2004) The Role of Theory in Disability Research – Springboard or Strait-jacket? *Scandinavian Journal of Disability Research*, 6 (1): 55–70.

affter, C. (1968) The Changeling: History and Psychodynamics of Attitudes to Handicapped Children in European Folklore, *Journal of the History of Behavioural Studies*, 4: 55–61.

ahn, H. (1994) The Minority Group Model of Disability: Implications for Medical Sociology, in R. Weitz and J.J. Kronenfeld (eds) *Research in the Sociology of Health Care: Agents of Health and Illness. Volume 11*, Greenwich, CT: JAI Press.

ahn, H. (2001) Adjudication or Empowerment: Contrasting Experiences with a Social Model of Disability, in L. Barton (ed.) *Disability Politics and the Struggle for Change*. London: David Fulton Publishers.

aller, B., Dorries, B. and Rahn, J. (2006) Media Labeling Versus the US Disability Community Identity: a Study of Shifting Cultural Language, *Disability & Society*, 21 (1): 61–75.

araway, D. (1991) *Siminans, Cyborgs and Women: The Reinvention of Nature*. London: Free Association Books.

arris, A., Cox, E. and Smith, C. (1971a) *Handicapped and Impaired in Great Britain*, vol. 1. London: HMSO.

arris, A., Cox, E. and Smith, C. (1971b) *Handicapped and Impaired in Great Britain, Economic Dimensions*. London: HMSO.

arris, J. (1995) *The Cultural Meaning of Deafness*. Aldershot: Avebury.

arris, J. (2003) 'All Doors are Closed to Us': A Social Model Analysis of the Experiences of Disabled Refugees and Asylum Seekers in Britain, *Disability & Society*, 18 (4): 395–410.

eath, C. (1981) The Opening Sequence in Doctor–Patient Interaction, in P. Atkinson and C. Heath (eds) *Medical Work: Realities and Routines*. Aldershot: Gower.

evey, D. (1992) *The Creatures Time Forgot: Photography and Disability Imagery*. London: Routledge.

ill Collins, P. (1990) *Black Feminist Thought: Knowledge, Consciousness, and the Politics of Empowerment*. London: Routledge.

ochschild, A.R. (1983) *The Managed Heart: The Commercialization of Human Feeling*. Berkeley, CA: University of California Press.

olden, C. and Beresford, P. (2002) Globalization and Disability, in C. Barnes, M. Oliver and L. Barton (eds) *Disability Studies Today*. Cambridge: Polity.

onneth, A. (1995) *The Struggle for Recognition – The Moral Grammar of Social Conflicts*. Cambridge: Polity.

owson, A. and Inglis, D. (2001) The Body in Sociology: Tensions Inside and Outside Sociological Thought, *The Sociological Review*, 49 (3): 297–317.

ubert, J. (ed.) (2001) *Madness, Disability and Social Exclusion*. London: Routledge (Taylor and Francis).

ughes, B. (1999) The Constitution of Impairment: Modernity and the Aesthetic of Oppression, *Disability & Society*, 14 (2): 155–72.

ughes, B. (2000) Medicine and Aesthetic Invalidation of Disabled People, *Disability & Society*, 15 (4): 555–68.

Hughes, B. (2002) Disability and the Body, in C. Barnes, M. Oliver and L. Barton (eds) *Disability Studies Today*. Cambridge: Polity Press.

Hughes, B. (2005) What Can a Foucauldian Analysis Contribute to Disability Theory?, in S. Tremain (ed.) *Foucault and the Government of Disability*. Michigan: The University of Michigan Press.

Hughes, B., McKie, L., Hopkins, D. and Watson, N. (2005) Love's Labours Lost? Feminism the Disabled People's Movement and an Ethic of Care. *Sociology*, 39 (2): 259–73.

Hughes, B. and Paterson, K. (1997) The Social Model of Disability and the Disappearing Body: Towards a Sociology of Impairment, *Disability & Society*, 12: 325–40.

Hughes, D. (1977) Everyday and Medical Knowledge in Categorizing Patients, in R. Dingwall, C. Heath, M. Reid and M. Stacey (eds) *Health Care and Health Knowledge*. London: Croom Helm.

Hunt, P. (ed.) (1966) *Stigma: The Experience of Disability*. London: Chapman.

Hunt, P. (1981) Settling Accounts with the Parasite People: a Critique of 'A Life Apart' by E.J. Miller and G.V. Gwynne, *Disability Challenge*, 1 (May): 37–50.

Hyden, L-C (1997) Illness and Narrative, *Sociology of Health and Illness*, 19(1): 48–69.

Illich, I. (1975) *Limits to Medicine: The Expropriation of Health*. London: Calder and Boyars.

Imrie, R. (1996) *Disability and the City: International Perspectives*. London: Paul Chapman.

Imrie, R. (2004) Demystifying Disability: A Review of *the International Classification of Functioning, Disability and Health. Sociology of Health and Illness*, 26 (3): 287–305.

Ingstad, B. (2001) Disability in the Developing World, in G.L. Albrecht, K.D. Seelman and M. Bury (eds) (2001) *Handbook of Disability Studies*. London: Sage.

Ingstad, B. and Reynolds-Whyte, S. (eds) (1995) *Disability and Culture*. Berkeley, CA: University of California Press.

James, N. (1992) Care = organisation + physical labour = emotional labour, *Sociology of Health and Illness*, 14 (4): 488–509.

Jeffreys, M. (2002) The Visible Cripple (Scars and Other Disfiguring Displays Included), in S.L. Snyder, B.J. Brueggeman and R. Garland Thomson (eds) *Disability Studies: Enabling the Humanities*. New York: The Modern Language Association of America.

Keith, L. (1992) Who cares wins? Women, caring and disability. *Disability, Handicap and Society*, 7 (2): 167–75.

Kelleher, D. (1988) *Diabetes*. London: Routledge.

Kelleher, D. and Leavey, G. (eds) (2004) *Identity and Health*. London: Routledge.

Kelly, M.P. (1996) Negative Attributes of Self: Radical Surgery and the Inner and Outer Lifeworld, in C. Barnes and G. Mercer (eds) *Exploring the Divide: Illness and Disability*. Leeds: The Disability Press.

Kelly, M.P. and Field, D. (2004) Medical Sociology, Chronic Illness and the Body, in M. Bury and J. Gabe (eds) *The Sociology of Health and Illness. A Reader*. London: Routledge. First appeared in *Sociology of Health and Illness*, 18 (1996): 241–57.

Kennedy, M. (1996) Sexual Abuse and Disabled children, in J. Morris (ed.) *Encounters with Strangers: Feminism and Disability*. London: The Women's Press.

Kerr, A. and Shakespeare, T. (2002) *Genetic Politics. From Eugenics to Genome*. Cheltenham: New Clarion Press.

Kleijn-De Vrankrijker, M.W. (2003) The Long Way from the International Classification of Impairments, Disabilities and Handicaps (ICIDH) to the International Classification of Functioning, Disability and Health (ICF), *Disability and Rehabilitation*, 25 (11): 561–4.

Kleinman, A. (1988) *The Illness Narratives. Suffering, Healing and the Human Condition*. New York: Basic Books.

Kristiansen, K. and Traustadóttir, R. (eds) (2004) *Gender and Disability Research in the Nordic Countries*. Lund: Studentlitteratur.

Lacan, J. (1977) *Ecrits: A Selection* (trans. A. Sheridan). London: Tavistock Publications.

Lapper, A. with Feldman, G. (2005) *My Life in My Hands*. London: Simon and Schuster.

Leach Scully, J. (2002) A Postmodern Disorder: Moral Encounters with Molecular Models of Disability, in M. Corker and T. Shakespeare (eds) *Disability/Postmodernity: Embodying Disability Theory*. London, Continuum.

Lemert, E. (1951) *Social Pathology*. New York: McGraw-Hill.

Linton, S. (1998a) Disability Studies/Not Disability Studies, *Disability & Society*, 13 (4): 523–40.
Linton, S. (1998b) *Claiming Disability: Knowledge and Identity*. New York: New York University Press.
Lloyd, M. (1992) Does She Boil Eggs? Towards a Feminist Model of Disability, *Disability, Handicap and Society* 7 (3): 207–21.
Lloyd, M. (2001) The Politics of Disability and Feminism: Discord or Synthesis?, *Sociology*, 35 (3): 715–28.
Locker, D. (1983) *Disability and Disadvantage. The Consequences of Chronic Illness*. London: Tavistock Publications.
Lonsdale, S. (1990) *Women and Disability*. London: Macmillan.
Lorber, J. (1997) *Gender and the Social Construction of Illness*. London: Sage.
Lorber, J. and Moore, L.J. (2002) *Gender and the Social Construction of Illness*, 2nd edn. Oxford: Rowman and Littlefield.
Lupton, D. (1995) *The Imperative of Health: Public Health and the Regulated Body*. London; Sage.
Lupton, D. (1997) Psychoanalytic Sociology and the Medical Encounter: Parsons and beyond, *Sociology of Health and Illness*, 19 (5): 561–79.
Lyotard, J.F. (1984) *The Postmodern Condition. A Report on Knowledge* (trans. Geoff Bennington and Brian Massumi). Manchester: Manchester University Press.
Mairs, N. (1996) *Carnal Acts*. Boston, MA: Beacon Press.
May, C.., Allison, G., Chapple, A., Chew-Graham, C., Dixon, C., Gask, L., Graham, R., Rogers, A. and Roland, M. (2005) Framing the doctor-patient relationship in chronic illness: a comparative study of general practitioners' accounts. *Sociology of Health and Illness*, 26 (2): 135–44.
Marks, D. (1999) *Disability. Controversial Debates and Psychosocial Perspectives*. London: Routledge.
Marmot, M. and Wilkinson, R.G. (eds) (1999) *Social Determinants of Health*. Oxford: Oxford University Press.
Martin, J., Meltzer, H. and Elliot, D. (1988) *OPCS Surveys of Disability in Great Britain: Report 1 – The Prevalence of Disability Among Adults*. London: HMSO.
Maynard, M. and Purvis, J. (eds) (1994) *Researching Women's Lives from a Feminist Perspective*. London: Taylor and Francis.
McFarlane, H. (2005) *Disabled Women and Socio-Spatial 'Barriers' to Motherhood*. PhD Thesis, Department of Geography and Geomatics, University of Glasgow.
McKeown (1979) The Role of Medicine: Dream, Mirage or Nemesis? Oxford: Blackwell.
MCLennan, G. (2003) Sociology's Complexity, *Sociology*, 37 (3): 547–64.
McNamara, J. (1996) Out of Order: Madness is a Feminist and a Disability Issue, in J. Morris (ed.) *Encounters with Strangers: Feminism and Disability*, London: The Women's Press.
McRuer, R. and Wilkerson, A.L. (2003) Desiring Disability: Queer Theory Meets Disability Studies, special issue of GLQ – the *Journal of Lesbian and Gay Studies*, 9 (1–2).
Mead, G.H. (ed.) (1934) Mind, Self and Society from the Standpoint of a Social Behaviorist, Chicago, IL: University of Chicago Press.
Mechanic, D. (1959) Illness and Social Disability: Some Problems of Analysis, *Pacific Sociological Review*, 2: 37–41.
Meekosha, H. (1998) Body Battles: Bodies, Gender and Disability, in T. Shakespeare (ed.) *The Disability Reader: Social Science Perspectives*. London: Continuum, pp. 163–80.
Meekosha, H. (2004) Drifting down the Gulf Stream: Navigating the Cultures of Disability Studies, *Disability & Society*, 19 (7): 721–34.
Mercer, G. (2002) Emancipatory Disability Research, in C. Barnes, M. Oliver and L. Barton (eds) *Disability Studies Today*. Cambridge: Polity.
Merleau-Ponty, M. (1962) *The Phenomenology of Perception*. London: Routledge and Kegan Paul.
Mertens, D.M., Truman, C. and Humphries, B. (2000) *Research and Inequality*. London: Routledge.
Miller, E.J. and Gwynne, G.V. (1972) *A Life Apart*. London: Tavistock Publications.
Milligan, C. (2003) Location or Dis-location? Towards a Conceptualization of People and Place in the Care-giving Experience, *Social and Cultural Geography*, 4 (4): 455–70.
Mitchell, D.T. (2002) Narrative Prosthesis and the Materiality of Metaphor, in S.L. Snyder, B.J. Brueggeman and R. Garland Thomson (eds) *Disability Studies: Enabling the Humanities*. New York: The Modern Language Association of America.

Mitchell, D.T. and Snyder, S.L. (eds) (2000) *The Body and Physical Difference: Discourses of Disability*. Ann Arbor, MI: University of Michigan Press.

Morgan, M., Calnan, M. and Manning, N. (1985) *Sociological Approaches to Health and Medicine*. London: Croom Helm.

Moore, M., Beasley, S. and Maelzer, J. (1998) *Researching Disability Issues*. Buckingham: Open University Press.

Morris, J. (1989) *Able Lives: Women's Experience of Paralysis*. London: The Women's Press.

Morris, J. (1991) *Pride Against Prejudice: Transforming Attitudes to Disability*. London: The Women's Press.

Morris, J. (ed.) (1992a) *Alone Together: Voices of Single Mothers*. London: The Women's Press.

Morris, J. (1992b) Personal and Political: a Feminist Perspective on Researching Physical Disability, *Disability, Handicap and Society*, 7 (2): 157–66.

Morris, J. (1993a) *Independent Lives? Community Care and Disabled People*. London: Macmillan.

Morris, J. (1993b) Gender and Disability, in J. Swain, V. Finkelstein, S. French and M. Oliver (eds) *Disabling Barriers – Enabling Environments*. London: Sage.

Morris, J. (1993c) Feminism and Disability, *Feminist Review*, 43 (Spring): 57–70.

Morris, J. (1995) Creating a Space for Absent Voices: Disabled Women's Experience of Receiving Assistance with Daily Living Activities, *Feminist Review*, 51 (Autumn): 68–93.

Morris, J. (ed.) (1996) *Encounters With Strangers: Feminism and Disability*. London: The Women's Press.

Morris, J. (1997a) Gone Missing? Disabled Children Living Away from Their Families, *Disability & Society*, 12 (2): 241–58.

Morris, J. (1997b) Care or Empowerment? A Disability Rights Perspective, *Social Policy and Administration*, 31 (1): 54–60.

Morris, J. (2001) Social Exclusion and Young Disabled People with High Levels of Support Needs, *Critical Social Policy*, 21 (2): 161–83.

Morris, J. (2004) Independent Living and Community Care: a Disempowering Framework, *Disability & Society*, 19 (5): 427–42.

Moss, P. and Dyck, I. (2003) *Women, Body, Illness. Space and Identity in the Everyday Lives of Women with Chronic Illness*. Oxford: Rowman and Littlefield.

Mulvany, J. (2000) Disability, Impairment or Illness? The Relevance of the Social Model of Disability to the Study of Mental Disorder, *Sociology of Health and Illness*, 22 (5): 582–601.

Murphy, R.F. (1990) *The Body Silent*. London: Norton and Company.

Navarro, V. (1976) *Medicine under Capitalism*. New York: Prodist.

Nettleton, S. and Gustavsson, U. (2002a) Introduction, in S. Nettleton and U. Gustafsson (eds) *The Sociology of Health and Illness Reader*. Cambridge: Polity Press.

Nettleton, S. and Gustafsson, U. (eds) (2002b) *The Sociology of Health and Illness Reader*. Cambridge: Polity Press.

Nettleton, S. and Watson, J. (1998) The Body in Everyday Life: An Introduction, in S. Nettleton and J. Watson (eds) *The Body in Everyday Life*. London: Routledge.

Nicholson, L.J. (ed.) (1990) *Feminism/Postmodernism*. London: Routledge.

Oakley, A. (1984) *The Captured Womb*. Oxford: Blackwell.

Oliver, M. (1983) *Social Work with Disabled People*. Basingstoke: Macmillan.

Oliver, M. (1990) *The Politics of Disablement*. London, Macmillan.

Oliver, M. (1991) Speaking Out: Disabled People and State Welfare, in G. Dalley (ed.) *Disability and Social Policy*. London: Social Policy Institute.

Oliver, M. (1992) Changing the Social Relations of Research Production?, *Disability, Handicap and Society*, 7 (2): 101–14.

Oliver, M. (1996a) *Understanding Disability: From Theory to Practice*. London, Macmillan.

Oliver, M. (1996b) Defining Impairment and Disability: Issues at Stake, in C. Barnes and G. Mercer (eds) *Exploring the Divide: Illness and Disability*. Leeds: The Disability Press.

Oliver, M. (1996c) A sociology of disability or a disablist sociology?, in L. Barton (ed.) *Disability And Society: Emerging Issues and Insights*. Harlow: Longman.

Oliver, M. (1997) Emancipatory Research: Realistic Goal or Impossible Dream?, in C. Barnes and G. Mercer (eds) *Doing Disability Research*. Leeds: The Disability Press.

Oliver, M. (2004) The Social Model in Action: if I had a Hammer, in C. Barnes and

G. Mercer (eds) *Implementing the Social Model of Disability: Theory and Research*. Leeds: The Disability Press.

Oliver, M. and Barnes, C. (1998) *Disabled People and Social Policy: From Exclusion to Inclusion*. London: Longman.

Oliver, M. and Sapey, B. (2005) *Social Work with Disabled People*, 3rd edn. Basingstoke: Palgrave Macmillan.

Oliver, M., Zarb, G., Silver, J., Moore, M. and Salisbury, V. (1988) *Walking into Darkness: The Experience of Spinal Cord Injury*. Basingstoke: Macmillan.

Omanski, G.B. and Rosenblum, K.E. (2001) Bringing Disability into the Sociological Frame: a Comparison of Disability with Race, Sex and Sexual Orientation Statuses, *Disability and Society*, 16 (1): 5–19.

Ong, B.N., Hooper, H., Dunn, K. and Croft, P. (2004) Establishing Self and Meaning in Low Back pain Narratives. *The Sociological Review*, 52 (4): 532–49.

Padden, C. and Humphries, T. (1988) *Deaf in America: Voices from a Culture*. Cambridge, MA: Harvard University Press.

Parker, G. (ed.) (1991) *Disability and Social Policy*. London: Policy Studies Institute.

Parker, G. (1993) *With this Body: Caring and Disability in Marriage*. Buckingham: Open University Press.

Parker, G. and Clarke, H. (2002) Making the Ends Meet: Do Carers and Disabled People Have a Common Agenda?, *Policy and Politics*, 30 (3): 347–59.

Parker, R. and Aggleton, P. (2003) HIV and AIDS-related stigma and discrimination: a conceptual framework and implications for action. *Social Science and Medicine*, 57 (1): 13–24.

Parr, H. (1999) Bodies and Psychiatric Medicine: Interpreting Different Geographies of Mental Health, in R. Butler and H. Parr (eds) *Mind and Body Spaces. Geographies of Illness, Impairment and Disability*. London: Routledge.

Parsons, T. (1951) *The Social System*. Glencoe: Free Press.

Parsons, T. (1975) The Sick Role and the Role of the Physician Reconsidered, *Milbank Memorial Fund Quarterly*, 53 (3): 257–78.

Paterson, K. and Hughes, B. (1999) Disability Studies and Phenomenology: the carnal politics of everyday life. *Disability and Society*, 14 (5): 597–610.

Pearson, C. (2004) Keeping the Cash under Control: What's the Problem with Direct Payments in Scotland?, *Disability & Society*, 19 (1): 3–14.

Petersen, A. and Bunton, R. (1997) *Foucault, Health and Medicine*. London: Routledge.

Pfeiffer, D. (2000) The Devils are in the Details: the ICIDH2 and the Disability Movement, *Disability & Society*, 15 (7): 1079–82.

Phillipson, C. (1982) *Capitalism and the Construction of Old Age*. London: Macmillan.

Pilgrim, D. and Rogers, A. (1999) *A Sociology of Mental Health and Illness*, 2nd edn. Buckingham: Open University Press.

Pinder, R. (1996) Sick-but-Fit or Fit-but-Sick? Ambiguity and Identity at the Workplace, in C. Barnes and G. Mercer (eds) *Exploring the Divide: Illness and Disability*. Leeds: The Disability Press.

Plummer, K. (2001) *Documents of Life 2. An Invitation to a Critical Humanism*. London: Sage.

Policy and Politics, Volume 30, Issue 3, 2002.

Price, J. and Shildrick, M. (1998) Uncertain Thoughts on the Dis/abled Body, in M. Shildrick and J. Price (eds) *Vital Signs: Feminist Reconfigurations of the Bio/logical Body*. Edinburgh: Edinburgh University Press.

Price, J.E. and Shildrick, M. (1999) *Feminist Theory and the Body: A Reader*. Edinburgh: Edinburgh University Press.

Price, J. and Shildrick, M. (2002) Bodies Together: Touch, Ethics and Disability, in M. Corker and T. Shakespeare (eds) *Disability/Postmodernity: Embodying Disability Theory*. London, Continuum.

Priestley, M. (1999) *Disability Politics and Community Care*. London: Jessica Kingsley Publishers.

Priestley, M. (ed.) (2001) *Disability and the Life Course: Global Perspectives*. Cambridge: Cambridge University Press.

Priestley, M. (2003) *Disability: A Life Course Approach*. Cambridge: Polity.

Putnam, H. (1981) *Reason, Truth and History*. Cambridge: Cambridge University Press.

Putnam, R.D., Leonardi, R., Nanetti, R.Y. (1993) *Making Democracy Work: Civic Traditions in Modern Italy*. Princeton, NJ: Princeton University Press.

Radley, A. (1989) Style, Discourse and Constraint in Adjusting to Chronic Illness, *Sociology of Health and Illness*, 11 (3): 230–52.

Radley, A. and Green, R. (1987) Chronic Illness as Adjustment: a Methodology and Conceptual Framework, *Sociology of Health and Illness*, 9 (2): 179–207.

Reeve, D. (2002) Negotiating Psycho-emotional Dimensions of Disability and their Influence on Identity Constructions. *Disability & Society*, 17 (5): 493–508.

Reeve, D. (2006) Towards a Psychology of Disability: The Emotional Effects of Living in a Disabling Society, in D. Goodley and R. Lawthom (eds) *Disability and Psychology: Critical Introductions and Reflections*. Basingstoke: Palgrave Macmillan.

Riddell, S. (1996) Theorising Special Educational Needs in a Changing Political Climate, in L. Barton (ed.) *Disability & Society: Emerging Issues and Insights*. Harlow: Longman, pp. 83–106.

Riddell, S., Pearson, C., Jolly, D., Barnes, C., Priestley, M. and Mercer, J. (2005) The Development of Direct Payments in the UK: Implications for Social Justice, *Social Policy and Society*, 4 (1): 75–85.

Rioux, M. and Bach, M. (eds) (1994) *Disability is Not Measles. New Research Paradigms in Disability*. New York, Ontario: Roeher Institute.

Robinson, I. (1988) *Multiple Sclerosis*. London: Routledge.

Robinson, C. and Stalker, K. (eds) (1998) *Growing Up with Disability*. London: Jessica Kingsley.

Robertson, S. (2004) Men and Disability, in J. Swain, S. French, C. Barnes and C. Thomas (eds) *Disabling Barriers – Enabling Environments*, 2nd edn. London: Sage.

Rose, N. (1990) *Governing the Soul: The Shaping of the Private Self*. London: Routledge.

Roulstone, A. (1998) *Enabling Technology: Disabled People, Work and New Technology*. Buckingham: Open University Press.

Roulstone, A. (2000) Disability, Dependency and the New Deal for Disabled People, *Disability & Society*, 15 (3): 427–43.

Rummery, K. (2002) *Disability, Citizenship and Community Care. A Care for Welfare Rights?* Aldershot: Ashgate.

Ryan, J. and Thomas, F. (1980) *The Politics of Mental Handicap*. Harmondsworth: Penguin.

Safilios-Rothschild, C. (1970) *The Sociology and Social Psychology of Disability and Rehabilitation*. New York: Random House.

Sapey, B., Stewart, J. and Donaldson, G. (2005) Increases in Wheelchair Use and Perceptions of Disablement, *Disability and Society*, 20 (5): 489–505.

Saussure, F. de (1974) *Course in General Linguistics*. London: Fontana.

Sayer, A. (1992) *Method in Social Science: a Realist Approach*. London: Routledge.

Sayer, A. (2000a) For Postdisciplinary Studies: Sociology and the Curse of Disciplinary Parochialism and Imperialism, in Eldridge *et al.* (eds) *For Sociology: Legacy and Prospects*. Durham, NC: The Sociology Press.

Sayer, A. (2000b) *Realism and Social Science*. London: Sage.

Scambler, G. (1984) Perceiving and Coping with Stigmatizing Illness, in R. Fitzpatrick, J. Hinton, S. Newman, G. Scambler and J. Thompson (eds) *The Experience of Illness*. London: Tavistock Publications.

Scambler, G. (ed.) (1987) *Sociological Theory and Medical Sociology*. London: Tavistock Publications.

Scambler, G. (1989) *Epilepsy*. London: Routledge.

Scambler, G. (2002) *Health and Social Change: A Critical Theory*. Buckingham: Open University Press.

Scambler, G. (2004) Re-framing Stigma: Felt and Enacted Stigma and Challenges to the Sociology of Chronic and Disabling Conditions, *Social Theory and Health*, 2: 29–46.

Scambler, S. (2005) *Exposing the Limitations of Disability Theory: The Case of Juvenile Batten Disease, Social Theory and Health*, 3: 144–64.

Scambler, G. and Higgs, P. (1998) *Modernity, Medicine and Health*. London: Routledge.

Scambler, G. and Hopkins, A. (1986) 'Being Epileptic': Coming to terms with Stigma, *Sociology of Health and Illness*, 8: 26–43.

Scambler, G. and Scambler, S. (2003) Realist Agendas on Biology, Health and Medicine, in

S.J. Williams, L. Birke and G.A. Bendelow (eds) *Debating Biology. Sociological Reflections on Health, Medicine and Society*. London: Routledge.

Scior, K. (2003) Using Discourse Analysis to Study the Experiences of Women with Learning Disabilities, *Disability & Society*, 18 (6): 779–95.

Schutz, A. (1953) Common-Sense and Scientific Interpretation of Human Action, *Philosophy and Phenomenological Research*, 14: 1–38.

Schutz, A. (1954) Concept and Theory Formation in the Social Sciences. *Journal of Philosophy*, 51.

Scotch, R. (1984) *From Good Will to Civil Rights: Transforming Federal Disability Policy*. Philadelphia, PA: Temple University Press.

Scott, R.A. (1969) *The Making of Blind Men*. New York: Russell Sage Foundation.

Scott, R.A. and Douglas, J.D. (eds) (1972) *Theoretical Perspectives on Deviance*. New York: Basic Books.

Seidman, S. (ed.) (1996) *QueerTheory/Sociology*. Oxford: Blackwell.

Sevenhuijsen, S. (1998) *Citizenship and the Ethics of Care: Feminist Considerations on Justice, Morality and Politics*. London: Routledge.

Shakespeare, T. (1996) Disability, Identity and Difference, in C. Barnes and G. Mercer (eds) (1996) *Exploring the Divide: Illness and Disability*. Leeds: The Disability Press.

Shakespeare, T. (1997a) Cultural Representation of Disabled People: Dustbins of disavowal?, in L. Barton and M. Oliver (eds) *Disability Studies: Past, Present and Future*. Leeds: The Disability Press.

Shakespeare, T. (1997b) Rules of Engagement: Changing Disability research, in L. Barton and M. Oliver (eds) *Disability Studies: Past, Present and Future*. Leeds: The Disability Press.

Shakespeare, T. (1999a) Art and Lies? Representations of Disability on Film, in M. Corker and S. French (eds) *Disability Discourse*. Buckingham: Open University Press.

Shakespeare, T. (1999b) Losing the Plot? Medical and Activist Discourses of Contemporary Genetics and Disability, *Sociology of Health and Illness*, 21 (5): 669–88.

Shakespeare, T. (2000) *Help*. Birmingham: Venture Press.

Shakespeare, T. (2003) Rights, Risks and Responsibilities. New Genetics and Disabled People, in S.J. Williams, L. Birke and G. Bendelow (eds) *Debating Biology. Sociological Reflections on Health, Medicine and Society*. London: Routledge.

Shakespeare, T. and Erikson, M. (2000) Different Strokes: Beyond Biological Determinism and Social Constructionism, in H. Rose and S. Rose (eds) *Alas Poor Darwin*. London: Jonathan Cape.

Shakerspeare, T., Gillespie-Sells and Davies, D. (1996) *The Sexual Politics of Disability: Untold Desires*. London: Casell.

Shakespeare, T. and Watson, N. (2001) The Social Model of Disability: An Outdated Ideology?, in *Research in Social science and Disability. Exploring Theories and Expanding Methodologies, volume 2*. Elsevier Science Ltd. pp. 9–18.

Sheer, J. and Groce, N. (1988) Impairment as a Human Constant: Cross-cultural and Historical Perspectives on Variation, *Journal of Social Issues*, 44 (1): 23–37.

Sherry, M. (2004) Overlaps and Contradictions between Queer Theory and Disability studies, *Disability & Society*, 19 (7): 769–84.

Shildrick, M. (1997) *Leaky Bodies and Boundaries. Feminism, Postmodernism and (Bio)ethics*. London: Routledge.

Shildrick, M. and Price, J. (1996) Breaking the Boundaries of the Broken Body, *Body and Society*, 2 (4): 93–113.

Shilling, C. (1993) *The Body and Social Theory*. London: Sage.

Shilling, C. (2001) Embodiment, Experience and Theory: In Defence of the Sociological Tradition, *The Sociological Review*, 49 (3): 327–44.

Shilling, C. (2005) *The Body in Culture, Technology and Society*. London: Sage.

Showalter, E. (1987) *The Female Malady*. London: Virago.

Silverman, D. (1981) The Child as a Social Object: Down's Syndrome Children in a Pediatric Cardiology Clinic, *Sociology of Health and Illness*, 3: 254–74.

Skritic, T.M. (ed.) (1995) *Disability and Democracy: Reconstructing (Special) Education for Postmodernity*. New York: Teachers College Press.

Sleeter, C.E. (1995) Radical Structuralist Perspectives on the Creation and Use of Learning Disabilities, in T.M. Skritic (ed.) *Disability and Democracy: Reconstructing (Special) Education for Postmodernity*. New York: Teachers College Press.

Small, N. and Rhodes, P. (2000) *Too Ill to Talk? User Involvement in Palliative Care*. London: Routledge.

Smith, B.G. and Hutchinson, B. (eds) (2004) *Gendering Disability*. New Brunswick, NJ: Rutgers University Press.

Smith, B. and Sparks, A.C. (2004) Men, Sport, and Spinal cord Injury: An Analysis of Metaphors and Narrative Types, *Disability & Society*, 19 (6): 613–26.

Snyder, S.L., Brueggeman, B.J. and Garland Thomson, R. (eds) (2002) *Disability Studies: Enabling the Humanities*. New York: The Modern Language Association of America.

Snyder, S.L and Mitchell, D.T. (2001) *Narrative Prosthesis: Disability and the Dependencies of Discourse*. Michigan: University of Michigan Press.

Sobsey, D. (1994) *Violence and Abuse in the Lives of People with Disabilities: the End of Silent Acceptance?* Baltimore, MD: Paul H. Brookes.

Social Policy and Society, Volume 4, Issue 1, January 2005.

Somers, M. (1994) The Narrative Construction of Identity: A Relational and Network Approach, *Theory and Society*, 23: 605–49.

SPA News (2002) *Newsletter of the UK Social Policy Association*.

Sparkes, A.C. and Smith, B. (2002) Sport, Spinal cord Injuries, Embodied Masculinities, and Narrative Identity Dilemmas, *Men and Masculinities*, 4 (3): 258–85.

Sparkes, A.C. (2004) Bodies, Narratives, Selves, and Autobiography. The Example of Lance Armstrong, *Journal of Sport and Social Issues*, 28 (4): 397–428.

Spelman, E. (1988) *Inessential Woman: Problems of Exclusion in Feminist Thought*. Boston, MA: Beacon Books.

Stacey, M. (1988) *The Sociology of Health and Healing*. London: Unwin Hyman.

Stacey, M. and Homans, H. (1978) The Sociology of Health and Illness: Its Present State, Futures and Potential for Health research, *Sociology*, 12: 281–307.

Stalker, K. (1998) Some Ethical and Methodological Issues in Research with People with Learning Difficulties, *Disability & Society*, 13 (1): 5–19.

Stewart, J., Harris, J. and Sapey, B. (1997) Disability and Dependency: Origins and Futures of 'special needs' Housing for Disabled People, *Disability & Society*, 14(1): 5–20.

Stone, D.A. (1984) *The Disabled State*. London: Macmillan.

Stone, E. (ed.) (1999) *Disability and Development: Learning From Action and Research on Disability in The Majority World*. Leeds: Disability Press.

Stone, E. and Priestley, M. (1996) Parasites, Pawns and Partners: Disability Research and the Role of Non-disabled Researchers, *British Journal of Sociology*, 47 (4): 699–716.

Strauss, A. and Glaser, B. (1970) *Anguish: Case History of a Dying Woman*. San Francisco, CA: Sociology Press.

Strauss, A. and Glaser, B. (1975) *Chronic Illness and the Quality of Life*. St Louis, MO: Mosby.

Strong, P.M. (1979a) *The Ceremonial Order of the Clinic: Parents, Doctors and Medical Bureaucracies*. London: Routledge and Kegan Paul.

Strong, P.M. (1979b) Sociological Imperialism and the Profession of Medicine, *Social Science and Medicine*, 13A: 199–215.

Stuart, O. (1993) Double Oppression: An Appropriate Starting-point?, in J. Swain, V. Finkelstein, S. French and M. Oliver (eds) *Disabling Barriers – Enabling Environments*. London: Sage.

Sutherland, A. (1981) *Disabled We Stand*. London: Souvenir Press.

Swain, J. and French, S. (eds) (1999) *Therapy and Learning Difficulties: Advocacy, Participation and Partnership*. Oxford: Butterworth-Heinemann.

Swain, J. and French, S. (2000) Towards an Affirmation Model of Disability, *Disability & Society*, 15 (4): 569–82.

Swain, J., French, S. and Cameron, C. (2003) *Controversial Issues in a Disabling Society*. Buckingham: Open University Press.

Swain, J., French, S., Barnes, C. and Thomas, C. (eds) (2004) *Disabling Barriers – Enabling Environments*. London: Sage.

Sussman, M. (ed.) (1966) *Sociology of Disability and Rehabilitation*. Washington: American Sociological Association.

Synnott, A. (1993) *The Body Social: Symbolism, Self and* Society. London: Routledge.

The Canadian Geographer (2003) Special issue: *Disability in Society and Space*. 47 (4).

Thomas, C. (1993) Deconstructing Concepts of Care, *Sociology* 27 (4): 649–69. (Note: Figure 1 in this issue was incorrectly formatted by the publisher. The corrected Figure was printed in the following issue of the journal as an erratum: *Sociology* 28 (1) 1994).

Thomas, C. (1996) Domestic Labour and Health: Bringing it All Back Home, *Sociology of Health and Illness*, 17 (3): 328–52.

Thomas, C. (1997) The Baby and the Bathwater: Disabled Women and Motherhood in Social Context, *Sociology of Health and Illness*, 19 (5): 622–43.

Thomas, C. (1999) *Female Forms: Experiencing and Understanding Disability*. Buckingham: Open University Press.

Thomas, C. (2001a) Medicine, Gender and Disability: Disabled Women's Health Care Encounters, *Health Care for Women International*, 22 (3) April–May: 245–62.

Thomas, C. (2001b) Feminism and Disability: The Theoretical and Political Significance of the Personal and the Experiential, in L. Barton (ed.) *Disability, Politics and the Struggle for Change*. London: David Fulton.

Thomas, C. (2004a) Developing the Social Relational in the Social Model of Disability: A Theoretical Agenda, in C. Barnes and G. Mercer (eds) *The Social Model of Disability – Theory and Research*. Leeds: The Disability Press.

Thomas, C. (2004b) How is Disability Understood? An Examination of Sociological Approaches, *Disability & Society*, 19 (6): 569–83.

Thomas, C. (2004c) The UK Social Model of Disability: Rescuing a Social Relational Understanding of Disability, *Scandinavian Journal of Disability Research*. 6 (1): 22–36.

Thomas, C. (2005) The Place of Death of Cancer Patients: Can Qualitative Data Add to Known Factors?, *Social Science and Medicine*, 60 (11): 2597–607.

Thomas, C. and Morris S.M. (2002) Informal Carers in Cancer Contexts, *European Journal of Cancer Care* 11 (3):178–82.

Thomas, C., Morris S.M. and Clark, D. (2004) Place of Death: Preferences Among Cancer Patients and Their Carers, *Social Science and Medicine* 58 (12): 2431–44.

Topliss, E. (1982) *Social Responses to Handicap*. Harlow: Longman.

Townsend, P. (1966) Foreword, in P. Hunt (ed.) *Stigma: The Experience of Disability*. London: Chapman.

Townsend, P. (1979) *Poverty in the United Kingdom*. Harmondsworth: Penguin.

Townsend, P. (1981) The Structural Dependency of the Elderly: The Creation of Social Policy in the Twentieth Century, *Ageing and Society*, 1 (May): 28.

Townsend, P. (1993) *The International Analysis of Poverty*. Hemel Hempstead: Harvester Wheatsheaf.

Townsend, P. and Davidson, N. (1982) *Inequalities in Health: The Black Report*. Harmondsworth: Penguin Books.

Traustadóttir, R. (2004) A New Way of Thinking: Exploring the Intersection of Disability and Gender, in K. Kristiansen and R. Traustadóttir (eds) *Gender and Disability Research in the Nordic Countries*. Lund: Studentlitteratur.

Traustadóttir, R. and Johnson, K. (eds) (2000) *Women with Intellectual Disabilities. Finding a Place in the World*. London: Jessica Kingsley.

Tremain, S. (2002) On the Subject of Impairment, in M. Corker and T. Shakespeare (eds) *Disability/Postmodernity: Embodying Disability Theory*. London: Continuum.

Tremain, S. (ed.) (2005) *Foucault and the Government of Disability*. Michigan: The University of Michigan Press.

Tronto, J.C. (1993) *Moral Boundaries: a Political Argument for an Ethic of Care*. London: Routledge.

Turner, B.S. (1984) *The Body and Society, Explorations in Social Theory*. Oxford: Basil Blackwell.

Turner, B.S. (1987) *Medical Power and Social Knowledge*. London: Sage.

Turner, B.S. (1992) *Regulating Bodies: Essays in Medical Sociology*. London: Routledge.

Turner, B.S. (2001) Disability and the Sociology of the Body, in G.L. Albrecht, K.D. Seelman and M. Bury (eds) *Handbook of Disability Studies*. London: Sage.

Twigg, J. (2000) *Bathing – the Body and Community Care*. London: Routledge.

Ungerson, C. (1997a) Social Politics and the Commodification of Care, *Social Politics*, 4 (3): 362–81.

Ungerson, C. (1997b) Give Them the Money: Is Cash a Route to Empowerment?, *Social Policy and Administration*, 31 (1): 45–53.

Ungerson, C. (1999) Personal Assistants and Disabled People: An Examination of a Hybrid Form of Work and Care, *Work, Employment and Society*, 13 (4): 583–600.

Ungerson, C. (2000) Thinking about the Production and Consumption of Long-term Care in Britain: Does Gender Still Matter?, *Journal of Social Policy*, 29 (4): 623–43.

Ungerson, C. (2004) Whose Empowerment and Independence? A Cross-national Perspective on 'Cash for Care' Schemes, *Ageing and Society*, 24: 189–212.

Union of the Physically Impaired Against Segregation (UPIAS) and The Disability Alliance (TDA) (1976) *Fundamental Principles of Disability*. London: UPIAS.

Urry, J. (2000) Mobile Sociology, *British Journal of Sociology*, 51 (1): 185–203.

Ussher, J. (1991) *Women's Madness: Misogyny or Mental Illness?* London: Harvester Wheatsheaf.

Ustun, T.B., Chatterji, S., Bickenbach, J.E., Trotter, R.T., Room, R., Rehm, J. and Saxena, S. (2001) *Disability and Culture: Universalism and Diversity*. Seattle, WA: World Health Organization, Hogrefe and Huber.

Vernon, A. (1997) Fighting Two Different Battles: Unity is Preferable to Enmity, in L. Barton and M. Oliver (eds) *Disability Studies: Past, Present and Future*. Leeds: The Disability Press.

Vernon, A. (2000) *User Defined Outcomes of Community Care for Asian Disabled People*. Bristol: The Policy Press.

Vincent, J. (1999) *Politics, Power and Old Age*. Buckingham: Open University Press.

Voysey, M. (1975) *A Constant Burden: The Reconstitution of Family Life*. London: Routledge and Kegan Paul.

Waitzkin, H. (1979) Medicine, Superstructure and Micropolitics. *Social Science and Medicine*, 13: 601–9.

Waitzkin, H. (1983) *The Second Sickness: Contradictions of Capitalist Health Care*. New York: Free Press.

Walby, S. (1990) *Theorising Patriarchy*. Oxford: Blackwell.

Walby, S. (1997) *Gender Transformations*. London: Routledge.

Walker, A. (1980) The Social Creation of Poverty and Dependency in Old Age, *Journal of Social Policy*, 9: 49–75.

Walker, A. and Townsend, P. (eds) (1980) *Disability in Britain: A Manifesto of Rights*. Oxford: Martin Robertson.

Walker, A. and Walker, L. (1991) Disability and Financial Need – The Failure of the Social Security System, in G. Dalley (ed.) *Disability and Social Policy*. London: Social Policy Institute.

Wallerstein, I. (2000) From Sociology to Historical Social science: Prospects and Obstacles, *British Journal of Sociology*, 51 (1): 25–36.

Walmsley, J. (1991) 'Talking to the Top People': Some Issues Relating to the Citizenship of People with Learning Difficulties, *Disability, Handicap and Society*, 6 (3): 219–31.

Walmsley, J. (1993) Contradictions in Caring: Reciprocity and Interdependence, *Disability, Handicap and Society*, 8: 129–42.

Walmsley, J. (2002) Normalisation, Emancipatory Research and Inclusive Research in Learning Disability, *Disability & Society*, 16 (2): 187–206.

Watson, N. (2002) Well, I Know this is Going to Sound Very Strange to You, but I Don't See Myself as a Disabled Person: Identity and Disability, *Disability & Society*, 17 (5): 509–27.

Watson, N., McKie, L., Hughes, B., Hopkins, D. and Gregory, S. (2004) (Inter)Dependence, Need and Care: The Potential for Disability and Feminist Theorists To Develop an Emancipatory Model. Sociology, 38 (2): 331–50.

Webb, B. and Stimson, G. (1976) People's Accounts of Medical Encounters, in M. Wadsworth and D. Robinson (eds) *Studies in Everyday Medical Life*. Oxford: Martin Robertson.

Wendell, S. (1989) Towards a Feminist Theory of Disability, *Hypatia* 4 (summer): 104–24.

Wendell, S. (1996) *The Rejected Body. Feminist Philosophical Reflections on Disability*. London: Routledge.

Whitehead, K. and Williams, J. (2001) Medical Treatment of Women with Lupus. The Case for Sharing Knowledge and Decision-making, *Disability & Society*, 16(1): 103–21.

WHO, 2001(a) *ICF Introduction. World Health Organization*. Retrieved September 2005 from http://www3.who.int/icf/intros/ICF-Eng-Intro.pdf. pp. 1–25.

WHO, 2001 (b) WHO Publishes New Guidelines to Measure Health. *World Health Organization Press Release*, 15 November, 2001. Retrieved September 2005 from http://www.who.int/inf-pr-2001/en/pr2001-48.html. pp. 1–2.

Wilde, A. (2004) *Disability Fictions: The Production of Gendered Impairments and Disability in Soap opera Discourses*. Unpublished PhD Thesis. Leeds: University of Leeds.

Williams, F. (2001) In and Beyond New Labour: Towards a New Political Ethics of Care, *Critical Social Policy*, 21 (4): 467–93.

Williams, G.H. (1984a) The Genesis of Chronic Illness: Narrative Reconstruction, *Sociology of Health and Illness*, 6: 174–200.

Williams, G.H (1984b) The Movement for Independent Living: an Evaluation and Critique, *Social Science and Medicine*, 17: 1000–12.

Williams, G.H. (1991) Disablement and the Ideological Crisis in Health Care, *Social Science and Medicine*, 32 (4): 517–24.

Williams, G.H. (1996a) Irving Kenneth Zola, (1935–1994): An Appreciation, *Sociology of Health and Illness*, 18 (1): 107–25.

Williams, G.H. (1996b) Representing Disability: Some Questions of Phenomenology and Politics, in C. Barnes and G. Mercer (eds) (1996) *Exploring the Divide: Illness and Disability*. Leeds: The Disability Press.

Williams, G.H. (2001) Theorizing Disability, in G.L. Albrecht, K.D. Seelman and M. Bury (eds) *Handbook of Disability Studies*. London: Sage.

Wilkinson, R.G. (1996) *Unhealthy Societies: The Afflictions of Inequality*. London: Routledge.

Williams, S.J. (1993). *Chronic Respiratory Illness*. London: Routledge.

Williams, S.J. (1999) Is Anybody There? Critical Realism, Chronic Illness and the Disability Debate, *Sociology of Health and Illness*, 21 (6): 797–819.

Williams, S.J. (2000) Chronic Illness as Biographical Disruption or Biographical Disruption as Chronic Illness? Reflections on a Core Concept, *Sociology of Health and Illness*, 22 (1): 40–67.

Williams, S.J. (2001a) Sociological Imperialism and the Medical Profession Revisited: Where are We Now? *Sociology of Health and Illness*, 23 (2): 135–58.

Williams, S.J. (2001b) *Emotion and Social Theory*. London: Sage.

Williams, S.J. (2001c) Reason, Emotion and Embodiment: Is 'Mental' Health a Contradiction in Terms?, in J. Busfield (ed.) *Rethinking the Sociology of Mental Health*. Oxford: Blackwell.

Williams, S.J. (2003) Beyond Meaning, Discourse and the Empirical World: Critical Realist Reflections on Health, *Social Theory and Health*, 1: 42–71.

Williams, S.J. (2005) Parsons Revisited: From the Sick Role to … ? *Health*, 9 (2): 123–44.

Williams, S.J. and Bendelow, G. (1998a) *The Lived Body: Sociological Themes, Embodied Issues*. London: Routledge.

Williams, S.J. and Bendelow, G. (1998b) In Search of the 'Missing Body': Pain, Suffering and the (Post)modern Condition, in G. Scambler and P. Higgs (eds) *Modernity, Medicine and Health*. London: Routledge.

Williams, S.J., Birke, L. and Bendelow, G. (eds) (2003) *Debating Biology*. London: Routledge.

Wolfensberger, W. (1980) The Definition of Normalisation: Update, Problems, Disagreements and Misunderstandings, in R.J. Flynn and K.E. Nitsch (eds) *Normalisation, Social Integration and Community Service*. Baltimore, MD: University Park Press.

Wolfensberger, W. (1983) Social Role Valorisation: A Proposed New Term for the Principle of Normalisation, *Mental Retardation*, 21 (6): 234–9.

Wolfensberger, W. (1994) The Growing Threat to the Lives of Handicapped People in the Context of Modernistic Values, *Disability & Society*, 9 (3): 395–413.

Wolfensberger, W. and Thomas, S. (1983) *Program Analysis of Service Systems Implementation of Normalisation Goals: Normalisation and Ratings Manual*, 2nd edn. Toronto: National Institute of Mental Retardation.

Wood, P. (1980) *International Classification of Impairments, Disabilities and Handicaps*. Geneva: World Health Organization.

Wood, R. (1991) Care of Disabled People, in G. Dalley (ed.) *Disability and Social Policy*. London: Social Policy Institute.

Wright, P. and Treacher, A. (1982) *The Problems of Medical Knowledge: Examining the Social Construction of Medicine*. Edinburgh: Edinburgh University Press.

Young, I.M. (1990) *Justice and the politics of difference*. Princeton, NJ: Princeton University Press.

Young, I.M. (2002) Autonomy, Welfare Reform, and Meaningful Work, in E.F. Kittay and E.K. Feder (eds) *The Subject of Care: Feminist Perspectives on Dependency*. Lanham, MD: Rowman and Littlefield.

Zarb, G. (1992) On the Road to Damascus: First Steps Towards Changing the Relations of Disability Research Production, *Disability, Handicap and Society*, 7(2): 125–38.

Zarb, G. and Nadash, P. (1994) Cashing in on Independence. Derby: The British Council of Organisations of Disabled People. Retrieved May 2005 from http:www. leeds.ac.uk/disability-studies/archiveuk/index.

Zitzelsberger, H. (2005) (In)visibility: Accounts of the Embodiment of Women with Physical Disabilities and Differences, *Disability & Society*, 20 (4): 389–403.

Zola, I.K. (1966) Culture and Symptoms: An Analysis of Patients Presenting Complaints, *American Sociological Review*, 31: 615–30.

Zola, I.K. (1972) Medicine as an Institution of Social Control, *Sociological Review*, 20: 487–504.

Zola, I.K. (1973) Pathways to the Doctor – From Person to Patient, *Social Science and Medicine*, 7: 677–89.

Zola, I.K. (1982a) *Missing Pieces: A Chronicle of Living With a Disability*. Philadelphia, PA: Temple University Press.

Zola, I.K. (1982b) *Ordinary Lives: Voices of Disease and Disability*. Watertown, MA: Applewood Books.

Zola, I.K. (1989) Toward the Necessary Universalizing of Disability Policy, *Milbank Memorial Fund Quarterly*, 67 (suppl.2): 401–28.

Zola, I.K. (1991) Bringing Our Bodies and Ourselves Back In Reflections on a Past, Present, and Future 'Medical Sociology', *Journal of Health and Social Behaviour*, 32 (March): 1–16.

Zola, I.K. (1993a) Self, Identity and the Naming Question: Reflections on the Language of Disability, *Social Science and Medicine* 36(2): 167–73.

Zola, I.K. (1993b) Disability Statistics, What We Count and What It Tells Us, *Journal of Disability Policy Studies*, 4(2): 9–39.

Zola, I.K. (1994) Towards Inclusion: The Role of People with Disabilities in Policy and Research Issues in the United States – A Historical and Political Analysis, in M. Rioux and M. Bach (eds) *Disability is not Measles*. North York, Ontario: Roeher Institute.

Index

CPSIA information can be obtained at www.ICGtesting.com
Printed in the USA
LVOW08s0244060614

388895LV00005B/94/P